Arab background series

Editor: N. A. Ziadeh, Emeritus Professor of History, American University of Beirut

Frankincense and Myrrh

A Study
of the Arabian Incense Trade

Nigel Groom

Longman London and New York
Librairie du Liban

Longman Group Limited,
Longman House,
Burnt Mill,
Harlow, Essex

Librairie du Liban,
Beirut, Lebanon

First published 1981

ISBN 0 582 76476 9

British Library Cataloguing in Publication Data
Groom, Nigel
    Frankincense and myrrh.— (Arab background series).
    1. Incense—History
    2. Arabia—Commerce—History
    I. Title   II. Series
    382'.45'6685   HD9769.I/

ISBN 0-582-76476-9

Printed in Great Britain by
Butler & Tanner Ltd
Frome and London

Contents

Acknowledgements

The author wishes to thank the following persons who kindly provided photographs for publication or assisted in their procurement:

Mr John Carter; Mr John Dayton; Dr Brian Doe; Mr William Facey; Dr Nigel Hepper; Professor Théodore Monod; Dr Jacqueline Pirenne; and Miss Rosalind Wade.

Acknowledgement is also given to the Directors and Curators of the following for permission to publish photographs:

The British Museum, London; the British Library, London; the Ashmolean Museum, Oxford; the Fitzwilliam Museum, Cambridge; the Victoria and Albert Museum, London; the Royal Geographical Society, London; the National Museum, Rome; the Roman-Germanic Museum, Cologne and the Cyprus Museum, Nicosia.

We are grateful to the following for permission to reproduce copyright material:

Harvard University Press for extracts from *Pliny's Natural History* translated by H. Rackham; extracts from *The Geography of Strabo* translated by H. L. Jones; extracts from *Theophrastus "Enquiry Into Plants" and "Concerning Odours"* translated by A. Hort.

Editor's Preface

The Arab World has, for some time, been attracting the attention of a growing public throughout the world. The strategic position of the Arab countries, the oil they produce, their sudden emancipation and emergence as independent states, their revolutions and *coups d'état*, have been the special concern of statesmen, politicians, businessmen, scholars and journalists, and of equal interest to the general public.

An appreciation of the present-day problems of Arab countries and of their immediate neighbours demands a certain knowledge of their geographical and social background; and a knowledge of the main trends of their history—political, cultural and religious—is essential for an understanding of current issues. Arabs had existed long before the advent of Islam in the seventh century AD, but it was with Islam that they became a world power. Arab civilization, which resulted from the contacts the Arabs had of this world power, and which reached its height in the ninth, tenth and eleventh centuries, was, for a few centuries that followed, the guiding light of a large part of the world. Its rôle cannot, thus, be ignored.

The Arab Background Series provides the English-speaking, educated reader with a series of books which attempt to clarify the historical past of the Arabs and to analyse their present problems. The contributors to the series, who come from many parts of the world, are all specialists in their own fields. This variety of approach and attitude creates for the English-speaking reader a unique picture of the Arab World.

N. A. ZIADEH

ix

Preface

A scholar who studies the ancient past of south Arabia needs some imposing skills, not least in his linguistic abilities. He must speak Arabic, of course, and understand its syntax, but go further than this and know something of the early language of south Arabia which preceded Arabic and of the dialects into which it was divided. In translating the ancient inscriptions he will encounter new words, and will therefore require a knowledge of other Semitic tongues, both ancient and modern, to help him to deduce their meaning. Because so much of the source material about the "incense kingdoms" of south Arabia derives from the classical authors, he needs a good acquaintance with both Latin and Greek in order to understand exactly what they said and what interpretations lie open to their words. On top of all this he must read the works of other scholars in the same field and to do so he will have to be familiar with the languages in which they are written, principally English, French and German but including others such as Italian and Russian.

I cannot claim enough of such qualifications nor any specialist academic expertise. The limitations of this book will therefore be readily apparent to the true scholar. None the less, I hope it will serve a useful purpose. First and foremost, it is designed to introduce the student and general reader to a fascinating subject on which little has yet been written and much remains to be discovered. But the scholar will, I hope, find it of value too, both as a stimulus, because it offers new thoughts and puts a number of points at issue, and as a reference compendium, because in particular it collects together most of the available information from the classical sources about incense and the areas where incense grew or the incense caravans trudged their weary way.

I have not hesitated to adopt a broad approach to my subject. One cannot look at the trade in frankincense and myrrh in complete isolation from the wider picture of Arabia Felix and the Horn of Africa presented by the Greek and Roman authors. I have described something of what is known about the states and peoples of Arabia at the time, from the incense kingdoms in the south to the Nabataeans and others in the north. In the early chapters I have attempted to analyse the historical information and traditions available in the classical writings, the Bible and other sources in order to see what clues they offer to the origins of the incense trade; this has led to a number of excursions away from the central theme. But apart from this search for a *terminus post quem* date I have thought it wise to keep well clear of the subject of chronology, over which scholars cannot yet agree.

The reader will find several maps in this book to illustrate the text. If he wishes to study points of geographical and topographical detail more closely he will find some areas well covered but others almost entirely without detailed cartography. For a general map of South-West Arabia showing the main pre-Islamic sites, that prepared by Professor Beeston and myself and published by the Royal Geographical Society is, I believe, the only one generally available where the topographical detail is of sufficient accuracy to be of value to historical study. For the enthusiast, there is an excellent small-scale map of ancient Arabia by Professor von Wissmann published in Grohmann, 1968 (see Bibliography), but this is not easy to obtain. The Ḥaḍramawt and the region west of it are thoroughly covered in the two sheets by Von Wissmann/Serjeant published by the Royal Geographical Society.

In transliterating Arabic names in this book I have followed customary spellings for some of the most common and well recognised place-names (e.g. Aden), but have otherwise used the conventional system of transcription using diacritics, the Arabic letter *'ayn* being portrayed by '. But I have not attempted to alter the transliterations of other authors quoted where these differ. Some difficulty arises in transcribing the letter *jīm* in Arabic place-names owing to its pronunciation as a soft "j" in the north of Arabia and a hard "g" in the south. This has led to the spelling "Nagrān" in the text whereas, for the sake of consistency with other spellings, this place is shown in the maps as "Najrān"; both pronunciations are valid.

The extract from Photius quoted at pages 68 to 72 has not, so far as I am aware, been published in English before and I am much indebted to Mr J. S. Hutchinson for his translation from the Greek.

My special thanks are due to Professor A. F. L. Beeston of St John's College, Oxford, who was kind enough to read this book in manuscript and gave his time and advice to me most generously, leading to a considerable number of improvements. His assistance included some scrutiny of the original texts of quotations from the Greek and Latin authors, resulting in several significant and important changes from the published translations normally used. I have acknowledged this help at various places in text and notes, but would like to record here how valuable it has been and how very much it is appreciated.

In preparing the botanical sections of this book, I have received substantial help and advice from Mr F. N. Hepper of the Royal Botanic Gardens, Kew. I hope this is adequately recognised in the text and notes and I am extremely grateful to him.

I must also acknowledge the help of the Director and Librarian of the Royal Botanic Gardens, who enabled me to study their records of the visit of William Lunt to South Arabia with the Bent expedition of 1893.

I am very grateful to Professor R. B. Serjeant, whose advice on several matters was incorporated in this book and who subsequently saw the manuscript and offered a number of other helpful comments.

I also have to thank Professor Dr W. W. Müller, who made a number of useful comments on certain of the chapters. His article on "Weihrauch" for Vol 15 of the *Realencyclopadie von Pauly-Wissowa* contains a most detailed and scholarly study of frankincense, but was unfortunately published after this book was written, and I have been unable to take full advantage of it.

In addition, my thanks are due to Dr Jacqueline Pirenne for information about the incense-bearing trees she found or heard of near Shabwah and to John Carter for information about incense in Oman.

An off-shoot of my work on this book was the paper I gave to the Arabian Seminar in 1976 suggesting that the frankincense region of South Arabia had extended very much further to the west than was supposed. Subsequently Professor Théodore Monod of the French National Museum of Natural History was able to validate this thesis by the discovery of many frankincense trees in South Yemen when he visited it on a botanical expedition. I did not see Professor Monod's published report on this important finding until he kindly sent me a copy in March 1980, by when the typescript of this book had been with the publishers for some time; in consequence there is some roughness in the relevant passages due to the limited amount of amendment which was practicable at that late stage.

I am grateful for the facilities provided by the Librarian and staff of the Library of the School of Oriental and African Studies; also to the Librarian and staff of the Kensington Public Library who, over the years, have courteously and efficiently handled my requests for so many obscure publications and rarely failed to find them for me; also for the assistance and courtesies of the Librarian and staff of the Royal Geographical Society.

In a work of this nature it is extremely difficult to keep abreast of new research and discoveries. In an attempt to do so, many parts of this book have been amended, some more than once, since it was first written. If there are still omissions and errors I can only apologize to those concerned and hope that they will nevertheless find interest and value in the parts which do not offend them.

N. St J. G.

List of Maps and Charts

List of Illustrations

xiv

List of Plates

Plate

ROME AND ARABIA
GENERAL MAP
SHOWING PLACES
MENTIONED IN
THE TEXT

Rome
Puteoli
Ephesus
Delos
Tyre
Alexandria — Gaza
Myos Hormos
Coptos
Berenice
Palmyra
Nineveh
Ur
al-Jawf
Thaj
Gerrha
Tayma
Dedan
Leuce Come
Yathrib
Hijra
Petra
Aelana
Makkah
Turabah
Tabala · as-Sulayyil
Tathlith
Najran Shabwah
Marib
Muza Sanaa
Aksum
Aden
Qana
Moscha
Socotra
Opone
Mundus

Chapter 1

Incense: The Food of the Gods

Incense has had a continuous religious significance through-out the entire expanse of history from the first civilisations to the present day. The Sumerians and Babylonians burned it to purify and to please their gods. From the earliest dynasties the Pharaohs used it as an offering to the gods of Egypt, sending out expeditions to the Land of Punt for the best materials. Balls of incense were found in the tomb of Tutankhamun. Harappan figures of the mother-goddess discovered in the Indus valley and dated to the third millennium BC show stains left by incense smoke. Ritual incense burners have been excavated from Minoan graves in Crete. The Assyrian sculptures at Nineveh depict incense being burned for the sun-god and in many Assyrian relief carvings tall incense stands separate the king from the gods and from his subjects. The very name of the principal Phoenician deity, Baal Hammon, signified "lord of the perfume altar". To the Hebrews the smoke of incense veiled the presence of the deity in the holy tabernacle. The Persians used incense and perfume in their worship and some of the monuments of Persepolis show the king offering incense. The Parthians employed it lavishly and its burning on small altars and incense stands is portrayed frequently in their sculpture. The Greeks and Romans, especially the latter, burned it in vast quantities in their temples. Christians took over the practice, after first abstaining from it, so that incense is used to this day in both the eastern and western churches. Although forming no authorized part of the religious rites of Islam, its use is permitted by the Traditions as a perfume for a corpse, while Muslims frequently offer incense in the shrines of their saints, and Doughty observed the people of al-Madīnah burning it before a sacrifice as "a pompous odour acceptable to God"—survivals, perhaps, of earlier, pagan customs of Arabia. In the religions of the Far East, especially in Buddhism, the burning of incense has formed an essential part of the ceremonials. Bronze incense burners found in China date back to the Shang dynasty (1600–1030 BC). Even in early America incense had a prominent part in religious rituals—the Mayas of Mexico, for example, burned balls of copal incense for their gods.

The spreading of the smoke and fragrance of incense and the visible movement of that smoke upwards towards the heavens has given it a symbolical relationship to prayer, making the offering synonymous with worship. This symbolism has sometimes been extended, so that the four basic components of the holy incense of the Hebrews have been variously held to signify the elements—water, earth, fire and air—or the products of the sea and of the inhabited and uninhabited earth, indicating that all things are God's.

Incense: The Food of the Gods

In ancient Egypt incense was presented to the gods by the king himself in all major ceremonies, sometimes with a libation of wine. Standing before the statue of the god, with a smoking censer in his hand, he can be seen in temple murals praying for help and favour and a long, pure and happy life. Sometimes he would offer two censers, together with oxen, birds, boxes of ointment, or even specially made cakes. Incense and libations were presented by the Pharaoh in the "procession of the shrines" and at the great ceremony of his coronation, when it was also burned by a priest to the sacred white bull. Incense was burned in the service of triumph which followed military successes and in the parading of the sacred boat. It was always burned before the opening of a shrine containing a deity. In Egyptian mortuary rituals the souls of the dead were thought to ascend to heaven in its flame. The "Book of the Dead", the earliest written record of religious and magical ceremonies, calls for the use of incense in many of the rites prescribed to ensure the safety of the departed in the after-life; other passages in that book enjoin the use of incense in ceremonial purification and in other magical activities: to ward off the enemies of the dead, for instance, it was to be burned in four clay troughs, the flame then being extinguished with the milk of a cow; "recite this chapter over the divine chaplet which is laid upon the face of the deceased and cast incense into the fire on behalf of Osiris triumphant", commands another passage, ". . . thus shalt thou cause him to triumph over his enemies . . . this chapter shall be said by thee at dawn and it is a never failing charm". Thus was incense not only a link with the gods but also a means of driving off evil demons.[1]

In the story in Chapter 16 of the Book of Numbers about the rebellion of Korah against Moses, incense is similarly given a magical property, here to bring down the vengeance of God. Each of the two hundred and fifty rebels was ordered by Moses to present himself before the temple carrying a censer of burning incense, so that the Lord could pass his own judgement on their action; "and the earth opened her mouth and swallowed them up . . . they and all that appertained to them went down alive into the pit . . . and they perished." But in the continuation of the story a new property is revealed for incense, when plague broke out among the people. Moses

3

then commanded Aaron to "take a censer and put fire therein from off the altar, and put on incense, and go quickly unto the congregation, and make an atonement for them." This Aaron did—"and he stood between the dead and the living; and the plague was stayed", although "fourteen thousand seven hundred people" had died before this early example of fumigation had taken effect.

Nowhere has the use of incense been more exactly prescribed than in the Jewish religion. In the Old Testament and certain Rabbinical texts we have detailed accounts of its composition and the ceremonies surrounding its use. The priests in the temple burned incense every morning when the lamps were trimmed and again at the time of the dawn sacrifice, when the lamps were lit in the evening and for the evening sacrifice. A special incense altar was located in front of the veil which separated the Holy Place from the Holy of Holies and some two pounds weight of incense was consumed in the temple every day. Originally only the high priest offered incense, but in course of time the role fell to a junior priest chosen by lot, a special merit being attached to this office. The chosen priest selected another to take the fire from the brazen altar, using a small silver shovel to collect the burning charcoals, which he then transferred into a smaller censer of gold. A third priest was appointed to clean the ashes of the previous offering away from the altar. The incense was stored in the House of Abtines and brought from there in a phial carried in a golden vessel, the temple being cleared of people before the priest bearing it entered the Holy Place. While the congregation outside observed complete silence, the priest then cast his incense on to the fire, bowed towards the Holy of Holies and withdrew backwards, avoiding delay in order not to alarm the congregation, for it was feared that if he performed the rite improperly he might be struck dead. On emerging, he would pronounce the blessing and the congregation then burst into song. On the Day of Atonement the priest carried a censer of live coals into the Holy of Holies, placed it on the Ark and sprinkled incense on the fire, remaining inside until the smoke had completely filled the room before he emerged backwards to offer prayers. In later times one of the quarrels between the Sadducees and Pharisees arose over a Sadducee contention that the priest ought to light the incense before he entered the Holy Place, lest he see the form of God before the incense smoke could veil it.

The burning of incense in the temple in New Testament times is attested by Luke in the story of Zacharias, where he records: "And it came to pass that while he executed the priest's office before God in the order of his course, according to the custom of the priest's office, his lot was to burn incense when he went into the temple of the Lord and the whole multitude of the people were praying without at the time of incense. And there appeared unto him an angel of the Lord standing on the right side of the altar of incense."

The early Greeks did not use incense in their rituals, although Homer (c.850 BC) refers in the *Odyssey* to an incense altar in the temple of Aphrodite at Paphos, in Cyprus. But the custom began to be favoured in the sixth century BC, when Pythagoras is said to have advocated worshipping the gods with incense rather than animal sacrifices, probably reaching Greece from the Persian-influenced Greek communities in Asia-Minor. Herodotus (c.485–425 BC) knew of frankincense, myrrh, cinnamon and other aromatics as Arabian produce apparently traded by the Phoenicians. In the play *Agamemnon* (c.475 BC), Aeschylus refers to "Syrian perfume sprinkled for the feast", while in Hermippus' comedy *The Basket Carriers* of about 430 BC a list of imports into Athens includes "incense from Syria". Sophocles referred to "the town . . . heavy with a mingled burden of sounds and smells, of groans and hymns and incense" in the opening lines of *Oedipus the King* (c.455 BC), while in his play *The Wasps* (c.422 BC) Aristophanes alludes to the custom of sprinkling incense for a sacrifice a pinch at a time with the thumb and two fingers. There is a story that Menecrates, a physician who had the effrontery to compare himself with Zeus, was effectively deflated by Philip of Macedon, who invited him to a banquet but, while other guests were being treated to a sumptuous meal, served him only with the food of a god—a censer of incense.

From the Roman travel-writer Pausanias we learn that, when the oracle at Patras was consulted, the priestess prayed and offered incense before gazing into a mirror in a sacred well to seek an answer. A Greek inscription of the third

5

century BC lists the gifts made to the temple of Apollo at Didyma, near Miletus, by Seleucos II of Syria; these include frankincense, myrrh, cassia, cinnamon and costum, all incense ingredients.[2]

The Greeks made much use of incense at public festivals. An inscription from Pergamum of about 158 BC recorded the honouring of a dignitary by a public celebration which included the burning of incense to him. Processions connected with the god Artemis at Ephesus were headed by persons bearing incense and, at ceremonies for the oracle at Delphi, Thessalian virgins carried baskets of incense and spices. Athenaeus, an Egyptian Greek of the third century AD, recorded an earlier description of a particularly ostentatious procession organised by Ptolemy II in about 278 BC to impress the Egyptian inhabitants of Alexandria. Near the head of the procession were women dressed as Victory, with golden wings, carrying nine-feet-high censers. These were followed by a double altar covered with gilded ivy leaves, behind which were "boys in purple tunics bearing frankincense and myrrh and saffron on golden dishes". Then, behind various allegorical figures, was carried a large, square, golden altar preceded and followed by other tall, gilded incense burners. Later, in a part of the procession which included chariots drawn by elephants, zebras and other animals (the account was probably exaggerated) came camels carrying "300 minae (pounds) weight of frankincense, 300 of myrrh and 200 of saffron, cassia, cinnamon, iris and other spices".[3]

In Italy incense was being burned by the Etruscans on elegant, long-stemmed incense stands before ever Rome was a city. The earliest historical reference to its use in Rome itself is found in an account by Dionysius of Halicarnassus (died 7 BC) of its offering by the citizens of Rome to greet a victorious returning general in 473 BC, but this may be an anachronism. However, the use of incense to propitiate the gods can be firmly observed from the beginning of the second century BC: Plautus (254–184 BC) mentions it frequently in connection with the worship of the household god and refers to its importation from Arabia. It was soon being burned widely on altars before the statues of deities. At public festivals and triumphs it was borne in procession in censers, while large quantities were burned in front of the temples and in niches

and doorways along the processional route. With the deifi-
cation of the emperors after Octavian it also became customary to burn incense in front of a statue of the reigning
emperor as if he were already a god.

Among the ancients the sacrifice was the principal means
by which the gods were worshipped—to propitiate, to show
gratitude or to induce a favour. Believing that the gods would
be most pleased with the offer of what was held most dearly,
the earliest people of both Greece and Italy made human
sacrifices, but by historical times only domestic animals were
used. In the classical period a small portion of the animal
sacrifice would be burned for the god and the rest consumed
in a festive meal. While the flesh was burning on the altar,
barley-meal, wine and incense were thrown on it to the
accompaniment of prayers and music. At lustrations (the
ceremonial purifying of land, buildings, people or armies)
and at other ceremonies a pig, a sheep and an ox (the
suovetaurilia or *solitaurilia* of the Romans and the *trittya* of
the Greeks) would be paraded and sacrificed in this way. In
course of time libations (the pouring of wine) and offerings of
incense came to be used on their own as sacrifices, as were
offerings of fruit and, in the case of the worshipping of certain
gods including Apollo, ritual cakes.

Incense for the sacrifice was usually kept in a small box
called by the Romans *acerra* (Greek *libanotris*), some of these
being also used as censers to be placed in front of a corpse. In
Greek ceremonies incense was sometimes carried by a virgin
on a flat circular basket on her head (the *kaneon* or *canistrum*)
on which was also laid a chaplet of flowers and the sacrificial
knife. Both the sacrificer and his victim would wear garlands.

The sacrifice was usually made on an altar, the *ara* (Greek
bomos or *thuterion*), the larger, higher altars found in temples
being known as *altare* (from *alta ara*). Some altars were cube-
shaped and others cylindrical, those used for burnt offerings
having recesses in their tops. They were usually elaborately
carved and would be decorated with garlands. Animal
sacrifices were made only on outside altars placed in front of
the temple, altars within the building being used for the
bloodless sacrifices, including the burning of incense. But
incense was also burnt in other vessels—sometimes in an
acerra as already noted; sometimes on a bronze tripod altar

(*tripos*), many of which imitated the table used by the priestess of the Delphi oracle; or in a portable censer called *turibulum* (Greek *thumiaterion*), which took many shapes from squat to tall and thin—these often had feet to enable incense to be burned in greater quantity than on an altar by allowing air to be drawn through the fire from below. In the homestead, where sacrifices were offered to the household spirits (*lares*), incense might also be burned on a brazier (Latin *foculus*, Greek *espia* or *eokhara*).

But even in very early days it was not just for religious purposes that incense was a highly desirable commodity. The ancient Egyptians understood the more practical properties of the material, so that after the sacking of Memphis in the eighth century BC the king appointed men to purify the city with natron and incense. Purification may have been behind the Assyrian custom, mentioned by Strabo, of offering incense immediately after sexual intercourse.[4]

The synoecism of communities from which the first civilisations developed brought about considerable sanitation problems which could be met only in most primitive ways. In the warm climates of the Mediterranean and Middle East, putrefaction of waste sets in quickly. Disagreeable smells pervaded the air. Pestilential insects, especially flies and mosquitoes, abounded and had to be kept at bay by a pleasant smoke. In such conditions incense and perfumes became very necessary for comfortable living and were used widely, the more effective of these substances becoming the expensive luxuries of the rich. Foremost among the materials used were frankincense and myrrh. These had an excellence of quality exceeding that of almost every other plant produce, not only for incense and perfumes but also for other applications, especially in medicine.

Demand exceeded the supply, and transport expenses were high. Consequently the cost of frankincense and myrrh was considerable. By the time of the Roman Empire the enormous demand for these rare products had so swelled the price that they could be equated with gold. Thus we find gold, frankincense and myrrh together as the gifts brought to the infant Jesus in the legend of the Magi. These gifts gave rise to a further symbolism, where gold represents the emblem of royalty, frankincense betokens divinity, and myrrh, a word

Incense: The Food of the Gods

derived from the Arabic for "bitter", signifies Christ's persecution and death. Myrrh, indeed, had a further place in the Christian story. It was a part of the last gift to Jesus, before he was crucified—"and they gave him to drink wine mingled with myrrh; but he received it not" (Mark 15.23)[5]— while, after the crucifixion, Nicodemus brought "a mixture of myrrh and aloes, about an hundred pound weight" (John 19. 39), with which the body of Christ was wound in linen cloth before burial.

Quite when frankincense and myrrh first came into general use in the ancient world is obscure and the problem is examined in more detail in later chapters. The trees from which true frankincense and myrrh were extracted grew only in southern Arabia, Somalia and parts of Ethiopia. Clearly, from what has already been said, the Greeks were using frankincense imported from Syria in the fifth century BC, but south Arabian aromatics seem to have been used by the Persians and others before then. In course of time a regular and eventually a substantial trade developed from south Arabia to meet the requirements of Egypt and Mesopotamia, Greece and Rome, India and even China. Huge camel caravans trudged seventeen hundred miles up the length of the Arabian peninsula along the great incense road, carrying these precious commodities, together with other valuable spices, to the temples and courts and markets of the north, while intrepid Greek and Roman sailors later ventured down

9

the Red Sea to augment the supply. This trade lasted for a thousand years. In that time the Arabs of south Arabia, who controlled it, gained a reputation for enormous wealth derived from its profits and their country became known as Arabia Felix—Happy Arabia or Arabia the Blessed.

At the very start of this work we must kill a myth. Undoubtedly the incense trade was important to the states of south Arabia, but the belief that the whole pre-Islamic civilisation of south Arabia was nurtured and developed on the incense profits can now be seen as without foundation. This belief has persisted ever since the glowing description of south Arabian wealth provided by the classical authors, who assumed that the very high cost of frankincense and myrrh in the Greek and Roman markets represented a vast profit to the growers. But that cost was in great measure due to the considerable expense of transporting the commodity over a very great distance through many different states and tribal areas, to each of which customs and service charges had to be paid. Much of the final sale price was thus expended over a wide area of Arabia and the people of south Arabia received only a portion. It was not an unimportant trade, particularly to the kings of Ḥaḍramawt who exercised a monopoly over frankincense, but the high cultural level achieved by the people of pre-Islamic south Arabia was the result of their own diligence. Some of their luxuries were obtained in exchange for frankincense and myrrh, the two main commodities they could offer which were in high demand elsewhere, but most of the population was concerned with farming and had very little to do with incense. They formed an agricultural society with a particular skill in the undertaking of highly organised irrigation schemes, a skill finding its zenith in the famous dam at Mārib, one of the great engineering achievements of early man. More than five thousand inscriptions are known from these ancient days, providing a wealth of detail about religious, military, agricultural and other matters, yet in none of them has any significant mention come to light about the incense trade.

To the outside world Arabia was synonymous with the incense lands. To the average south Arabian of those days agriculture and irrigation were the key to economic survival. Yet the people of Arabia Felix gained significantly from the incense trade in a more subtle way. It gave them a direct and continuous contact with the Mediterranean lands. At an early stage in the formulation of the alphabet in the area of the Fertile Crescent the idea was conveyed down the sub-continent to south Arabia, leading to the development there of a script of exceptional elegance. While this spreading of a manner of writing may have been due more to population movements than to regular trading connections, it was down the incense route that there later flowed the great cultural influence of classical Greece and Rome, so that new ideas were blended with local conceptions, producing a distinctive form of art and architecture which is an important feature of the early south Arabian civilisation and was to spread both to other parts of Arabia and into Ethiopia.

Just what were frankincense and myrrh and how do they relate to incense? Before we can go further an explanation is necessary of the terminology used, some looseness in which will already be apparent, while a more precise description must be provided of the commodities we are discussing and how they are scientifically distinguished.

The term "incense" is used in a variety of ways. In its widest sense it is the material which emits fragrant fumes by burning or by volatilization (i.e. rapid evaporation caused by heat or exposure). Often it means the odours created by that process. The material so used may be compounded of a variety of gums, resins and spices. In ancient times, as already shown, it was usually sprinkled on lighted charcoal on an incense altar or in a censer, or it could be applied to the person in the form of an unguent. In modern times it is invariably burned rather than applied as an unguent.

In a narrower meaning "incense" refers to the gums and resins which formed the principal ingredients of this material, the main ones being frankincense and myrrh. When we talk of the "incense trade", the "incense road" and the "incense lands" it is in this sense.'

But there is a still narrower meaning, because "incense" is often used to signify "frankincense", the produce of a tree of the genus *Boswellia*, as distinct from "myrrh", which comes from the genus *Commiphora*. In this sense there is a further confusing factor, because frankincense is sometimes held to be only the "true frankincense", also called "commercial frankincense", which is derived from species of *Boswellia* found only in south Arabia and Somalia. This was the frankincense most sought after in the days of classical Greece and Rome. But other varieties of frankincense deriving from other species of *Boswellia* are found elsewhere, in India and Africa, as we shall see. When "frankincense" is held to mean the "true" or "commercial" frankincense, then the other varieties may be called simply "incense" to distinguish them.

In the same way that the term "incense" will be found loosely and sometimes confusingly used, the words "gum" and "resin" are often used quite synonymously, when in fact there is a scientific difference between them. Certain trees exude a liquid from their bark either as a result of natural causes or when incisions are made in them. Some of these excretions remain liquid, usually thick and syrupy, and are known as oleo-resins (e.g. turpentine) or balsams. Others soon harden and may eventually become solid. These are the gums and resins and what are known scientifically as "gum-resins". Resins (ladanum and mastic are examples) will not dissolve in water, but are usually wholly or largely soluble in alcohol, whereas gums will not dissolve in alcohol, but are either soluble in water or capable of absorbing sufficient water to form a mucilage. Gum Arabic, which derives from several species of the acacia tree, is an example of the latter. But it is the third group, the "gum-resins", which interest us most here. These, as the name implies, are a mixture of both gum and resin and contain a small portion of volatile oil. They include various bdelliums and also frankincense and myrrh. Unfortunately, in studying the ancient trade in incense and the uses to which it was put, we have to recognize that this scientific differentiation was not properly understood in ancient times and the terms were used then with as much confusion as is found today.[6] Moreover, in modern Arabic parlance some similar looseness of terminology exists and this can add to the confusion.

Both myrrh and frankincense contain a small quantity of volatile oil, which gives the material its fragrance. There is considerably more oil in myrrh, up to 17 per cent of total volume, and naturally the quantity is greatest (and hence the fragrance more pronounced) when the material is fresh.[7] In ancient times a process was developed for extracting the oil from myrrh, producing the highly prized myrrh-oil also known as stacte. Theophrastus, a botanist, and Dioscorides, a physician, have both left descriptions of this process from classical times, but the methods they quoted differ and neither would appear to have portrayed the process accurately. Pliny refers to stacte as the liquid which exuded naturally from the myrrh tree before the gum was collected from man-made incisions; possibly he did so because this exudation contained more oil than the later excretions and was therefore more suitable for the extraction process. But however obscure may be the accounts of how stacte was obtained, its importance in ancient times in the manufacture of perfume cannot be disputed.

Frankincense, also known as "olibanum", was the pre-eminent material for creating fragrant smoke by burning. Although sometimes compounded with other materials, as we have already seen in the case of the holy incense of the Hebrews, it was much used on its own, especially by the Greeks and Romans. In Arabic the usual word for frankincense is *lubān*, from the Semitic root signifying whiteness which also conveys an inference of purity. This name is repeated in the Hebrew *lebōnāh*, in Akkadian *lebanatu* and, derivatively, in the Greek *libanos* or *libanotos*. The Latin for it is *tus*.[8]

In ancient south Arabia frankincense was a sacred commodity and its harvesters worked under ritualistic restraints. It was stored in the temples and burned as offerings to the gods, particularly in conjunction with sacrifices. South Arabian incense burners of these times were small cube-shaped altars with a cavity in the top surface and usually with four short legs. Incense burners were often placed in tombs.[9]

Besides using frankincense to create aromatic smoke, the Hebrews also placed it on other religious offerings to give them an additional sanctity. Thus, in Leviticus 2. 14–16 we find it instructed: "if thou offer a meat offering of thy first fruits unto the Lord . . . thou shalt put oil upon it, and lay frankincense thereon . . . and the priest shall burn the memorial of it, part of the beaten corn thereof and part of the oil thereof, with all the frankincense thereof; it is an offering made by fire unto the Lord". Again, in Leviticus 24. *et seq.*, the shew-bread was to be set out on the altar "and thou shalt put pure frankincense upon each row, so that it may be on the bread for a memorial, even an offering made by fire unto the Lord. . . . And it shall be Aaron's and his sons'; and they shall eat it in the holy place."

We have already talked of the place of incense in ordinary life to combat the bad smells of primitive urban conditions. Frankincense was of special importance here to those who could afford it, especially in Greece and Rome. At funerals it not only had a religious significance, to propitiate the gods, but when cremation replaced interment it also served the more practical purpose of disguising the odour of burning flesh. The Romans began to use it increasingly lavishly for this purpose, until vast sums were being squandered on it. "(Arabia's) good fortune has been caused by the luxury of mankind even in the hours of death," Pliny said laconically, "when they burn over the departed the products which they had originally understood to have been created for the gods. Good authorities declare that Arabia does not produce so large a quantity of perfume in a year's output as was burned by the Emperor Nero in a day at the obsequies of his consort Poppaea. Then reckon up the vast number of funerals celebrated yearly throughout the entire world, and the perfumes such as are given to the gods a grain at a time, that are piled up in heaps to the honour of dead bodies! Yet the gods used not to regard with less favour the worshippers who petitioned them with salted spelt." [10] An earlier example of this profligacy is found in Plutarch's description of the funeral in 79 BC of the infamous tyrant Sulla: "The women contributed so great a quantity of aromatics . . . that without including what was conveyed in two hundred and ten litters, there was enough to make a large figure of Sulla, and also to make a lictor out of costly frankincense and cinnamon." [11]

But frankincense also had a considerable part to play in the medicine of the ancient world, especially in Greek and Roman times. We find much evidence of this in the work of Celsus—*De Medicina*—where there are prescriptions for its use in medicines for pains in the side and chest, bruises, paralysed limbs, ulcers and abscesses, wounds and "broken heads", haemorrhages in mouth and throat, haemorrhoids, and as an antidote to hemlock. Dioscorides, in his *Materia Medica* of about AD 65, includes frankincense in his lists. [12]

Theophrastus also mentioned it as an antidote to poisoning by hemlock.[13] Cato had a veterinary use for it, in his work on agriculture, recommending it to cure worms in animals.[14]

In the fourth or fifth century AD (probably) an eminent Greek physician in Alexandria who has not been identified gave a series of lectures on medical matters which were later translated into Syrian for the benefit of Syrian doctors and medical students. Part of a manuscript containing this work has survived and is known as "The Syriac Book of Medicine". In it frankincense has substantial mention. It is an ingredient in various prescriptions for headache, nose-bleeding, catarrh (by inhalation of the smoke), diseases of the eyes and ears, general pain, gout, palsy, spasms, dropsy, laxness of the joints, ailments affecting the voice, throat and lungs, dysentery, colic, haemorrhage, diarrhoea, coughing, pleurisy, stomach pains, diseases of the liver, kidney and bladder, jaundice, hardness of the spleen, nausea and ailments of the anus; in addition frankincense berries were recommended for clearing the throat, frankincense bark as an ingredient in a medicine for haemorrhage and "dust of frankincense" as an ingredient in an all-purpose unguent called Fillet of Musk.[15]

Frankincense continued to be used for medicines in the Middle Ages. The great tenth-century Persian physician and poet Avicenna, for example, recommended it for tumours, ulcers on the head, ears and breast, vomiting, dysentery and fever, while the *Tāj al-'Arūs* described it as useful for stopping phlegm and as a dispeller of forgetfulness.[16] It is still used medicinally in south Arabia today. In Yemen a beverage prepared with pounded frankincense was thought to combat inflammation of the urethra, phthisis and shock paralysis.[17]. In Somaliland it has been used for venereal complaints[18] and as an external application on carbuncles, boils and gangrenous sores. In India it has been applied to swellings, used as a local astringent, detergent, fumigant and detersive and to promote menstruation.[19] In China it has been regarded as a remedy for leprosy. In south Arabia it is still used for purifying and sweetening drinking water[20] and as a fumigant.

Frankincense has had and still has other uses in recent times. The Jews of Yemen used to burn it at funerals and to assist labour during childbirth. Arab women of south Arabia have used it during the celebrations following a birth, partly to appease evil spirits.[21] South Arabian beduin have used it to fumigate the hair, and in some parts of south Arabia it is burned at the time of taking an oath. In Zufār it is used as a wax depilatory and burned to keep away "jinns". In Yemen and Ḥaḍramawt it provides a deodorant, a chewing-gum, a tooth-filling and even a means of sealing cracks in household utensils,[22] while in parts of Ḥaḍramawt a custom exists under which it is burned by a tribesman guilty of a crime as part of a ritual designed to prevent his guilt falling on the rest of the tribe.[23]

We have good examples of the more normal use of frankincense by burning in the writings of the nineteenth-century travellers, the Bents. Of the Arabian "palaces" they visited in the Ḥaḍramawt they wrote: "Every guest room has . . . also carved censers in which frankincense is burnt and handed round to the guests, each one of whom fumigates his garments with it before passing it on. It is also customary to fumigate with frankincense a tumbler before putting water in it, a process we did not altogether relish as it imparts a sickly flavour to the fluid."[24] Later Mrs Bent visited the *harem* and recorded: "Presently the women who had prepared the frankincense brought it down in a small chafing dish, continuing the same chant and handing it round. I wondered if I should be left out, or left to the last, but neither happened and when my turn came, like the rest, I held my head and hands over the fumes and we were all fumigated inside our garments."[25] But the ancient use of frankincense to combat bad smells also continued into modern times and the Bents had cause to be glad of it; of their journey in a dhow they wrote: "In our little cabin in the stern the smell of bilge-water was almost overpowering, and every silver thing we had turned black. . . . These pungent odours were relieved from time to time by burning huge chafing dishes of frankincense, a cargo of which was aboard for transport to Bombay."[26]

Wyman Bury, a Political Officer in the Aden Protectorate early in the twentieth century, described his visit to a saint's tomb which was attended by an aged woman: "Within the gloomy precincts of the shrine . . . stood a tall-ridged tomb of clay . . . at the foot of (which) were two or three shallow receptacles hollowed out in a clay plinth. Into these we put our offerings in cash and frankincense. The old lady brought some live charcoal, and as the sickly-sweet fumes of the incense arose in that close, stifling atmosphere, she took the cash offering in her clenched fist, wherewith she smote the flank of the tomb thrice."[27]

A later traveller, the entomologist Dr Hugh Scott, described the use of frankincense at a meal in a mountain village north of Aden: "A large earthenware vessel with glowing charcoal and incense was passed round, and each person made a movement of taking a handful of smoke and putting it up his nostrils. . . . Later, in the Arab quarter of San'a, an old man was seen to be carrying a smoking censer suspended from an iron arm on a long staff with a spike at the bottom. Apparently he visited tea-houses or hired himself out to parties, planting his pole and censer in the earthen floor."[28]

The word "myrrh" derives, as we have said, from the Semitic root *murr*, meaning "bitter" (Arabic *murr*, Hebrew *mor*, Akkadian *murru*). Classical Greek used the words *murra* and *smyrna*, while the Latin word was *murra* and also *myrrha*.

Myrrh, like frankincense, was a major ingredient of most compounded incenses in ancient times. There is some indication in Theophrastus that the Greeks may have burned it on its own as an incense ("some fragrant solids . . . need . . . to be subjected to fire, as myrrh, frankincense and anything that is burnt as incense.")[29] In Assyria, it has been stated, myrrh was burned in a censer, which was placed at the head of a sick person's bed, perhaps as a fumigant.[30] But in classical times, when frankincense came to be used on its own for incense, the most important uses of myrrh were in the making of perfume and in pharmacy.

The special qualities of myrrh for the manufacturing of perfumes were explained by Theophrastus in his treatise "Concerning Odours". Whereas most materials faded rapidly, myrrh would last ten years, even improving with time. Myrrh-oil, or stacte, had the longest life of any perfume known. Once applied to the person, the scent of stacte was one of the longest lasting. Theophrastus also noted that myrrh could be steeped in sweet wine to make the perfume itself more fragrant. The perfume known as "megaleion", highly rated at the time of Theophrastus, included myrrh among its primary ingredients, the others being "burnt resin", cassia and cinnamon.

Pliny described the manufacture of different unguents, observing that: "resin or gum are added to retain the scent in the solid part, as it evaporates and disappears very quickly if these are not added." They kept best, he noted, in alabaster boxes. Of the many perfumes in which myrrh was found, Pliny named: Mendes scent, made of behen-oil, resin and myrrh; Egyptian metopium; some "cheaper kinds of oil"; sisinum; oil of Cyprus; unguent of cinnamon, "the thickest in consistency of all the unguents" and fetching enormous prices; spikenard or leaf-unguent; and the great royal unguent of the kings of Parthia. He also noted that there were nine species of plant resembling the Indian nard which were used for adulterating; these could be rendered "thicker in consistency and sweeter by means of myrrh". He added that: "myrrh even when used by itself without oil makes an unguent, provided that the stacte kind is used—otherwise it produces too bitter a flavour."[31] A Roman official named Theophanes, travelling in Egypt early in the fourth century AD, listed myrrh among his luggage, probably to apply as a lotion after washing.[32]

The fragrance of myrrh is referred to several times in the Old Testament. "Thy God hath anointed thee with the oil of gladness above thy fellows. All thy garments smell of myrrh,

and aloes, and cassia . . . whereby they have made thee glad" (Psalms, 45. 7–8). "Who is this that cometh out of the wilderness . . . perfumed with myrrh and frankincense, with all powders of the merchant?" (Song of Solomon, 3. 6). "I have perfumed my bed with myrrh, aloes and cinnamon" (Proverbs, 7. 17). "A bundle of myrrh is my well beloved unto me" (Song of Solomon, 1. 13). "I rose up to open to my beloved; and my hands dropped with myrrh and my fingers with sweet smelling myrrh, upon the handle of the lock" (Song of Solomon, 5. 5). "His cheeks are a bed of spices, as sweet flowers; his lips like lilies, dropping sweet smelling myrrh" (Song of Solomon, 5. 13). In Esther 2. 12 the girls selected for the Persian court of King Ahasuerus were prepared over a twelve-month period "to wit, six months with oil of myrrh, and six months with sweet odours and with other things for the purifying of women". However, in some of these passages there is an inference that the perfume in question was a liquid one and we cannot be too sure whether the reference is to stacte or to another oil made with myrrh or perhaps even to the rare perfume called Balm of Gilead, which was produced in Palestine.

"Pure myrrh" was one of the main ingredients of the holy anointing oil of the Jews, as laid down in Exodus, other components being cassia, sweet cinnamon, sweet calamus and olive oil. This was used to anoint not only the high priests ("Aaron and his sons") but also objects in the temple, including the tabernacle, the ark, the table, the candlestick, the altar of incense and the altar of burnt offerings.[33]

Theophrastus noted that myrrh was sometimes added to wine to give it "point" by the touch of astringency which it imparted. Aristotle, according to Athenaeus, wrote that myrrh and aromatic rush and other similar materials were boiled in water, the resultant liquid being added to wine to diminish drunkenness. Athenaeus also recorded a note by Antiphanes about the use of myrrh in cooking: "into the appetizer these ingredients were also put—pepper, a salad leaf, myrrh, sedge and Egyptian perfume."[34]

Herodotus described the use of myrrh by the Egyptians of his time for embalming. Three processes were available, varying in cost. In the most expensive of these the body, emptied of its organs and cleansed, would be "filled with pure bruised myrrh, cassia and every other aromatic substance with the exception of frankincense," then sewn up again and left to soak in dry natron for seventy days.[35] A rather different process was described by Diodorus, in which myrrh was rubbed on to the eviscerated and cleansed body in order to preserve and perfume it.[36] It is uncertain how far back in history pure myrrh, as opposed to some other similar material, was used for embalming. The matter of the use of myrrh in ancient Egypt is examined in greater detail in the next chapter.

The use of myrrh in medicine was extensive in Greece and Rome and throughout the Middle East. Assyrian cuneiform texts show that in Mesopotamia myrrh was used in making poultices for the head, for treating blains and chilblains and ailments of the eye, nose, ear, and anus; it was also mixed with alum for a mouthwash, prescribed for strangury and used as an enema. Myrrh oil was used for mouth infections and as a medium for other drugs.[37] According to Celsus, myrrh was used internally in medicines to cure dropsy and quartan fever and as an antidote to poison, while it was an ingredient in prescriptions applied externally for the relief of pain in the side and liver, for inflammation of the ears and earache, for treating eye diseases, for haemorrhoids, bladder-stones, inflammation of the uvula and genitals, for inducing menstruation, for abscesses and in plasters for "broken heads". In many of these prescriptions it was used together with frankincense. It has been suggested that it was as an analgesic that myrrh added to wine was offered to Jesus at the Crucifixion.

In the Syriac *Book of Medicine*, which has already been described, myrrh features in a large number of prescriptions for a wide variety of ailments, again frequently in conjunction with frankincense. In addition to those mentioned by Celsus, these include headache, delirium, falling sickness, paralysis, fatigue, spasms, palsy, gout, coughs, many ailments of the chest, throat and mouth, toothache, stomach pains, diarrhoea, haemorrhages, phthisis, dropsy, pleurisy, palpitations, hiccoughs, insect bites and stings, constipation, dysentery, nausea, jaundice and ailments of the digestion, liver, spleen, colon and anus. In addition stacte appears in prescriptions for a number of other ailments.[38] Eighteenth-century Arab lexicographers knew myrrh only as a medicine "useful for coughs when sucked in the mouth and for the sting of the scorpion when applied as a plaster, and for worms of the intestines when taken in the mouth in a dry state or licked up from the palm of the hand".[39]

In modern times myrrh has continued to be used for local medicines in the myrrh-growing areas. In Somalia it has been given in a diluted emulsion to newly born children and also used for venereal complaints and, in animal husbandry, to improve the yield of milch camels.[40] Different varieties of myrrh have also been used as a stimulant, astringent and purgative, for rheumatism, to induce sweating, to heal wounds, as a chewing gum, as a shampoo, as a fumigant and as a tooth-powder. Sometimes myrrh was added to food. The Bents wrote of their journey to the west of Aden: "The sultan sent to our camp some bowls of food, soup and a fowl cut up and cooked in gravy, very rich with oil and onions. It would have been good but for the stuffy, bitter taste of myrrh, which they like so much to put in their food."[41]

The confusion with the bdelliums makes it difficult to determine the uses of myrrh very precisely and the different types of myrrh undoubtedly had different applications in ancient times just as they have had nearer to the present day. The commercial value of myrrh in modern times has been based mainly on its use in perfumery and for making incense and incense sticks rather than for its medicinal use. But myrrh still has a place in Western pharmaceuticals, mainly in mouthwashes and gargles, for ulcers in the mouth and pharynx and in special toothpastes.[42]

Chapter 2

When the
Trade Began

In about 1500 BC the walls of the great Egyptian temple at Deir al-Bahari, near Thebes, were decorated with a series of coloured relief frescoes commemorating the journey of a fleet which the queen of Egypt had sent to "God's Land"—the Land of Pwenet or Punt.[1]

Formerly, according to the text on these frescoes, the Land of Punt had been known of only "from mouth to mouth by hearsay of the ancestors. . . . The marvels brought thence under thy fathers, the Kings of Lower Egypt, were brought from one to another, and since the time of the ancestors of the kings of Upper Egypt, who were of old, as a return for many payments; none reaching them except thy carriers."

The Egyptian force had journeyed by land and sea, it is recorded, until it reached the incense terraces. "But I have led them on water and on land, to explore the waters of inaccessible channels, and I have reached the *incense* terraces." It brought back quantities of incense, together with trees in tubs, ebony, ivory, gold ("green gold of Emu"), cinnamon, eye-paint, apes, monkeys, dogs and leopard skins, even some natives and their children. "Never was brought the like of this for any king who has been since the beginning." Some of the incense trees appear to have been planted in the temple courtyard as an offering to the god Amon.

Five ships are depicted in these reliefs, piled high with the treasures obtained for Queen Hatshepsut. One of the pictures shows the Egyptians bartering with the chief of Punt, named Perehu, who wears rings on one of his legs and is accompanied by a remarkably fat wife named Eti. The village of

22

this chief consists of round huts on piles, with ladders leading up to the doors, and it has been observed that the people shown are partly negroes and partly persons of Hamitic stock. Thirty-one small incense trees are being carried on board in tubs. There are date palms with baboons climbing them and, in fragmentary remains, giraffes, a lioness, cheetahs on leashes and even what appears to be a rhinoceros or hippopotamus (only his legs and tummy still remain). Other baboons swarm over the ships while they are being loaded.

In fact Queen Hatshepsut was not the first Egyptian monarch to send an expedition out for treasures from the Land of Punt. Early ritual texts show that incense was in use many centuries before, being mostly brought overland to the Upper Nile by traders ("brought from hand to hand") and not sought out by the Pharaohs. But during the fifth dynasty, around 2800 BC, an expedition had been sent to Punt by King Sahure and another by King Isesi, which latter brought back a dancing dwarf; inscriptions refer to an expedition to Punt under Mentuhotep III (eleventh dynasty, 2100 BC); in the twelfth dynasty (2000 BC) under Amenemhat II a royal officer named Khenketwar recorded his safe return from Punt; another expedition is recorded as having gone there under Sesostris II.

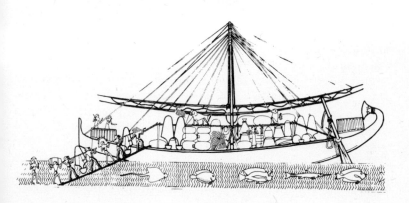

The expeditions of Queen Hatshepsut and the powerful Pharaohs of the eighteenth dynasty may for a while have become almost a seasonal affair, but the great expansion of Egyptian power which these monarchs initiated led to a wealth derived from trade and tribute which made further treasure-seeking journeys unnecessary. Despite bitter quarrelling over the succession, which led to the names of Hatshepsut and her supporters being excised from some of the inscriptions, the temple of Amon was richly endowed and incense began to be used most extravagantly. Hormeheb received "tribute" (perhaps this would be better termed "gifts on exchange") from the chiefs of Punt in the form of gold, ostrich plumes and *incense*.

In the quotations given above the italicized word *incense* represents the ancient Egyptian word '*ntyw*. In fact that word is usually translated as "myrrh"[2], another word *sntr* being held to mean "incense" in its wider sense, although *sntr* is sometimes translated as "frankincense".[3] But a number of authorities dispute the translation of '*ntyw* as "myrrh" and contend that it means "frankincense", arguing from this that, as frankincense came only from south Arabia and Somalia, so the Land of Punt must have been in one or the other of those territories.[4]

In the Deir al-Bahari inscriptions it is quite clear that one variety of incense alone was the most sought after and that was '*ntyw*. The caption to the scene depicting the loading of the ships lists the goods being taken on board in the order: '*ntyw* and '*ntyw* trees, then ebony, ivory, gold, cinnamon wood and *khesyt* wood, then *ihmut* incense and *sntr* incense. This is the only place in the whole of the inscriptions where any kinds of incense other than '*ntyw* are mentioned and it is clear that, coming last in the list, the *ihmut* and *sntr* incenses were in no way so highly regarded. In all the other inscriptions quoted only '*ntyw* is mentioned. *Sntr* here seems to be a name for a specific variety of incense; if it was frankincense, as it is sometimes held to be, then it was clearly not valued as was "true frankincense" in later times.

One of the Deir al-Bahari drawings shows '*ntyw* being measured as an offering to the god Amon, with the queen assisting in the ceremony. "Her majesty herself is acting with her two hands, the best of the '*ntyw* is upon all her limbs, her fragrance is divine dew, her odour is mingled with Punt." In a scene showing the formal ceremony announcing the success of the expedition before Amon, the call from the oracle to send out the expedition is recalled: "a command was heard from the great throne, an oracle of the god himself, that the ways of Punt should be searched out, that the highways to the *'ntyw* terraces should be penetrated." In the final scene, the queen's formal announcement to the court, the sole stated purpose of the expedition is to procure *'ntyw* trees; "a decree of my majesty commanding to send to the *'ntyw* terraces . . . trees were taken in God's Land and set in the ground in (Egypt) . . . for the king of the gods. They were brought bearing *'ntyw* therein for expressing ointment for the divine limbs, which I owed to the lord of gods." In the weighing and measuring scene seven incense trees can be seen in tubs, as they were brought from Punt. In the queen's words: "I have hearkened to my father [i.e. the god Amon] . . . commanding me to establish for him a Punt in his house, to plant the trees of God's Land beside his temple, in his garden, just as he commanded me, for Thebes."

An important feature which emerges twice in these extracts is that the *'ntyw* was to be used as "an ointment for the divine limbs". Nowhere is there mention of burning it as incense. This suggests very strongly that it was a myrrh. The process of obtaining stacte from myrrh seems to have been known in ancient Egypt, where the stacte was called *mdt*; this essence appears to have been mixed with balanos oil, obtained from a tree common in Egypt, which then became perfumed, providing an anointing oil which was used generally and lavishly.[5] Frankincense could not be processed in this manner and was not used in unguents.

In geographical terms it is certainly much more probable that the material brought from Punt would be myrrh rather than frankincense. As we shall see later, the frankincense trees on the African continent grow, with the exception of *Boswellia papyrifera*, only in the eastern region of Somalia, whereas myrrh trees are found very much further to the west, extending, on the evidence of classical as well as of modern authorities, westwards along the Somali coast at least to the area of modern Djibouti and inland to the high plateau area of Dulbahanta, Haud and Ogaden, and to the more northerly region of Wahash in Ethiopia. By coasting down the Red Sea, the Egyptian ships would have reached the myrrh-bearing region long before they reached the main frankincense-bearing region. They could have found myrrh without finding high-class frankincense, but they could not have found such frankincense without also finding myrrh.

The trees depicted in the Deir al-Bahari reliefs being carried on board ship in tubs are sometimes described as "saplings", but in fact they could well be fully grown myrrh trees of the type which grew in the Somali coastal regions: such trees rarely exceed four or five feet in height.[6] But depicted in one panel of the frescoes are three large trees, lush with foliage and drawn as about twenty to twenty-five feet high. It has been held that these are too large to be myrrh trees and that in any case their foliage resembles that of the frankincense tree. This provides support for the contention that it was frankincense which the Egyptians sought from Punt. These trees could represent the Somali frankincense trees, which are of taller species than the Arabian ones, or the tall frankincense tree of the species *Boswellia papyrifera*, which is found in Ethiopia, Sudan and East Africa as well as, it may be supposed, Somalia. But as these pictures are of the trees planted in the courtyard of the temple of Amon it must be expected that the artist would have shown them growing with a luxuriousness fit for a god; the size should not therefore be regarded as botanically significant. In any case all the trees in the Punt frescoes are drawn very stylistically; there is really no differentiation between the incense trees and the trees shown being chopped up to produce ebony logs, while the palm trees are not accurate representations. No safe conclusions can therefore be drawn about the species involved by studying the pictures.[7]

Nor can we be too sure that the myrrh so prized by the Egyptians was the same variety as the myrrh of classical perfumery and pharmacy. West and north of the main myrrh-bearing regions of Somalia and extending into Ethiopia is found the tree *Commiphora erythraea*, which produces a bdellium known as "sweet myrrh" and "perfumed bdellium" and which, as is suggested later, was possibly the "scented myrrh" of Pliny. This product would have been met by the ancient Egyptians long before they reached modern Somalia.

It then becomes questionable whether the Egyptian fleets ever went so far as the Somali coast in their visits to the Land of Punt, since both "sweet myrrh' and an inferior frankincense were available much closer to their shores, on the coast of Eritrea. The possibility that Punt was a part of Ethiopia is demonstrated in the journey made by Sebni, an official of the Pharoah Pepi II, in about 2600 BC, for he went overland to what is thought to have been the Tigre highlands, where he "descended to Wawat and Uthek, and sent on the royal attendant Iri, with two others, bearing '*ntyw*, clothing, one tusk and one hide," presumably to provide his ruler with samples of the products of the land he had discovered; it is demonstrated too in other evidence that the Egyptians received incense overland through the Upper Nile; it is also

27

displayed in the African features of the Deir al-Bahari frescoes—the giraffes and hippopotomus, for example, which completely rule out Arabia—while the Hamitic appearance of the inhabitants of Punt matches that of the Ethiopians.

Punt seems indeed to have been related geographically to Nubia, the ancient Land of Kush, in Sudan. In the scene in the Deir al-Bahari frescoes showing the presentation of tribute to the queen, the chiefs of Punt are seen handing over their gifts together with the chiefs of "Irem" and "Nemyew". Irem, from its mention elsewhere, appears to be a southern region of Nubia and, although Nemyew does not occur in any other inscription, its chiefs are shown as negroes. Other parts of the inscriptions also suggest that Nubian produce was brought back by the expedition. The Pharaoh Thutmose III commemorated his victories in Nubia at a later period in an inscription in which Punt is listed among the districts conquered—a propaganda claim, perhaps, but nevertheless one displaying association of the names geographically.[8]

It would seem that the Pharaohs, knowing that incense was obtained from distant lands to the south of Kush, on the far side of the great mountain mass of Abyssinia, sent their ships down the Red Sea to reach those lands more easily. These ships, sometimes referred to as the "ships of Gebal", were built at the head of the Gulf of Suez and travelled the entire length of the Red Sea, no mean achievement in itself in those early days.[9] The Deir al-Bahari drawings show that they were motivated by a combination of thirty oarsmen and a single broad sail. Almost certainly they will have coasted down the Egyptian side of the Red Sea, for even at the time of frequent Roman sailings to India in the second century AD the eastern coastline was still regarded as dangerous to navigators, "without harbours, with bad anchorages, foul, inaccessible because of breakers and rocks, and terrible in every way".[10] They probably found the coast of Punt in what is now southern Eritrea, perhaps around Assab, and may never have passed through the Bab al-Mandab straits into the more difficult waters of the Arabian Gulf, which they were ill equipped and ill constructed to navigate.[11] Thus south Arabia may not have featured at all in this early search for incense. Certainly there is no historical or archaeological evidence to support the notion sometimes put forward that an organized commerce between south Arabia and Egypt existed in those early times.

But the Land of Punt may never have been a very precisely defined geographical area. The well known *Hymn of Amon*, inscribed on a stela for Amenhotep II, refers to the chiefs of Kush in the south, then to "the countries of the ends of Asia" in the north, the "Tehanu" in the west and, finally, "when I turn my face to the orient, I work a wonder for thee; I cause to come to thee the countries of Punt, bearing all the pleasant sweet woods of their countries, to crave peace with him and breath of thy giving." Here, whatever the poetical license over accuracy of direction, "Punt" seems to be used, much as the term "ends of Asia", to signify a general, distant region rather than any particular country.[12] It may vaguely have included Arabia even though it would seem most questionable whether the Egyptian fleet of Hatshepsut ever landed there.

The Egyptians were not, of course, the only users of incense in these very early days. Inscriptions of Thutmose III, who reigned not long after Hatshepsut and waged vigorous campaigns which conquered Palestine, the ancient "Retenu", record the tribute of the chiefs of Retenu. This included "823 jars of incense" on one occasion[13] and "dry myrrh" and "693 jars of incense" on another.[14] Elsewhere there is mention of "incense" as part of "the harvest of the Lant of Retenu".[15] Incense came from other areas too, for instance in the Syrian tribute paid after a later expedition.[16] The incense of Retenu could be the Balm of Gilead which Pliny mentions as growing in that area and which on some authority is the resin of the terebinth tree[17], but the quantity quoted seems rather too great for a product which, on Pliny's evidence, was exceedingly rare. We have no clear idea of what is meant by "dry myrrh", but any variety of genuine myrrh would have needed to be imported into the Palestine/Syria area. Possibly a trickle of myrrh was traded from hand to hand northwards from south Arabia until it came within reach of the early Phoenicians of Retenu, although there is no firm evidence for such trade at so early a date. In the Amarna letters, myrrh and oil of myrrh are said to have been included among the gifts of Tushratta, the King of Mitanni, to Amenhotep III and possibly to Akhnaton of Egypt.[18]

But the term "incense" in these early Egyptian inscriptions may have signified the wider sense of any gum or resin or other material which, either on its own or in a compound, created a pleasing odour when burned or mixed in an unguent. The ancient perfumes and unguents were often elaborate concoctions. *Metopium*, which had become popular as a scent in Pliny's time, was compounded, from his description, out of "an oil made in Egypt, pressed out of bitter almonds, with the addition of omphacion, cardamom, rush, flag, honey, wine, myrrh, seed of balsam, galbanum and terebinth-resin",[19] while the Royal Unguent of the kings of Parthia was made, according to Pliny, out of "behen-nut juice, costum, amomum, Syrian cinnamon, cardamom, spikenard, cat-thyme, myrrh, cinnamon-bark, styrax-tree gum, ladanum, balm, Syrian flag and Syrian rush, wild grape, cinnamon-leaf, serichatum, cyprus, camel's-thorn, all-heal, saffron, gladiolus, marjoram, lotus, honey and wine".[20] Theophrastus describes the collection of resin from trees in Syria, from the terebinth, which "sets firm, is the most fragrant and has the most delicate smell" and also from the silver-fir and Aleppo pine.[21] Pliny talks about styrax, coming from "the region of Syria beyond Phoenicia nearest to Judaea . . . its tears have a pleasant, almost pungent scent"[22] and refers to galbanum, the smell of which would drive away snakes and which was also produced in Syria, as was *malobathrum*, used for unguents, of which Pliny observed that "its scent, when it is put in slightly warmed wine, surpasses all others."[23]

Although Theophrastus and Pliny have left details of the composition of early perfumes and unguents, neither described the preparation of incense burned to produce odours. By Pliny's time, in fact, it is clear that to the Romans the only incense worthy of the name was frankincense on its own—the pure, commercial frankincense which came from south Arabia and Somalia. Nor do we know much about the composition of the incense burned by the Egyptians in these earlier days, although murals survive depicting the censers used, which were held with one hand while small balls of incense were thrown on them with the other.[24] But in the Old Testament we are given complete details not only of the composition of the holy anointing oil—myrrh, cinnamon, sweet calamus, cassia and olive oil[25]—but also of the preparation and use of incense. In the rituals of the tabernacle the fragrant smoke of incense was held to veil the presence of the Deity and its preparation was therefore minutely prescribed. The basis was laid down in Exodus 30.34–36: "And the Lord said unto Moses, take unto thee sweet spices, stacte and onycha and galbanum; these sweet spices with pure frankincense: of each there shall be a like weight; and thou shalt make it a perfume, a confection after the art of the apothecary, tempered together, pure and holy: And thou shalt beat some of it very small and put of it before the testimony in the tabernacle of the congregation, where I will meet with thee: it shall be unto you most holy." In later times numerous other ingredients have been added to the basic four—myrrh, cassia, spikenard, saffron, costus, cinnamon, sweet bark, salt, amber of Jordan, and a secret herb known as "the smoke raiser". As we shall see, this passage from Exodus does not provide historical evidence for the use of frankincense and myrrh from south Arabia at the time of Moses, because the Pentateuch was not compiled until very much later and contains many such anachronisms;[26] but it demonstrates the use of material such as galbanum, which grew in Syria and Palestine, in the preparation of incense for burning. The locally grown incense given as tribute to Thutmose III by Retenu and Syria was more probably a material such as this than imported frankincense.

Some confusion exists over the nature of galbanum, uncertainty about the plant which produced it in ancient times being complicated by the conflicting statements from Pliny that its smell was repellent to snakes (with a possibly erroneous assumption therefrom that it would be repugnant to human beings)[27] and that it was used in making perfume, as well as by its use as one of the "sweet spices" in the incense of the Hebrews. Galbanum derives from the botanical genus *Ferula*, of which there are well over a hundred species, and the confusion seems to be due to there being several varieties of galbanum. The roots of *Ferula rubicaulis* and *Ferula assa-foetida* yield a gum used in ancient times (Pliny referred to it as "laser") and in Persia and Afghanistan in modern times to flavour food and also medicinally; the root of *Ferula sumbul*, which has similar medicinal uses, is heavily scented and is

31

used in Iran to this day as a perfume and incense; the gum from *Ferula galbaniflua*, or all-heal, appears to have been the "true" galbanum; Theophrastus, calling this gum "khalbane", listed some of its medicinal uses[28] and it is still used widely for medical purposes. But other species of *Ferula* also yield gums.[29]

There is archaeological evidence for the use of incense in Palestine and Syria in the second millennium BC. At Hazor, for example, in a stratum dated to the fifteenth century BC, a unique drainage channel was found made up in part of disused incense stands; in a temple of a slightly later stratum was found a basalt incense altar in the form of a square pillar bearing a relief carving showing the divine symbol of the sun god; in a fourteenth century BC stratum were discovered alabaster incense vessels and other ritual objects. At Megiddo elaborate pottery incense bowls on tall stands were found in a stratum dated to the eleventh century BC, while a horned limestone incense altar is attributed to a stratum of 1050–1000 BC.[30]

These and many other discoveries clearly confirm the use of incense in the Fertile Crescent outside of Egypt long before the days of Solomon, but they do not establish that the incense used was frankincense or that it came from south Arabia. In Mesopotamia incense was used in even earlier

times in the religious ritual of the Sumerians, but here the evidence points to the burning of aromatic woods, such as cypress and cedar, rather than gums.[31] In his work on Assyrian botany, R. Campbell Thompson identified those plants mentioned in Assyrian texts which exuded oils or gums used medicinally for fumigation. These include galbanum, storax, pine, juniper, cedar, fir and wormwood. Frankincense is not included, unless the word *kanaktu* might mean frankincense (olibanum) rather than opoponax as has been more generally supposed; but that alternative is proposed in order to find a place in the list for frankincense, on the assumption that it ought to be there, rather than because of any evidence that *kanaktu* had properties identifying it as frankincense.[32] Myrrh is identified in many Assyrian medical texts as an incense or fumigant, and also as a medicine taken internally, but myrrh would not necessarily need to have come from south Arabia. The use of incense in Mesopotamia, Palestine and Syria in these early years cannot therefore be held as evidence for the existence of the incense trade with south Arabia. But there is another factor of considerable significance in determining when that incense trade commenced. That is the date of the domestication of the camel.

The domestication of the camel was one of the most significant economic developments of the ancient Middle East. It enabled tribal groups to move into or pass through arid areas where life could not previously be sustained; it enabled raiding and warfare to be undertaken over previously impossible distances; it enabled heavy loads of goods to be carried considerable distances through waterless and previously unpassable tracts; and it brought into being a new way of life, that of the desert nomad.

In 1940 the distinguished American biblical archaeologist, Professor W. F. Albright, suggested that the earliest certain evidence for the domestication of the camel could not antedate the end of the twelfth century BC; in the thousands of cuneiform texts from Mesopotamia the earliest reference to an Arabian camel dates to the ninth century BC; in the Cappadocian and Mari tablets there is mention only of caravans of asses.[33] In the Deir al-Bahari reliefs, as we have seen, the Egyptian artist depicted a donkey as the means of transport for the chief of the Land of Punt and in the pictures of animals from that country no camel is portrayed, nor was the camel known in Egypt in those days.

Albright's view has since had to be modified. There is evidence that the camel was being used by man in the Omān peninsula area of south Arabia during the second half of the fourth millennium BC and reason to believe that it was tamed and domesticated in that region over the following millennium.[34] It appears to have been effectively domesticated there by the second millennium. A number of archaeological finds also give some indication of the knowledge if not the existence of domesticated camels in Mesopotamia, Palestine and North Arabia in the third millennium.[35]

Recently Richard Bulliet has suggested that the camel was originally domesticated in south Arabia as a milk animal and form of wealth, its general use as a pack animal coming about later and as a riding animal much later still. In Somalia to this day camels are owned almost entirely for the first of these functions and ridden only very rarely. Bulliet has also demonstrated the difficulties other communities outside south Arabia would have faced in retaining and, more particularly, in breeding domesticated animals brought from south Arabia. Domestication was clearly a very long process and for a very long period it seems probable that the domesticated camel was bred only in south Arabia, with small numbers being brought into Mesopotamia, Syria, Egypt and north Arabia in the course of trade.[36]

The earliest literary reference to a camel is in Genesis 12.16, where, on Abraham reaching Egypt, the Pharaoh gave him "sheep and oxen and he-asses and menservants and maid-servants and she-asses and camels". In Genesis 24, Abraham's servant, sent to collect Rebekah as a wife for Isaak, took with him camels belonging to Abraham on which the bride and her cortège were brought back. A generation later Jakob "set his sons and his wives upon camels" (Genesis 31.17) and was pursued by Laban the Syrian, who failed to find stolen property which Rachel had hidden "in the camel's furniture" (Genesis 31.34). In a subsequent story Joseph was rescued from the pit by a "company of Ishmaelites from Gilead with their camels bearing spicery . . . to Egypt" (Genesis 37.25). These few references may look historically convincing but they lie in a mass of text in which it is clear that the camel had no part to play in the general life of the Israelites. "Thou shalt not covet thy neighbour's ox, nor his ass", it was commanded, without mention of his camel. In all the history and the detail of social and administrative laws in Genesis, Exodus and Leviticus the only animals mentioned elsewhere are the ox, ass, sheep and goat, with the isolated exceptions that the camel is listed among the beasts threatened by murrain during the plagues (Exodus 9.3) and among the unclean animals which cannot be eaten (Leviticus 11.4). Elsewhere Abraham was "very rich in cattle, silver and gold" (Genesis 13.2), but not apparently in camels, while he "rose up early in the morning and saddled his ass" (Genesis 22.3) rather than a camel, as, of course, did the prophet Balaam. These references to camels may in fact be later insertions in the text. An intriguing aspect of them is that camels appear to be used as riding animals only for women and children, possibly reflecting the custom at the time when the references were interpolated.

The patriarchal period can now be dated fairly firmly on historical and archaeological grounds to around 2000–1800 BC.[37] Albright held that all these references to the camel in the Pentateuch must therefore be anachronisms because of the stronger evidence that the domesticated camel was not known at this period.[38] As the Pentateuch did not even begin to take shape as a unified written document for another ten centuries the chances of such anachronistic insertions being made were considerable. Moreover there are other aspects of fable in the stories of Sarah, Rebekah and Rachel. But at the very least it is apparent that the camel was an extremely rare animal in Egypt at this time and was no better known in the Fertile Crescent and north Arabia. Albright noted that the first historical evidence for the camel as a significant factor in the biblical lands was to be found in the raids of the camel-riding Midianites from north Arabia into Palestine around 1100 BC[39] and from this it is concluded that camels cannot have emerged into prominence in north Arabia much before 1200 BC.

Because of the assumption that incense used in Mesopotamia and the Fertile Crescent from earliest days was true frankincense, which could come only from south Arabia and Somalia, it has been held that the south Arabian incense trade must have existed before the camel came into use as a pack animal and that the loads of incense must therefore have been conveyed northwards on the backs of donkeys and, perhaps, mules. This necessarily pre-supposes a route divided into well protected and easy stages, for the donkey, mule and horse cannot travel far without water. While the incense route had become well-defined by Pliny's time, that would seem due in great part to the very importance of the camel-borne trade, which encouraged the digging of wells and the provision of staging posts along the route. In the earliest days the long journey would have been much more difficult and it is doubtful whether donkey caravans could possibly have accomplished it because of the long waterless stretches. But we have now seen that incense used in the north in these times was derived from locally grown plants and trees and is unlikely to have come at all from south Arabia in any quantity.

A study has been made of primitive rock drawings in central Arabia in an area north of Nagrān through which, for reasons of topography, the spice and incense traffic would probably have been funnelled on its journey north. These drawings were left by a people who inhabited the area from the third to the early part of the first millennium BC. The camel appears in them but rarely, and then only as a wild creature which is hunted and speared to death. The ostrich, the ox and an unusual fat-tailed sheep are the most commonly depicted animals (the ox and, in the later phases, the sheep being domesticated); the ibex and lion also appear, together with the wild ass (onager). There is no sign of a domesticated camel or donkey in these drawings and nothing to suggest the passage of trading caravans through the area, although there are graffiti of passing caravans of later eras superimposed over the earlier drawings.[40]

As far as the evidence permits one to draw conclusions at present, it may be supposed that domesticated camels from south-east Arabia were finding their way northwards in small numbers from late in the third millennium BC and that some of them may have been used as pack animals carrying produce from that area for trade. This movement seems likely to have been northwards from Omān round the eastern border of the Empty Quarter to start with, with movement round the southern and western borders of that great desert barrier developing as the area of camel domestication expanded westwards from Omān. The introduction of the camel as a beast of burden would have made the south Arabian incense trade feasible, but there is no reason to suppose that this trade was of any significance before the first millennium BC.

Chapter 3

Bible Stories and the Queen of Sheba

Before one can begin to examine the references in the Bible to incense and the incense lands, some understanding is necessary of how the many books of the Old Testament came to be assembled and of the difficulties and problems of making historical interpretations from their contents.

Much of the early material of the Old Testament derives from oral tradition which was given literary form at a time when writing itself was still being developed. The beginnings of writing date to the fourth millennium BC in Egypt; the literature of Mesopotamia, etched in cuneiform script on tablets of fine clay, dates from about 3500 BC, with ideograms beginning to supplement pictograms by about 2900 BC. But the earliest sign which has yet come to light of the alphabet as we know it dates from about 1500 BC, when Phoenician labourers left inscriptions in a temple in Sinai which were discovered by Petrie in 1904; however, the Phoenician alphabet, with its Egyptian affinities, must already have gone through a long process of development before the turquoise miners of Sinai inscribed their votive dedications. In course of time, by about 800 BC, it was adapted to the Greek tongue and developed into the Greek and Latin alphabets, while another development of it led to the elegant monumental script of south Arabia.

The earliest Old Testament manuscripts were written in Hebrew using the Phoenician script, and it was not until about the second century BC that the "square", or "Assyrian" script, which we would now recognize as "Hebrew" script, was adopted by the Jews in Palestine—paradoxically coming into use when Aramaic, the language of Syria, began to replace Hebrew as their vernacular.

No example survives of any part of the Old Testament written in the ancient Phoenician script, although there are connected pieces, such as the well-known Moabite stone, discovered in 1868, which records the Moabite version of a war with Israel in about 850 BC mentioned in II Kings. The Dead Sea scrolls, the first of which was discovered in 1947, are remnants of a library concealed by the Qumran sect not long before the final suppression of the Jewish revolt of 73 AD; they consist of manuscripts copied in the "square" script over the preceding two centuries, with the earliest fragments dating from the third century BC. Until the Dead Sea scrolls were found, the oldest surviving Hebrew manuscript of any substantial part of the Old Testament dated from about 900 AD.

It is because of the inevitable uncertainty about the original text, due to the change from Phoenician to "Assyrian" script, coupled with the errors which creep in over centuries of copying from one manuscript down to another, that bible scholars attach so much importance to the Septuagint, the Greek translation of the Old Testament, which was sponsored by Jews in Alexandria knowing only the Greek tongue, and which was commenced in about 250 BC.

The Jews recognize the Old Testament as being composed of three parts: the Law, the Prophets and the Hagiographa. The books of the Law (the Torah) are the five books of Moses, known as the Pentateuch, which are the earliest part of the Old Testament and the first to be formally recognized as sacred. The earliest portions of the Pentateuch are variously assigned to dates between 950 BC and 750 BC, but derive from oral tradition and written material of even earlier years, as we have seen in discussing the domestication of the camel. The book of Deuteronomy is thought to be the book discovered in the temple by Hilkiah (II Kings 22.8) in about 621 BC and was probably written in the preceding half century. The Jews attribute the canonization of the Pentateuch, its recognition as the Law, to Ezra in about 400 BC (as recorded in Nehemiah 8).

The books of the Prophets are the historical records of Joshua, Judges, Samuel and Kings as well as the prophetic books of Isaiah, Jeremiah and Ezekiel and the twelve "minor

Prophets". They vary considerably in age and origin. Joshua is probably as old as the Pentateuch; Judges, Samuel, and I and II Kings were assembled together from various materials probably some time after the sacking of Jerusalem and the fall of the monarchy in about 586 BC; Isaiah probably dates, in part, from the eighth century BC. The canonization of these books took place before 180 BC, but the precise date is not known. They were translated into Greek for the Jews of Alexandria by about 150 BC.

Of the Hagiographa, which includes Psalms and Proverbs, it may be noted that the two books of Chronicles date from the fourth century BC. Canonization of the Hagiographa occurred at some time between about 200 and 150 BC and the first Greek translation was made at about the time of Christ's birth.

The significance of canonization in our context is that from the date of it the books in question were copied under tight rabbinical controls with a strict attention to accuracy, making errors in the text less likely to be found, although existing mistakes could of course be perpetuated. Very probably the copy would be required because the existing scroll had become damaged with age, when letters or whole words might even have disappeared. Once the replacement was complete the imperfect original was consigned to the "Geniza", the lumber-room attached to a synagogue, and might later be buried. But research has indicated that there were divergent forms of parts of the canonized text in different rabbinical schools, adding to the difficulties of determining exactitudes of the original text.[1]

The existence of the south Arabian incense trade with the north is testified by Greek historians and by archaeological evidence (for example, the discovery of south Arabian script in Eilath) back to the sixth century BC. Evidence to support the belief that it had existed for long before then is usually derived from passages in the Old Testament, some of which have already been quoted. But the accuracy of these references, particularly the very early ones, as historical evidence is clearly open to question; each needs to be examined with some care to assess the true value which can be placed on it.

We have already observed that the inclusion in Exodus of

frankincense and myrrh among the ingredients of the holy anointing oil and incense seems to be a late insertion and cannot be held to prove the use of these materials in patriarchal times. We have also noted, in the discussion about camels, the story from that period of Joseph, who was sold to "a travelling company of Ishmaelites (who) came from Gilead, with their camels, bearing spicery and balm and myrrh, going to carry it down to Egypt" (Genesis 37. 25). "Balm of Gilead" was possibly a gum drawn from the terebinth tree[2], but here the word used for "myrrh" in the Hebrew text is not the normal *môr* but a word not found elsewhere—*lôt*—which is now thought to mean "ladanum". The belief that this passage provides evidence for the existence of the incense trade at the time of Joseph (i.e. around 1750 to 1550 BC) therefore derives purely from a mistranslation into the English language.[3] There would seem in fact to be no evidence in the Old Testament which establishes the existence of the incense trade at any earlier date than that known through archaeological finds and Greek literature. But what we do appear to find in the Old Testament are references to the people of south Arabia as the people of "Sheba" (being the Hebrew form of the Arabic *Saba'*) long before that name first appears in the work of any Greek writer. This name is used generically to describe all south Arabians, although more properly it designates the people of what was the most prominent of the south Arabian kingdoms.

In chapter 45 of the Book of Isaiah it is recorded:

"1. Thus saith the Lord to his anointed, to Cyrus, whose right hand I have holden, to subdue nations before him. . . .

14. Thus saith the Lord, The labour of Egypt, and merchandise of Ethiopia and of the Sabaeans, men of stature, shall come over unto thee, and they shall be thine. . . ."

In chapter 60 we find the following:

"6. The multitude of camels shall cover thee, the dromedaries of Midian and Ephah; all they from Sheba shall come; they shall bring gold and incense; and they shall shew forth the praises of the Lord."

In the first of these two passages, verse 14 is a portion of a long eulogy of the Persian king Cyrus the Great, whose reign commenced in 559 BC. Isaiah lived in the period of Hezekiah, around 700 BC. However, both passages are contained in the final twenty-seven chapters of the Book, which it is now accepted are not the prophetic utterances of Isaiah at all but the work of another prophet, known as "the second Isaiah", and date from the time of the Babylonian exile, which ended in 538 BC.

A slightly earlier reference may be found in the Book of Jeremiah, who probably lived around 600 BC:

> "To what purpose cometh there to me incense from Sheba, and the sweet cane from a far country? Your burnt offerings are not acceptable, nor your sacrifices sweet unto me." (Jeremiah 6. 20).

In the Book of Ezekiel, another prophet from the time of the Babylonian exile, there is a passage in chapter 27 which is often quoted as a striking reference to trade with south Arabia:

> "1. The word of the Lord came again unto me saying
> 2. Now, thou son of man, take up a lamentation for Tyrus:
> 3. And say unto Tyrus, O thou that art situate at the entry of the sea, which art a merchant of the people for many isles, thus saith the Lord God; O Tyrus, thou hast said, I am of perfect beauty. . . .
> 22. The merchants of Sheba and Raamah, they were thy merchants: they occupied in thy fairs with chief of all spices, and with all precious stones, and gold.
> 23. Haran, and Canneh, and Eden, the merchants of Sheba, Asshur and Chilmad, were thy merchants.
> 24. These were thy merchants in all sorts of things, in blue clothes, and broidered work, and in chests of rich apparel, bound with cords, and made of cedar, among thy merchandise."

The south Arabian connection is argued by equating Sheba with Saba, Canneh with Qana, the south Arabian frankincense port, and Eden with Aden. The reference is then held to be confirmed not only by the mention of "spices" (although there is no mention of "incense") but also by the allusion to "blue clothes", which are claimed to signify the indigo-dyed garments still found in south Arabia in modern times. Were these points firmly based, the reference would be of some importance to historical study, indicating a sea-borne trade with south Arabia from very early times and providing the earliest date by some centuries for "Aden" as the name of the port termed by the classical authors "Eudymon Arabia" or "Arabia Emporium". But this interpretation does not stand up to close analysis. The passage is part of a much longer one in which Ezekiel inveighed against the Phoenician city of Tyre, then threatened by Nebuchadnezzar, and it concerns the trading links of Tyre, which were with Palestine and Mesopotamia rather than with south Arabia. While it is difficult to correlate any of the other names with places in south Arabia, all the names quoted can be correlated with northern cities: Harran is the town on the Euphrates from which Abraham migrated to Ur; Canneh may be Calneh, one of the cities of Nimrod, or Kannu, an Akkadian city; Eden may be Bayt 'Adini, an Assyrian town (Isaiah 37. 12 mentions its conquest by Assyria, together with Harran); Asshur is well known as the city from which the country Asshur, or Assyria, derived its name; Chilmad is thought to be Kilwadha, a place near Baghdad. The place called Sheba in Verse 23 of this passage is now believed by Old Testament scholars to be an interpolation (the Authorized Version is quoted here but in the New English Bible it has been omitted). Moreover, the "blue clothes" are much more likely to refer to the purple dye made from murex shells for which both Tyre and Sidon were famous, while both "broidered works" and cedar chests were exports from Tyre.[4]

In chapter 10 of Genesis there appears a lengthy genealogical tree. This is not simply a list of fathers and sons, but represents the tradition of national and tribal origins throughout the Middle East on the basis of a common ancestry from Noah. The names in it and similar references elsewhere have a geographical as well as a tribal connotation and much Arab tradition stems back to them. Thus Arabs regard the inland regions of south Arabia which border the Empty Quarter as the ancient kingdom of Uz, whose son was Ad,[5] while many south Arabian tribes to this day claim descent from Qahtan, who is identified with Joktan, one of the descendants of Noah's son Shem. Sheba appears in the list as one of Joktan's sons. But another Sheba is to be found in an entirely different line, that descended from Noah's grandson Cush, the son of Ham. One of Cush's sons was Raamah, himself the father of Sheba and Dedan; another was Seba and in this Hebrew spelling the name is thought to refer to the Sabaeans from Arabia who colonized Ethiopia. The plurality of the name is recognized in the sentence "The kings of Sheba and Saba shall offer gifts" (Psalms 72. 8–10). In the passage from Ezekiel quoted above "Sheba and Raamah" may represent tribes or tribal areas in Arabia.

In Genesis 25. 3 there is another reference to Sheba. Here the family of Abraham included, through his wife Keturah, a son Jokshan—"and Jokshan begat Sheba and Dedan." As these ancient genealogical trees frequently miss out many generations (hence the vast ages of many of the patriarchs) these could even be the same two brothers who are listed in Genesis as the sons of Raamah. We can recognize the name Dedan as the ancient city state sited at al-'Ula, near Madā'in Ṣāliḥ, in northern Arabia. Nineteenth-century biblical scholars concluded that the "Cushite Sheba" carried the great Indian trading traffic from the Arabian Gulf to Palestine in conjunction with the "Keturahite Sheba", the former living at the eastern and the latter at the western end of the trade route.[6] There is possible support for the historicity of a northern group of Shebans, or Sabaeans, in non-biblical sources. In 728 BC the Assyrian emperor Tiglath Pileser III recorded that "the inhabitants of Mas'ai, Tema, the Sabaeans . . . (etc) . . . bowed to my yoke," while in 715 BC Sargon II recorded the receipt of gifts (including "aromatic substances") from "Pir'u (i.e. Pharoah), the king of Musru (i.e. Egypt), Samsi, the queen of Arabia and It'amra the Sabaean".[7] Pliny mentions, specifically in the context of the Arabian Gulf area, "a number of islands belonging to the Sabaei" and "the Sabaei, a tribe of the Scenitae (i.e. the tent-dwelling Arab nomads), owning many islands",[8] while Strabo records: "The first people above Syria who dwell in Arabia Felix are the Nabataeans and the Sabaeans. They often overran Syria before they became subject to the Romans."[9]

Clearly it was the people of northern Sheba who appear in the book of Job, despite various arguments for a south Arabian connection. It is apparent that Job was a wealthy tribal chief living in a desert region, but although tradition places Uz in south Arabia and there is a Jobab listed among the sons of Joktan, he seems more likely to be the ruler of Edom called

Jobab who is mentioned in Genesis 36. 33. The pertinent passages are:

"... there came a messenger unto Job, and said, The oxen were plowing, and the asses feeding beside them; And the Sabaeans fell upon them and took them away;" (Job 1. 14–15)

and:

"The troops of Tema looked, the companies of Sheba waited for them." (Job 6. 19).

In their context both of these passages must refer to northern Arabia, the first because the subsequent verses take the story of Job's afflictions a further stage with another messenger who announces a raid by the Chaldeans, the second because Tema would seem to be either Teman, an Edomite district containing the city of Bozrah, or, more probably, Tayma. The linking of Tema with Sheba (Sabaeans) both here and in the text of Tiglath Pileser III quoted above will be noted.

The possibility that there were separate tribes of Sabaeans, or people of Sheba, in the north and south of Arabia is of considerable importance, but has tended to be overlooked, in examining the Old Testament story most closely associated with early south Arabia, that of the visit of the Queen of Sheba to the court of Solomon.[10] This famous story, which is found in I Kings 10 and repeated almost word for word in II Chronicles 9, is linked with an account of Solomon's use of the fleet of Hiram, King of Tyre, for overseas trading ventures and, in quoting it below, the Hiram story is included to show how the two have been interwoven. Solomon's dates are thought to be about 960–930 BC, but the Books of Kings were not compiled until after the fall of the monarchy in 586 BC, Chronicles being put together more than a century later, so that the story had some eight hundred years of development before canonization some time between 200 and 150 BC.

The version in Kings reads as follows:

Chapter 9. "26. And King Solomon made a navy of ships in Ezion-Geber, which is beside Eloth, on the shore of the Red Sea, in the land of Edom.

27. And Hiram sent in the navy his servants, shipmen that had knowledge of the sea, with the servants of Solomon.

28. And they came to Ophir, and fetched from thence gold, four

hundred and twenty talents, and brought it back to King Solomon."

Chapter 10. "1. And when the Queen of Sheba heard of the fame of Solomon concerning the name of the Lord, she came to prove him with hard questions.

2. And she came to Jerusalem with a very great train, with camels that bare spices, and very much gold and precious stones: and when she was come to Solomon, she communed with him of all that was in her heart.

3. And Solomon told her all her questions: there was not anything hid from the king, which he told her not.

4. And when the Queen of Sheba had seen all of Solomon's wisdom, and the house that he had built,

5. And the meat of his table, and the sitting of his servants, and the attendance of his ministers, and their apparel, and his cupbearers, and his ascent by which he went up unto the house of the Lord; there was no more spirit in her.

6. And she said to the king, It was a true report that I heard in my own land of thy acts and of thy wisdom.

7. Howbeit I believed not the words, until I came, and mine eyes had seen it: and, behold, the half was not told me; thy wisdom and prosperity exceedeth the fame which I heard.

8. Happy are thy men, happy are these thy servants, which stand continually before thee, and that hear thy wisdom.

9. Blessed be the Lord thy God, which delighted in thee, to set thee on the throne of Israel; because the Lord loved Israel for ever, therefore made he thee king, to do judgement and justice.

10. And she gave the king an hundred and twenty talents of gold, and of spices very great store, and precious stones: there came no more such abundancy of spices as those which the queen of Sheba gave to King Solomon.

11. And the navy also of Hiram, that brought gold from Ophir, brought in from Ophir great plenty of almug trees, and precious stones.

12. And the king made of the almug trees pillars for the house of the Lord, and for the king's house, harps also and psalteries for singers; there came no such almug trees, nor were seen unto this day.

13. And king Solomon gave unto the queen of Sheba all her desire, whatever she asked, beside that which Solomon gave her of his royal bounty. So she turned and went to her own country, she and her servants.

14. Now the weight of gold that came to Solomon in one year was six hundred three score and six talents of gold.

15. Beside that he had of the merchantmen, and of the traffick of the spice merchants, and of all the kings of Arabia, and of the governors of the country."

Alongside this story we must set two rival traditions, the Arab and the Ethiopian one. The visit to Solomon is referred to in the 27th Surah of the Qur'ān with much ornamentation: the existence of the queen in Saba (her name is not quoted in the Qur'ān) is notified to Solomon by a lapwing; after persuading her to visit him, Solomon arranges for the queen to step over a glass floor; mistaking this for water, she lifts her skirt and reveals her legs. Arab legend maintains that this was a ruse of Solomon's to verify a report that her legs were covered with hair like those of a donkey.[11] Traditionally she was called Bilqis (Balkis), a name known to mediaeval Arab writers which may simply be derived from a Hebrew word meaning "concubine".[12] Her capital was Mārib and she is believed to have been buried in the ancient town of Ṣirwāḥ nearby. The ruins of a large temple near Mārib are now known as Maḥram Bilqis ("the sacred place of Bilqis"), but there appears to be no real basis for associating that building with anyone of that name.

The Ethiopian legend is enshrined in the fourteenth-century Kebra-Negast, which is reputedly copied from a third-century manuscript found in the cathedral library of Saint Sophia, in Constantinople. This holds that the Queen of Sheba was named Makeda and ruled over Tigre; on visiting Solomon she fell a victim to his wiles and on the journey home she gave birth to a son. The boy was called Ebna-Hakim ("the son of the wise one"). In due course he was sent back to Jerusalem to be blessed by his father and just before setting out for home he managed to appropriate the Ark of the Covenant, which was brought back secretly to Ethiopia. There are other associated Ethiopian legends.[13]

To the extent that they are credible at all, neither the Arab nor the Ethiopian traditions appear to have any historical basis of fact over and above the Hebrew story on which they are based, and it is unnecessary to consider them here in any greater detail.

Although they are interwoven in the telling, the Old Testament stories of the Queen of Sheba and of Hiram, King of Tyre, run quite separately, with no connecting link except that both monarchs were in contact with Solomon. The factual information offered about the queen is slender. We are not given her name, we are supplied with no geographical information about her realm other than that it was called Sheba, and we are provided with no reason for her visit to Solomon except that it was "to prove him with hard questions". The compilers of the two books of Kings[14] may have tied the stories together because they believed there was a geographical connection or simply because the stories provided two good examples to illustrate Solomon's foreign policy.

To explore the possibility of a geographical connection one needs to know the whereabouts of the land or port of Ophir. In the genealogical list in Genesis 10 Ophir is associated with Sheba and Havilah as one of the sons of Joktan. In Genesis 2. 11 Havilah is cited as one of the four lands into which flowed rivers out of the Garden of Eden, two of the others being named as Ethiopia and Assyria; Havilah is described there as producing gold, bdellium and onyx stone. Hiram built ships for Solomon in what is now the Gulf of Aqaba[15] and the journey to Ophir therefore quite clearly commenced southwards down the Red Sea. The ships returned from Ophir with gold, "almug" trees and precious stones. In a later verse it is recorded: "For the king had at sea a navy of Tharshish with the navy of Hiram: once in three years came the navy of Tharshish, bringing gold, and silver, ivory, and apes and peacocks" (1 Kings 10. 22). It is frequently held from this passage that the round voyage to and from Ophir took three years, but there is no justification for such conclusion, and various other Bible references to Tharshish clearly relate to Phoenician trading in the western Mediterranean. We do however know for a fact that Ophir was not legendary and was a genuine source of gold, because an inscribed tablet has been excavated near Jaffa which is dated to the eighth century BC and which reads: "gold of Ūfīr to Beth-horon 30 shekels".[16] Various theories about the location of Ophir have advocated south-western Arabia, south-eastern Arabia, Eritrea, East Africa, India and even Malaysia.

Protagonists for placing Ophir in India point out that "almug" (or "algum" as it appears in Chronicles) was probably sandalwood and that this word, as also the words used for "apes" and "peacocks", appear to be of Sanskrit origin. Moreover, the Coptic word for India is "Sifir" and the Septuagint uses "Sophir" instead of "Ophir". A strong candidate for the actual site is ancient Suppara, near Bombay,[17] but Ptolemy's "Abiria", near the Indus, and the "Sovira" coast of Buddhist writing have also been proposed.[18] Josephus is quoted in support of this claim when he states: "the land that was of old called Ophir, but now Aurea Cersonesus, which belongs to India."[19]

The case for placing Ophir in Malaysia has been propounded by Innes Miller and rests on the unconvincing suggestion that a figure on one of three carved stone megaliths on the coast of the Malacca Strait resembles in appearance and dress a Phoenician as portrayed in Phoenician reliefs; it is therefore argued that these megaliths may have been set up by Hiram's men.[20]

Those who advocate Omān, in south-east Arabia, argue that the area was once famous for its gold (which is not in fact correct, although copper came from that region) and that, as there was trade between Omān and India, the other items could have been acquired there. They also point out that as Ophir was one of the sons of Joktan, the place of that name is likely to be found in Arabia. Ẓufār is sometimes proposed as a word etymologically close to Ophir, while the nineteenth-century traveller Von Wrede observed that the Mahra of

south Arabia, who live adjacent to Ẕufār and whose language has very ancient origins, used the word "ofir" to mean "red" and called themselves the tribes of Ofir, meaning the "red country".

The East African claim relied principally on the theory that the Phoenicians had a particular interest in the African continent and at a later date established a trading link with the East African coast (a contention by no means proven). But this theory died when the ruins at ancient Zimbabwe, in Mashonaland, were proved to be only of mediaeval origin.

We have a very good idea of the probable appearance of the sea-going ships which Hiram would have built for the journey to Ophir, because a relief discovered in the site of the palace of Sennacherib and depicting the flight of a King of Tyre and Sidon in 701 BC showed such ships clearly. Although using a small sail from a central mast, the main propulsion was by a double bank of oars.[21] The extremely humid heat at sea level during high summer in tropical latitudes may therefore have affected mobility as much as the rough weather of the monsoon, forcing crews to spend long periods in harbour awaiting favourable conditions. At this period sailors did not navigate by the stars and ships clung to the coast, travelling only when they could see. Nor did these ships carry provisions and water for extended periods at sea.

Herodotus gives an account of an epic Phoenician voyage supposedly made under the sponsorship of Pharoah Necho II in about 600 BC; this was the circumnavigation of Africa, which Herodotus observed was made in something over two years, the crew stopping each autumn to sow and harvest their seed for provisioning.[22] If Hiram had anticipated a comparable voyage three centuries earlier by sending a fleet to India, one might expect that some tradition of it would have survived, yet Herodotus had clearly never heard of it. Moreover, on such a journey the ships would have had to call in at harbours along the south Arabian or Somali coast and it is almost inconceivable that they would then have returned without frankincense and myrrh in their cargoes. But no such goods are mentioned in the Bible story.

In fact the journey made by Hiram's fleet would seem to have been a much more modest one than is supposed by those who see Ophir in India, Malaysia, eastern Arabia or east Africa, and it is improbable that his ships reached as far as the incense lands of south Arabia. The sea journey to the southern end of the Red Sea, "a voyage of forty days under oars" according to Herodotus,[23] was itself considerable for that age. Gold could have been obtained from the coast of 'Asīr, being found in the area of Wādī Dhahabān (a word meaning "gold"); it was noted there by the classical authors and some mining is carried on there today. This has been proposed as the location of Ophir in conjunction with the hypothesis that Havilah might be the area to the south of it now called Khawlān, which is also gold-bearing.[24] But whereas Arabia may not have produced all three of the items secured from Ophir—gold, precious stones and some sort of wood—they could all have been obtained from Eritrea, with its rich Ethiopian hinterland, and it is there that this elusive place would seem most likely to have been. In these early centuries, trading contact with Ethiopia was mainly overland through Nubia and Egypt along the course of the Nile. Herodotus (Book 3 section 97) reported that gold was found in abundance there and that every two years the Ethiopians paid Darius a voluntary tribute of "about two quarts of unrefined gold, two hundred logs of ebony, and twenty elephants tusks", thereby suggesting the possible identity of the "almug" tree.

The gifts brought to Solomon by the Queen of Sheba were gold, spices and precious stones. The voluntary tribute paid to Darius by the Arabians consisted, according to Herodotus, solely of frankincense. We have seen that the gold found in Arabia comes from 'Asīr; it is not found anywhere in the incense regions of the south. No precious stones are found in south Arabia. Although frankincense and myrrh are included under the term "spice", the Hebrew word used here, *besamin*, also embraces the seasoning with which food is flavoured.[25] We cannot therefore infer that frankincense and myrrh were necessarily part of the queen's gifts to Solomon. There is then nothing in the Old Testament story of the Queen of Sheba to connect her positively with south Arabia. Josephus, compiling his "Antiquities of the Jews" in about 93 AD, did not even know her as "queen of Sheba", but described her as "queen of Egypt and Ethiopia".[26]

Other difficulties also arise in accepting the popular view that the queen came from south Arabia. In the first place, nothing has yet been discovered in the archaeological investigation of south Arabia, admittedly so far very limited, or in the much more considerable epigraphical study of south Arabia's history, to indicate that any developed and organised kingdom existed there as early as the time of Solomon. The earliest south Arabian rulers so far known from epigraphical testimony do not seem, on the latest reasoning, to have lived much before 500 BC.[27] Secondly, the epigraphical testimony, drawn from monumental inscriptions and providing considerable information about the monarchic system of the time, contains no trace of any reigning queen and the monarchies appear to have been exclusively male, although the title "queen" was used for the queen-consort.[28]

Thirdly, it is difficult to accept that any such state visit would have been made over so exceptionally long a distance. The reason now generally suggested for the visit is that it was to secure some sort of commercial agreement with Solomon over the incense trade, but there is really no reason to suppose that the incense trade was so well developed by Solomon's time as to occasion this or that the political and economic conditions were appropriate for such a deal. The most probable reason for any ruler to visit Solomon would have been to secure safe passage through his realm or protection from his expansionist policies, perhaps by offering some form of voluntary tribute. No threat existed to distant south Arabia from Solomon, whose power was rather less than the bible account would imply.[29] But the traders conveying goods to Tyre and the other Phoenician cities would have been obliged to pass through Israelite territory and therefore concerned to maintain good relations with Solomon.

In the quotation already given from Ezekiel (chapter 27 verses 22–24) the merchants trading with Tyre (which fell to Nebuchadnezzar in 574 BC) came from Sheba and Raamah and brought spices, precious stones and gold. These are precisely the same goods that the queen of Sheba gave Solomon, suggesting a trading pattern rather more than mere co-incidence. The books of Kings were not put together until after the fall of the monarchy (586 BC), so that the process of assembling them would have been nearly contemporaneous with the composition of Ezekiel.[30] If the Sheba of Ezekiel belonged to north Arabia it would seem that the Sheba of Kings whose queen visited Solomon may have had the same northern origin.

While the existence of a queen is only partially compatible with the situation in south Arabia in so far as can be judged from current knowledge (and we cannot totally dismiss the possibility that the visit was from a queen-consort), there is a tradition of reigning queens in northern Arabia which is historically attested. In 742 BC Tiglath-Pileser III exacted tribute from Zabibi, a queen of "Aribi" land; six years later he conquered the forces of another queen, Samsi; in 715 BC Sargon II received tribute from another Samsi, an Arabian queen; in 688 BC Sennacherib reduced 'Aduma, the "fortress of Arabia", and took the queen Telkhunu a prisoner.[31] Although these examples are all after the time of Solomon, they show evidence of a system of female tribal chiefs which may well have stretched back to the Solomon era.

We must maintain caution over any interpretation of the story of the Queen of Sheba, but the available facts do seem to suggest that she was not a queen from south Arabia, as is popularly supposed, but the head of a tribe of Sabaeans of north Arabia who engaged in commerce with Tyre through Israelite territory. These people may have carried incense, including some frankincense and myrrh which had been traded through from south Arabia, but there is no evidence of the highly organised incense trade of later centuries in this account from the Book of Kings and no reason to think that any direct trading existed between Solomon's Israel and the far-distant Sheba, or Saba, of the south at so early a date.

Chapter 4

The Greek
Geographers

From the fifth century BC, Greek and Roman scholars started to compile encyclopaedic works about the world in which they lived with a remarkable concern for accuracy and comprehensiveness. The difficulties facing the classical geographers, who usually combined geographical with historical studies, when they tried to establish the facts about distant lands were substantial: the only extant written source material might be decades or even centuries old; travellers to or from the outer edges of the known world were few and of these even fewer could be relied on as accurate reporters; most of the information in circulation was fable rather than fact.

At the start of Book 15 of his Geography, Strabo ruminated on these problems before commencing to write about India:

"It is necessary to hear accounts of this country with indulgence, for not only is it furthest away from us, but not many of our people have seen it; and even those who have seen it have seen only parts of it, and the greater part of what they saw is from hearsay; and even what they saw they learned on a hasty passage with an army through the country" (i.e. the army of Alexander the Great, which had marched into India over 250 years before Strabo was born). "Wherefore they do not give out the same accounts of the same things, even though they have written these accounts as though their statements had been carefully confirmed. . . . Moreover most of those who have written anything about this region in much later times, and those who sail there at the present time, do not present any accurate information either. . . . As for the merchants who now sail from Egypt by the Nile and the Arabian Gulf as far as India, only a small number have sailed as far as the Ganges and even these are merely private

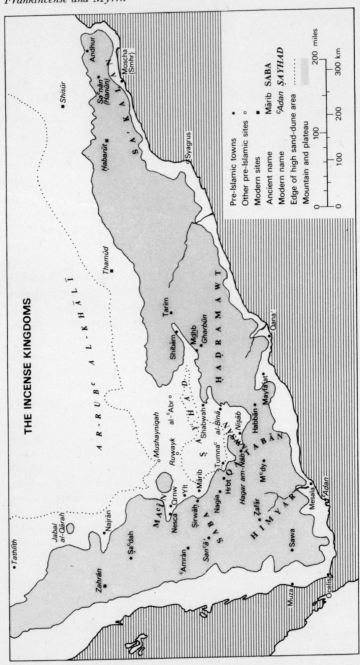

THE INCENSE KINGDOMS

A R - R U B ͨ   A L - K H Ā L Ī

Tathlith

Jabal
al-Qārah

Zehrān

Şaͨdah

ͨAmrān

Najrān

Mushayniqah

al-ͨAbr

Ruwayk

Ylt

MāͨIN

Ornw

Nescā

Şirwāh

Sanͨāͨ   ŞABA

Hrbt

Nagīa

ͨAdan

Shisūr

Andhur

Şaͨnān
(Hanūn)

Moscha
(Smhr)

Habarūt

Syagrus

Thamūd

Tarīm

Shibām

Majib

Gharbūn

H A D R A M A W T

Qana'

Mushayniqah

al-ͨAbr

Y H A D

Shabwah

Tumnaͨ

Hagar am-Nāb

al-Bīnā'

Nişāb

M A Y N

Mayfaͨat

Habbān

T A B Ā N

Zafār

Mͨdy

H I M Y A R

Sawa

Mesala

ͨAdan

Muza

Ocelis

56

citizens and of no use as regards the history of the places they have seen. . . . So . . . one must accept everything that is nearest to credibility."[1]

An understanding of this problem of the ancient scholars and their approach to it is necessary if one is to understand the problem faced by modern scholars in studying and analysing their work; in attempting to discover what set of facts and conditions relate to a particular period of history, ancient writings must be dissected so that material from the different sources can be separated, examined and, if deemed valid, placed in correct chronological sequence alongside other material of the same period. It is a process not unlike sorting out a pack of playing cards into the correct suits and sequences, with the added complications that the markings on the cards will often be almost illegible, that many of the cards will be missing and that the pack will contain duplicates. The missing cards are a particularly difficult feature of the process. Only a portion of the original texts of many of these ancient savants has survived; this portion contains scribal errors made during copying, for the original manuscripts have long ago perished; much has vanished altogether.

Early accounts of Arabia are particularly scarce. The cultural centre of the Hellenistic world became Alexandria, but the vast library assembled there by the Ptolemies, which contained some 700,000 volumes, was partly destroyed during Julius Caesar's campaign; although augmented by some 200,000 volumes from its great rival at Pergamum,[2] it was to meet destruction again in AD 389, apparently on an edict of the Emperor Theodosius.[3] These events were major catastrophes to the whole of culture and learning, but knowledge of Arabia must have been especially affected, for it was in the depositories of the Alexandria library that the earliest writings about that land were most likely to be found.

The earliest of the classical authors whose work survives to give us information about the incense lands is Herodotus, the "father of history", who was born in a Greek town in Asia-Minor in about 485 BC and travelled widely around the Greek world of the day and into northern parts of Arabia, Egypt and Africa. At least part of his "Histories" were written by 446 BC and he died in 425 BC.

Herodotus recorded that in about 500 BC the Persian

emperor Darius the Great sent out an expedition of Ionian Greeks under Scylax of Caryanda from the north-west of India to explore the delta of the Indus and beyond. From the Indus this expedition had coasted westwards, passed by the entrance to the Arabian Gulf and skirted round the south of Arabia into the Red Sea and so up to the port of Arsinoe, near modern Suez, which it reached after 30 months.[4] If Herodotus is correct, this was probably the first journey round the south of Arabia made by a Greek crew, although he seems to have learned little from it. While one may suppose that Herodotus had access to a few chronicles about voyages such as this, he mentions only one written source (the historian Hecataeus of Miletus—*c*.500 BC—who is not referred to in an Arabian context) and there is no doubt that his primary source of information was his own observation and enquiry. His geographical information, which he was at pains to make as complete as possible, is therefore mostly a statement of what he saw or was told about, including travellers' tales and local beliefs which he realised might not be true, in around 450 BC. To the Greek world of that time Arabia, outside of the

northern region adjoining the Mediterranean lands where Cyrus of Persia was waging his campaigns, was far away, unvisited and little known, and its southern extremity was "the most southerly country of the inhabited world". Herodotus had nothing to say about the incense trade as such, but he knew Arabia as "the only place that produces frankincense, myrrh, cassia, cinnamon and the gum called ledanon".

Herodotus noted that the above products "excepting the myrrh, cause the Arabians a lot of trouble to collect." The cassia plant, for example, grew in a shallow lake "infested by winged creatures like bats, which screech alarmingly and are very pugnacious". The dry sticks of cinnamon were believed to be collected from some unknown district by large birds who carried them to mud nests on the edge of mountain precipices in Arabia; the Arabians, he reported, would lay out heavy chunks of meat which the birds seized and conveyed to their nests; the weight of the meat would break the nests, allowing the cinnamon sticks to fall to the foot of the cliffs, from whence they were recovered. Ledanon, "an ingredient in many kinds of perfumes" and also stated to be "what the Arabians chiefly burn as incense", was a sweet-smelling substance thought to be gathered off the beards of he-goats which had browsed among the bushes on which it grew.[5]

Despite the confusion and tall story in some of his accounts, Herodotus also picked up accurate facts. For example, he correctly reported the fat-tailed sheep known from rock-drawings to have existed in ancient Arabia and found in Somalia to this day.[6] However, his description of the problem which faced the persons collecting frankincense is perplexing: "When they gather frankincense they burn storax (the gum of which is brought into Greece by the Phoenicians) in order to raise a smoke to drive off the flying snakes; these snakes . . . are small in size and of various colours and great numbers of them keep guard over all the trees which bear the frankincense and the only way to get rid of them is by smoking them out with storax."[7]

There have been various explanations for this story of the flying snakes. They may have been a species still found in south Arabia which leaps when it strikes and might therefore be said to fly.[8] Strabo, quoting Artemidorus, recorded that there were found in the country of the Sabaeans "serpents a span in length, which are dark red in colour (and) can leap even as far as a hare and inflict an incurable bite."[9] Pliny suggested the story was just an invention of wily Arabian traders who wished to deter outsiders from incursions into the source of their wealth. But another origin for the tale could be the desert locust. "The Arabians say that the whole world would swarm with these creatures were it not for a certain peculiar fact," Herodotus continued, revealing that the female was believed to kill the male after copulation. The breeding and movement of locusts are governed by climatic factors, the swarms drifting with the prevailing wind.[10] In south Arabia there would be swarms during the period of the frankincense harvest and smoke may have been used to protect the trees. Possibly Herodotus was confusing information about two separate pests, snakes and locusts, in his account.

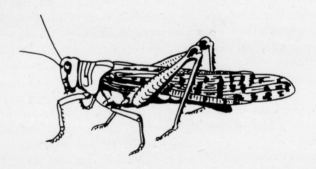

Another fact provided by Herodotus illustrates the importance of the incense trade by his time. In listing the tribute each of the twenty provinces of the kingdom paid to Darius, he added that a voluntary tribute was also paid by the Arabians, whom Darius had not subjected in recognition of their assistance when he attacked Egypt. This tribute was one thousand Babylonian talents (about $24\frac{1}{2}$ tons) of frankincense yearly. While the volume may have been exaggerated for propaganda reasons, it is evident from this that by the fifth century BC the export of frankincense from south Arabia was substantial. Herodotus reported nothing of any recognized incense road, but it is apparent that by this time the trade was becoming an organised one, with south Arabian merchants beginning to appear at the northern end of the route. Fragments of jars with south Arabian lettering on them found in Eilath are dated to the fifth or sixth century BC, the earliest archaeological evidence for the trade.[11]

Herodotus wrote of the great wars of conquest of the Persians, but within a century of his death the Persian tide had been turned and Alexander the Great had crossed the Hellespont into Asia Minor and rolled up the empire of Darius in a series of swift campaigns. In 332 BC Egypt fell; five years later Alexander invaded India; and in 323 BC, when he died suddenly in Babylon, he was preparing to subjugate Arabia.

Quoting Aristobulus, who had taken part in these campaigns, Strabo observed that: "Alexander alleged as the cause of war that the Arabians were the only people on earth who did not send ambassadors to him, but in truth (he) was reaching out to be lord of all."[12] But Arrian (*c.* 90–175 AD), who wrote a seven-volume history of Alexander's campaigns based on contemporary accounts, added:

> "Moreover, the wealth of their country was an additional incitement—the cassia in the oases, the trees which bore frankincense and myrrh, the shrubs which yielded cinnamon, the meadows where nard grew wild; of all this report had told him. Arabia, too, was a large country, its coast (it was said) no less in extent than the coast of India; many islands lay off it and there were harbours everywhere for his fleet to ride in and to provide sites for new settlements likely to grow to great wealth and prosperity."[13]

According to Arrian, Alexander had sent out oared reconnaissance vessels to explore the Arabian coasts southwards from the Arabian Gulf. One of these, under Hiero of Soli, had even been ordered to try to navigate round the south of Arabia and so back to Egypt, but had returned after determining that the peninsula was of immense size.[14]

Alexander's sudden death of a fever in 323 BC brought all his preparations for an Arabian expedition to an immediate end, but his vast and dramatic conquests had turned the attention of the Greeks to new areas and entirely changed and broadened their outlook. Arabia now lay within the knowledge of Greek scholars; they were aware of its shape and they were beginning to learn something more about its products and its people. In Egypt, Greek rule was continued by Alexander's Macedonian companion, Ptolemy, who took the throne and founded a dynasty. Over the ensuing period an ancient canal from the Nile to the Gulf of Suez, commenced by the Pharaoh Necos and finished by Darius,[15] was reconstructed, ports were built on the Red Sea coast (at Myos Hormos, Berenice and Cosseir), piracy was suppressed and Greek vessels began to trade with "Arabia the Blessed" and to feel a tentative way through the Bab al-Mandab into the wide, uncertain reaches of the Indian Ocean.

The earliest mention of Arabia in surviving Greek literature after Herodotus is contained in a botanical book *An Enquiry into Plants* written by Theophrastus (372–287 BC), a philosopher who had studied under Plato and Aristotle. This book, thought to have been written in about 295 BC, contains a section on frankincense and myrrh and the other Arabian products. It is clear that his main source was the evidence of Greek sailors "on the coasting voyage which they made from the Bay of Heroes" (i.e. the Gulf of Suez) who had "landed to look for water on the mountains and so saw these trees and the manner of collecting their gums."[16] This expedition may have been one sent out from Heroönopolis (Suez) under the command of Anaxicrates[17] at about the same time as Hiero's voyage from the Arabian Gulf. Strabo, quoting Eratosthenes, gives a measurement of the length of the Red Sea "as recorded by Alexander's associates and by Anaxicrates".[18]

Of the account given by Theophrastus about the nature and cultivation of the incense trees we shall make mention later. Regarding the country itself he had little to say but the following passage:

"Now frankincense, myrrh, cassia and also cinnamon are found in the Arabian peninsula about Saba, Hadramyta, Kitibaina and Mamali. The trees of frankincense and myrrh grow partly in the mountains, partly on private estates at the foot of the mountains; wherefore some are under cultivation, others not; the mountains, they say, are lofty, forest-covered and subject to snow, and rivers from them flow down into the plain. . . . The whole range, they said, belongs to the portion of the Sabaeans; for it is under their sway and they are honest in their dealings with one another. Wherefore no-one keeps watch; so that these sailors greedily took, they said, and put on board their ships some of the frankincense and myrrh, since there was no-one about, and sailed away."[19]

This passage by Theophrastus contains the first recorded mention in these classical works of the main south Arabian peoples—those of Saba, Ḥaḍramawt, Qatabān and Maʿīn, though scholars differ about the last named, which is certainly corrupted in the surviving text and has also been given other interpretations, such as "Mahri".[20] The "lofty, forest-covered mountains subject to snow" would seem to refer to the Yemeni highlands, where snow and ice do occasionally occur; these were unquestionably Sabaean at the time but they did not produce frankincense, which grew much further to the east. Possibly the Greek sailors landed for water and saw incense trees growing at a point on the southern coast, but made their disreputable theft from a Sabaean port to which incense had been brought for trading. But there are other reasons for thinking that in about the fifth century BC the Sabaeans may have been in some sort of control over the whole area and this passage may reflect that position.

Theophrastus was followed a century later by one of the greatest of all the Greek savants, Eratosthenes of Cyrene (276–196 BC), who wrote books on astronomy, geometry, philosophy, history, geography and grammar, not one of which has survived. Eratosthenes was appointed head of the library at Alexandria by Ptolemy and while there, in 225 BC, he even evolved a method of measuring the circumference of the earth which proved accurate to within 200 miles.[21] His most important work was his *Geography*, which was in three books, the first on the form and nature of the earth, the second on the "mathematics" of geography and the third on "political geography", possibly in the form of a gazetteer.

Some fragments of what Eratosthenes wrote survive as extracts quoted, probably in a summarized form, by Strabo two centuries later. Fortunately Strabo is meticulous in quoting his sources, so that these are fairly readily defined. From Eratosthenes, Strabo provided the following description of the incense lands of Arabia as they were known to the Greeks of 225–200 BC:

"The extreme parts towards the south, lying opposite to Ethiopia, are watered by summer rains and are sowed twice, like India; and the rivers there are used up in supplying plains and lakes. The country is in general fertile and abounds in particular with places for making honey; and, with the exception of horses and mules and hogs, it has an abundance of domesticated animals; and with the exception of geese and chicks, has all kinds of birds. The extreme part of the country above mentioned is occupied by the four largest tribes; by the Minaeans on the side towards the Red Sea, whose largest city is Carna or Carnana; next to these by the Sabaeans, whose metropolis is Mariaba; third by the Cattabanians, whose territory extends down to the straits and the passage across the Arabian Gulf, and whose royal seat is called Tamna; and, farthest towards the east, the Chatramotitae, whose city is Sabota. All these cities are ruled by monarchs and are prosperous, being beautifully adorned with both temples and royal palaces. And the houses are like the Egyptians' in respect to the manner in which the timbers are joined together. The four jurisdictions cover more territory than the Egyptian delta. . . .

Cattabania produces frankincense, and Chatramotitis produces myrrh; and both these and the other aromatics are bartered to merchants. These travel to Minaea in seventy days from Aelana (Aelana is a city on the other recess of the Arabian Gulf, the recess near Gaza called Aelanites, as I have stated before) but the Gabaioi arrive at Chatramotitis in forty days. The part of the Arabian Gulf along the side of Arabia, beginning at the Aelanites recess, is, as recorded by Alexander's associates and by Anaxicrates, fourteen thousand stadia, though this figure is excessive. . . ."[22]

In the above translation the name "Gabaioi", which appears in the original text, is used instead of "Gerrhaeans", which is generally substituted. The significance of this will be seen later.

At this stage something may be said about the nomenclature of the seas surrounding Arabia, which can be confusing. The northern part of the Gulf of Suez was, as already noted, sometimes called the Bay of Heroes. The Gulf of Aqaba was known as the Aelanites (or Leanites) Gulf. What is at present the Red Sea used to be termed the Arabian Gulf (Sinus Arabicus), although the name Red Sea (Mare Rubrum or Erythraean Sea) was also used at times to describe its southern part before it came to apply to the whole. The present Gulf of Aden and Arabian Sea were formerly the Red Sea and this could be held to include the Indian Ocean. Sometimes the Persian Gulf was also regarded as a part of the Red Sea, although the name Persian Gulf (Sinus Persicus) was more general, with the expanse south of Bahrayn sometimes being called the Persian Sea. This nomenclature will be more readily understood if it is appreciated that in earliest days the Greeks had no proper conception of the size or shape of Arabia and visualised its southern shores as a vast semi-circle lapped by one sea, the Erythraean Sea, into which the Arabian Gulf led on the western side and the Tigris and Euphrates flowed on the eastern side.

With Eratosthenes we obtain a clearer picture of the kingdoms of Arabia the Blessed and, for the first time, a list of their capitals. There is no longer doubt about the Minaeans as one of the four peoples, although the statement that they were "on the side towards the Red Sea" is not easy to understand, the original Greek being obscure; it may simply mean that they lived on the western side of Arabia.[23] More important is a mistake which can be attributed to scribal error and which reverses the true facts about the incense production areas; the text should have read "*Cattabania* produces myrrh and *Chatramotitis* produces frankincense." We will come to the significance of this in a later chapter.

It is evident that the source for the greater part of what Eratosthenes recorded here was not a sailor. The final passage about Anaxicrates probably has a separate origin, but the rest is clearly written by someone familiar with the inland route rather than the voyage down the coast. This person describes the country through which he has passed not only in south

Arabia but also, in an earlier passage not quoted here, on the way south through the rest of Arabia. The principal source of the information provided by Eratosthenes seems in fact to be someone who had travelled along the incense route itself.

In the second century BC a Greek grammarian from Cnidus named Agatharchides came to live in Alexandria as tutor of one of the Ptolemaic princes. Besides writing books on history, he made a study of the lands bordering the Erythraean Sea and wrote a description of the area in a work of five books called *Concerning the Erythraean Sea*. This was probably produced near the end of his life in about 132 BC.[24] No copy of it survives, but considerable extracts from the first and fifth books and some information drawn from other parts have come down to us in the writings of later geographers.

In the first place, Agatharchides' work was used in an eleven-volume geography produced around 100 BC by Artemidorus of Ephesus. That work too is lost, but Strabo quoted from it, noting that the information he had already derived from Eratosthenes was also to be found in it. The passage taken from Artemidorus which can be attributed to Agatharchides is as follows:

"Bordering upon these people" (i.e. the Debae to the north) "is the very fertile country of the Sabaeans, a very large tribe, in whose country myrrh and frankincense and cinnamon are produced; and on the coast is found balsam, as also another kind of herb of very fragrant smell, which quickly loses its fragrance. There are also sweet-smelling palms, and reeds; and serpents a span in length, which are dark red in colour, can leap even as far as a hare, and inflict an incurable bite. On account of the abundance of fruits the people are lazy and easy-going in their modes of life. Most of the populace sleep on the roots of trees which they have to cut out of the ground. Those who live close to one another receive in continuous succession the loads of aromatics and deliver them to their next neighbours, as far as Syria and Mesopotamia; and when they are made drowsy by the sweet odours they overcome the drowsiness by inhaling the incense of asphalt and goats' beard.

The city of the Sabaeans, Mariaba, is situated upon a well-wooded mountain; and it has a king who is authority in lawsuits and everything else; but it is not lawful for him to leave the palace, or if he does, the rabble, in accordance with some oracle, stone him to death on the spot. Both he himself and those about him live in effeminate luxury; but the masses engage partly in farming and partly in the traffic of aromatics, both the local kinds and those from Ethiopia; to get the latter they sail across the straits in leathern boats. They have these aromatics in such abundance that they use cinnamon and cassia and the others instead of sticks and firewood. In the country of the Sabaeans is also found larimnum, a most fragrant incense. From their trafficking both the Sabaeans and the Gerrhaeans have become richest of all; and they have a vast equipment of both gold and silver articles, such as couches and tripods and bowls, together with drinking vessels and very costly houses; for doors and walls and ceilings are variegated with ivory and gold and silver set with precious stones.''[25]

Factually not a great deal more seems to have been learned about south Arabia in the period of nearly a century which divided Eratosthenes and Agatharchides, nor, evidently, was learned in the further period of some thirty years between Agatharchides and Artemidorus. Clearly there are some errors. The Sabaean capital of Marib, for example, lies in a plain, and not on "a well-wooded mountain". But the account of the luxurious life and great wealth of the Arabians reveals the exaggerated ideas which were spreading in the Mediterranean world, notions which had already gripped Alexander and which were soon to delude the Romans into making their ill-fated attempt at acquiring the riches of Arabia by conquest.

Second of the sources which provide material taken from the work of Agatharchides is Diodorus Siculus (*c*.80–20 BC), who wrote an enormous world history, *The Library of History*, in forty books, of which fifteen and a few fragments survive. Diodorus compiled this by assembling excerpts from various authors in an uncritical manner and, although he attempted to make use only of reputable writers, he needs to be read with caution. His Third Book, which is extant, covers the Ethiopians and Arabians and provides the first detailed account available of the early Nabataeans. At two points in his text Diodorus acknowledges Agatharchides as his main source for this information.

Third of the extant works from which the text of Agatharchides can be derived is Photius, a Byzantine ecclesiastic of the ninth century AD and a man of immense erudition. For most of the time between AD 857 and 886 he was Patriarch of Constantinople, until banished on an accusation of conspiring against the life of Leo VI. His *Myriobiblium seu Biblioteca* is an analysis of some 280 works of ancient Greek literature with which he was familiar and contains many extracts from them. From him we learn something of Agatharchides' own sources, for he noted that Agatharchides had access to written reports in the king's archives in Alexandria, to eye-witnesses whom he questioned and to the report of one Ariston, who explored the west coast of Arabia for one of the Ptolemies (probably Ptolemy II, who reigned between 285 and 246 BC).[26]

The text of the passages about Arabia quoted by Photius is remarkably similar to that of Diodorus Siculus and it is unnecessary for the purposes of this book to quote both of them, although the differences will be of specialist interest to scholars. Photius has not previously been published in English translation. A translation of the relevant passages, prepared for this volume by Mr J. S. Hutchinson, is as follows:

"86. In the Palm-grove the regions which are seen from the interior are covered with rocks of varying heights; while those who travel across toward the sea are presented with a long, narrow shore.

87. There is joined to the said seashore a place which they call the Land of Ducks (Nessa) because of their great abundance. This Land of Ducks borders upon a thickly wooded promontory and it stretches, if one follows along it in a straight line, towards the town called Petra and Palestine. To this land (Palestine) the Gerrhaei and the Minaei and all those Arabs with dwellings nearby convey, so it is reported, from the upper country frankincense and cargoes connected with spices. . . .

89. After the gulf which is called Leanites around which the Arabs live, is the land of the Bythemanei. It is vast and flat, well watered and fertile. Only coarse grass, Persian clover and lotus, which is as tall as a man, grow. This describes all the vegetation there is; nothing else grows. Thus here there are many wild goats, camels, many herds of deer and gazelle, numerous flocks of sheep and an uncountable number of mules and cattle. To these advantages is joined an equal disadvantage. For the land also supports a great number of lions, wolves and leopards. So, the natural advantages of the land are responsible for the misfortunes of its inhabitants.

90. Immediately after these shores there is a gulf which cuts deep into the land. One discovers that its depth is no less than 500

stades. Those who live around the gulf are called Batmizomanes: they are hunters of land animals.

91. After the land just mentioned come three islands which provide many harbours. The first of these is called the Sanctuary of Isis, the second Soukabya and the third Salydo. They are all desert islands and are shaded by olive trees—not the ones which grow in our country but the ones which grow in those parts.

92. After these islands, which lie out to sea, it is possible to see a long, rocky coast. This is the land of the Thamoudenian Arabs. Sailing past this is extremely hazardous for more than 1000 stades. For there is no, I repeat no, harbour with good anchorage, no roadstead for anchoring, no bay for protection, no trace of a breakwater to receive the sailors as a place of refuge in an emergency. . . .

94. After this—not immediately, but after some distance—there is an extensive and exceedingly well watered shore and the mountain called Laenus, which exhibits a vast and extensive perimeter. It is clothed in forests of every kind of tree.

95. The Debae inhabit the land which borders upon this mountainous land. Some are nomads, others are farmers. Down through the middle of their country there flows a river which has three courses. It carries down gold-dust in such great profusion that the mud which accumulates at the mouth shines in the distance. The inhabitants of the place are ignorant of how to work this metal. They are extremely hospitable, not to all men but to those who cross over from the Peloponnese and Boeotia. This is because of some mythical story connected with Hercules.

96. The neighbours of these people are the Alilaei and the Cassandres. They occupy a land in no way similar to those mentioned before. For the air is neither chill nor dry nor fiery but exhibits soft, thick clouds from which come showers and temperate storms even in summer. The land for the most part produces everything, but not all receives cultivation because the people lack the experience. However, they find the gold in flat underground passages in the region and dig it out in great quantities. It is not gold which has been fused together from gold-dust as a result of their knowledge and experience; it is natural gold which is called 'unfired' by the Greeks because of the way it is formed. The smallest of these nuggets is the size of a fruit pip. The medium ones are the size of the fruit of the medlar tree. The largest could be compared with Persian walnuts. They perforate these and wear them alternately with transparent stones around their wrists and necks. They take them to neighbouring peoples and sell them cheaply. In fact, they exchange for bronze, gold three times its weight; for iron, they exchange gold twice its

weight and silver is worth ten times as much as gold. Price is fixed by plenty or scarcity in those products which all life looks to not for the nature of them but out of desire to have them.

97. Immediately after these people come the Carbae, who occupy the mainland. There follows a deep harbour where many springs discharge their waters. Straightway after this come the Sabaean race, which is the greatest throughout Arabia and the possessor of all kinds of blessedness. For the land produces everything which we regard as important for our lives. The bodies of the inhabitants are rather striking. They are well supplied with countless numbers of cattle. A fragrance fills the whole coastal region, providing newcomers with a pleasure past seeing and telling. For along the same coast grow large numbers of balsam, cassia and another kind of plant: when it is freshly picked it provides the sweetest pleasure to the eyes, but after a while it suddenly withers away to nothing, so that the usefulness of the plant disappears before such power can reach us.

In the interior of the land there are large, unbroken tracts of forest. There tall trees rise up which produce myrrh and frankincense, in addition to cinnamon trees, palms, reeds and others of like nature, so that no word can express what happens to those who have undergone the experience of such a kind in their senses. For it is not the pleasure one takes in spices which are old and have been kept stored away, nor the pleasure in spices which are separated from the plant on which they grew and by which they are kept alive. It is the pleasure in spices which are in the peak of their bloom and which send out their extraordinary perfume from their own natural locations. It so happens that many forget mortal pleasures and secretly suppose that they are partaking of ambrosia, since that is the substance the name of which expresses what is appropriate to its superlative qualities.

98. In the spice forests there is a kind of snake which is the most peculiar of all. It is as if fortune were jealous of the vast numbers of advantages (in this land) and had mingled what is harmful with what is good, so that no-one might end by being insolent and conceiving a titanic pride, having despised divine providence, but that he might be schooled by the example and remembrance of adversity. This kind of snake has a red colour, is about a span in length and has an incurable bite if it draws blood higher than the flanks. It inflicts its wound by leaping in the air.

99. Among the Sabaei themselves the perception of spicy smells is very keen but the appreciation (of them) is less. When something has persisted continuously from childhood, it excites the senses less. Rather it makes them blunt when no change in the way of life is proposed. However, since they cannot direct their

life so that it is in a state of balance—because the body is permeated by a strong and penetrating odour with a proportionate condensation, so as to cause extreme debility—they remove the excessively sweet onslaught of the odour and moderate the harmful part of the pleasure by fumigating with a little bitumen and 'goat's beard', mixing what seems to be disagreeable. So, every pleasure which is controlled by moderation and order promotes life, but if devoid of due proportion and proper timing, it is not an advantageous possession.

100. The capital of the Sabaei, which is called Sabas, takes its name from the whole people. It is situated upon a small mountain and is the most beautiful town throughout Arabia. The ruler of all the tribes holds his office from the people. Though it is prized, it is nevertheless very hazardous. It is prized because the king gives orders to many and he does whatever he wills in accordance with his judgements, which are not open to question; it is hazardous because, although he has received the whole oversight, he is not able to leave the palace. Otherwise he is stoned by everyone in accordance with an ancient oracle. Thus the position is exceedingly perilous.

101. Among the men there are those who are destined to spend their lives at home with scarcely any more bravery than the women. They have become effeminate through a life of constant ease. All the other men train for war and work the land. They export their goods using large rafts. They transport, among other things, the aromatic fruit which grows in the hinterland (called in Arabic 'larimna'); it has the strongest perfume of all the other aromatic spices; they say that this has a great deal of power over certain body ailments.

Since the land has no other wood, they are forced to burn cinnamon and cassia trees for their day to day purposes and to use them for the other needs in life. Thus has Fortune apportioned unequally her gifts, giving to some a paucity of necessities, to others a superfluity. Not a few of the Sabaei use boats made of leather; they have learned how to exploit the tide when using these, even though they are living in the lap of luxury.

102. No race seems to be more prosperous than the Sabaei and the Gerrhaei, since they act as the warehouse for everything from Asia and Europe which goes under the name of distinction. These people have made Ptolemy's Syria rich in gold. These, by the activities of the Phoenicians, have, amongst a thousand other things, procured lucrative markets. Their luxury consists not only in their wonderful embossed work and in their intricate drinking vessels, but also in the size of their beds and tripods. It reaches its height in the other domestic items which are common

with us. Many of them, so it seems, possess a royal fortune. It is said that they have built many columns covered in gold or made of silver. In addition, their ceilings and doors have been decorated with sunken recesses set with close-packed gems. In the same way the spaces between the columns are wonderful to behold. In short, there exists a great difference between their riches and those of other peoples. This is what has been reported about them up to our time. If they had not had their dwellings at such a distance, taking their forces in all directions, foreign administrators would have become the masters of such a prize, since the soft living (of these people) would not have safeguarded their liberty for long.

103. All along this country the sea appears white, just like a river, so that one asks in astonishment the reason for this phenonemon. The Blessed Isles lie close by. Here all the cattle are white and none of the female beasts have horns growing. In these islands it is possible to see merchant vessels at anchor. Most come from the place where Alexander established an anchorage on the Indus river. A considerable number come from Persia and Carmania and all around." [27]

One learns something of the character of Agatharchides himself from this extract copied down by Photius. It contains several passages with which neither Artemidorus nor even Diodorus could be bothered, suggesting a tutor who missed no opportunity to point a moral to his princely young pupil. Moreover the long sections regarding the ambrosia-like quality of the incense trees and the surpassing wealth of the Sabaeans show that he was rather carried away by the descriptions given to him—a little gullible, perhaps. Not that the fragrance of the Arabian air was entirely imagined. "In parts of the mountains and in particular in the valley which leads down to the town . . . (frankincense and myrrh) trees grow in abundance", wrote a modern traveller, Douglas Botting, of a journey to the island of Socotra; "in the summer they blossom and fill the entire valley with a magnificent scent." [28]

When the text of Agatharchides, as quoted by Strabo/Artemidorus, Diodorus and Photius, is compared with the Strabo/Eratosthenes passage, it becomes apparent that the sources are of a different kind. While most of the information in Eratosthenes seems to have come from someone familiar with the land route, that of Agatharchides derives quite clearly from sailors who knew only the coast and had picked up some wild tales and exaggerations about the inland areas. But Artemidorus also had another source not available to Agatharchides. Strabo quotes a passage from Artemidorus which details the islands, headlands and beaches passed on the journey south down the Arabian west coast. This would seem to have derived from Eudoxus of Cyzicus, a geographer who lived at the end of the second century BC. Eudoxus is known to have been employed by Ptolemy Evergates on voyages to India between 120 and 110 BC. He fell foul of Ptolemy Lathyrus, however, who confiscated his possessions, whereupon he is reputed to have sailed off down the Red Sea and eventually arrived in Gades (Cadiz) after making the first (unless we accept the Phoenician claim mentioned by Herodotus) circumnavigation of Africa.

Although stressing the wealth of the incense lands, Agatharchides has little to say about the incense trade itself.[29] He noted, as both Photius and Diodorus reveal, that the Minaei and the Gerrhaei conveyed frankincense and other cargoes to Palestine "so it is reported" and he had obviously heard that they did so very profitably. But that is about all. Clearly the trade at this time was almost entirely an overland one, following the traditional inland route, and first-hand details about it were not available to Agatharchides. In the coastal areas of the Red Sea it was probably heard of hardly at all. Incense was not being conveyed northwards by sea at this time, while Alexandria, where Agatharchides lived, had not yet become the great incense-processing centre which it was to be later under the Romans.

So far we have mentioned Strabo of Pontus, another Asiatic Greek, only in regard to his quotations from other geographers. His dates are approximately 64 BC to AD 25. He wrote a monumental history, which has been lost, but we are concerned here with his famous *Geography*, which filled seventeen books and is one of the comparatively few classical works to have survived intact to the present day. Strabo travelled widely before producing this great study, visiting areas as far apart as Italy, the Black Sea, Egypt and even, it is believed, Ethiopia.

Book 16 of Strabo's *Geography* deals with Mesopotamia and Arabia. Strabo never visited Arabia and was therefore dependent on other people's accounts of it, although he took some care to define his sources. On top of the information he derived from early authors like Eratosthenes and Artemidorus he was able to add a valuable, up-to-date account received from a person who had accompanied the ill-fated expedition of Aelius Gallus, which set out from Egypt in 25 BC to conquer the incense lands. His section on Arabia was therefore completed after 24 BC and in it, for the first time, we get a Roman view of Arabia:

> "Many of the special characteristics of Arabia have been disclosed by the recent expedition of the Romans against the Arabians made in my time under Aelius Gallus as commander. He was sent by Augustus Caesar to explore the tribes and places, not only in Arabia, but also in Ethiopia, since Caesar saw that the Troglodyte country which adjoins Egypt neighbours upon Arabia, and also that the Arabian Gulf, which separates the Arabians from the Troglodytes, is extremely narrow. Accordingly he conceived the purpose of winning the Arabians over to himself or of subjugating them. Another consideration was the report, which had prevailed from all time, that they were very wealthy, and that they sold aromatics and the most valuable stones for gold and silver, but never expended with outsiders any part of what they received in exchange; for he expected either to deal with wealthy friends or to master wealthy enemies."[30]

After describing at some length the preparations and the nearly disastrous hardships and delays which afflicted the army once it was on the march (misfortunes attributed to the treachery of their Nabataean guide), Strabo went on to relate the story of the campaign in Arabia Felix itself:

> "The next country . . . traversed belonged to nomads and most of it was truly desert; and it was called Ararene; and its king was Sabos; and in passing through this country, through parts that had no roads, he spent fifty days, arriving at the city of the Negrani and at a country which was both peaceful and fertile. Now the king had fled and the city was seized at the first onset; and from there he arrived at the river in six days. Here the barbarians joined battle with the Romans, and about ten thousand of them fell, but only two Romans; for they used their weapons in an inexperienced manner, being utterly unfit for war, using bows and spears and swords and slings, though most of them used a double-edged axe; and immediately afterwards he took the city called Asca, which had been forsaken by its king; and

thence he went to a city called Athrula; and, having mastered it without a struggle, he placed a garrison in it, arranged for supplies of dates and grain for his march, advanced to a city called Marsiaba, which belonged to the tribe of the Rhammanitae, who were subject to Ilasarus. Now he assaulted and besieged this city for six days, but for want of water desisted. He was indeed only a two days' journey from the country that produces aromatics, as informed by his captives, but he had used up six months' time on his marches because of bad guidance, and he realised the fact when he turned back, when at last he had learned the plot against him and gone back by other roads; for on the ninth day he arrived at Negrana, where the battle had taken place, and thence on the eleventh day at Hepta Phraeta . . . on his return he accomplished the whole journey within sixty days, although he had used up six months in his first journey.''[31]

One of the most debated points in this description of the expedition of Aelius Gallus is how far he really penetrated into the incense lands. The argument has not been concluded, although most scholars now accept that Marsiaba, the furthest town noted by Strabo, was Mārib, the capital city of the Sabaeans. The "Res Gestae" of the Emperor Augustus, inscribed on his tomb, recorded that the army advanced into Sabaean territory to the town of "Mariba". Pliny gave the furthest point reached as "Caripeta" (cf. Arabic "kharibat" meaning "ruins"), but this may simply have been the result of a reconnaissance while the main force tried to besiege "Marsiaba". Certainly Negrana, nine days away on the return journey, must have been modern Nagrān, and the other names have identifiable counterparts. Yet it is extraordinary that this expedition should have failed for want of water at Mārib, a most fertile area where there were numerous and copious wells, and we can by no means be sure that the identification of "Marsiaba" with Mārib is correct. Professor Beeston has recently proposed that Gallus may indeed never have advanced to Mārib; instead, from Athrula, which seems to be Yathul, now called Barāqish, he may have tried to march direct to the incense land itself by a difficult northern crossing of the Ṣayhad desert towards Ḥaḍramawt, meeting his defeat at the oasis now called al-'Abr, two days' journey north of Shabwah.[32] There may in any case have been more to the story of Aelius Gallus' failure than Strabo was able to record. Syllaeus, the treacherous Nabataean guide, "paid the penalty at Rome, since, although he pretended friendship, he was convicted, in addition to his rascality in this matter, of other offences too, and was beheaded." One senses that Syllaeus may have been a scapegoat. The third century Roman historian Cassius Dio, possibly with Livy as his source, could only attribute the failure to a disease brought about by "the desert, the sun and the water".[33]

Chapter 5

Pliny, Ptolemy and the "Periplus"

By far the most important single source of information about the incense trade is the *Natural History* of Gaius Plinius Secundus, known as Pliny the Elder, who was born in north Italy in AD 23 and perished during the Vesuvius eruption in AD 79. Pliny spent his younger days in the army in Germany and afterwards practised as a lawyer in Rome. At the time of his death he was in command of a Roman fleet. He was a man of wide interests and insatiable curiosity who read avidly and wrote a number of books, of which only the *Natural History*, completed in AD 77, survives.

In the thirty-seven sections of the *Natural History* Pliny assembled a vast mass of facts about geography, ethnography, anthropology, zoology, botany, agriculture, horticulture, medicine, gems and other subjects. He was not a critical writer, so his information is an undiscriminating mixture of the true and the false, but he took care to list his sources, although not always against the information they had provided, and there is much in his work which is not found elsewhere. Of particular interest to students of ancient south Arabia are Book 6, which deals with the "sites, races, seas, towns, harbours, mountains, rivers, dimensions and present and past populations" of various areas including "Arabia" and the "Gulf of the Red Sea", and Book 12, which is the section on Trees.

In Book 1, Pliny provided a summary of the contents of the subsequent Books, together with a list of the sources he had used for each. He quoted sixteen Latin writers and thirty-seven "foreign authorities" as his sources for Book 6 and sixteen Latin and forty-one "foreign" authorities for Book

12, although only a portion of these provided information about Arabia and the incense trade. They include the Greek writers Herodotus, Theophrastus, Eratosthenes and Artemidorus, but Pliny does not appear to have had direct access to Agatharchides.

In the fifth century AD a Constantinople grammarian named Stephanus of Byzantium wrote a geographical lexicon called *Ethnica*; that work is lost but a summary of it survives from which we learn of another lost work, a geography in five books called *Arabica* written by one Uranios, who lived at some time between about 80 BC and AD 10 (these dates have been worked out through references in the summary to the names of certain Nabataean kings whose dates are known). This book by Uranios is thought to have been used as a source by Livy (59 BC–AD 17) in writing his immense *History of Rome* when he came to cover the Arabian campaign of Aelius Gallus, and it is even possible that Uranios fought in that campaign. Unfortunately there are many sections of Livy's work too which have been lost and the section on the Arabian campaign is among them. Pliny of course had access to the whole of Livy's work, which he lists as one of his sources. A short description of the campaign by the third-century historian Cassius Dio may also have derived from it. But Uranios' *Arabica* is also thought to have been used by Juba (*c.*50 BC–AD 19), a king of Mauretania, brought up in Italy, who married the daughter of Anthony and Cleopatra and achieved distinction for his great erudition. None of Juba's works survive, but he too was a source for Pliny, who quotes extensively from his geographical work when dealing with Arabia. Thus information from Uranios about Arabia may have reached Pliny from two of his acknowledged sources—Livy and Juba; there is some suggestion that it may also have been known to Strabo.[1] This information would seem most likely to date between about 20 BC and AD 10.

In the previous chapter we mentioned Eudoxus of Cyzicus, who voyaged on journeys to India on behalf of the Ptolemys in the period around 120–110 BC. What he wrote about these journeys is not known, but Pliny lists him as one of the sources for Book 6 of the *Natural History*. Either with Eudoxus or possibly in some other Greek ship sailing into the Erythraean Sea then or a little later, there travelled a Greek named Hippalus who was to make a discovery of immense significance. Hippalus realised how a sailing ship could use the strong monsoon winds for a trading voyage to India. We shall deal further with that discovery in Chapter 8, but the effect of it is at once apparent when one reads Pliny, for by his time the journey from Egypt to India, once, as Strabo had recorded,[2] undertaken by fewer than twenty ships a year, was being made by numerous sea captains. Pliny described the journey to India and back and his description reveals the route by which sea-borne incense was carried to Alexandria after it had become the processing centre for the Roman empire, although, as we shall see, the main trade continued to be an overland one. Pliny wrote about it as follows:

"It will not be amiss to set out the whole of the voyage from Egypt now that reliable knowledge of it is for the first time available. It is an important subject in view of the fact that in no year does India absorb less than fifty million sesterces of our empire's wealth, sending back merchandise to be sold with us at a hundred times its prime cost."

Starting from Alexandria, the merchants sailed up the Nile for twelve days and then moved overland through a series of caravanseries (known as *hydreuma*, or "watering places") for another twelve days to Berenice, on the Red Sea coast. From there:

"travelling by sea begins at midsummer before the dogstar rises or immediately after its rising, and it takes about thirty days to reach the Arabian port of Ocelis, or Cane in the frankincense-producing district. There is also a third port named Muza, which is not called at on the voyage to India, and is only used by merchants trading in frankincense and Arabian perfumes. Inland there is a town, the residence of the king of the district, called Sapphar, and another called Save. But the most advantageous way of sailing to India is to set out from Ocelis; from that port it is a forty days' voyage, if the Hippalus is blowing, to the first trading station in India, Muziris—not a desirable port of call on account of the neighbouring pirates. . . . Travellers set sail from India on the return voyage at the beginning of the Egyptian month of Tybis, which is our December, or at all events before the sixth day of the Egyptian Mechir, which works out at before January 13 in our calendar—so making it possible to return home in the same year. They set sail from India with a south-east wind, and after entering the Red Sea, continue the voyage with a south-west or south wind."[3]

In this passage Pliny gives a sailor's account and the information about inland Arabia is scanty. Presumably when calling at the port of Muza, on the Yemeni Red Sea coast, or Ocelis, which lay on the same coast near the Straits of Bāb al-Mandab, this sailor had learned of the inland capital of Sapphar (or Zafār), the centre of the Himyarite tribe which was by then beginning to make an appearance in south Arabia. The ruins of Zafār lie on the Yemeni plateau not far from modern Yarīm, while Save, the other town mentioned by Pliny, is thought to be a ruin site close to the present city of Ta'izz and would have been on the route to the capital from either Muza or Ocelis, Strabo, too, knew the name Ocelis, recording in regard to the straits that according to Artemidorus "the promontory on the Arabian side opposite to Deire is called Acila",[4] which suggests that, at that earlier time of somewhere around 150 BC, there was no port. In the account of the *Periplus*, which we shall come to and which followed about a century or more after Pliny, Ocelis was described as an anchorage and watering place rather than a port; it seems to have developed for this purpose with the growth of the trade between the Mediterranean and India.

In a subsequent section of Book 6, Pliny provides a long list of tribes and places on the Arabian mainland, seemingly with King Juba (and hence perhaps Uranios) as his main source and possibly Artemidorus as one of his secondary sources:

"The remaining tribes on the mainland situated in the south ('*a noto*') are the Autarides, seven days' journey into the mountains, the Larendani and Catapani tribes, the Gebbanitae with several towns, of which the largest are Nagia and Thomna, the latter with sixty-five temples, a fact that indicates its size. Then a cape the distance between which and the mainland in the Cave-Dwellers' territory is fifty miles; then the Thoani, the Actaei, the Chatramotitae, the Tonabaei, the Antiadelai and Lexianae, the Agraei, the Cerbani and the Sabaei, the best known of all the Arabian tribes because of their frankincense—these tribes extend from sea to sea. Their towns on the coast of the Red Sea are Merme, Marma, Corolia, Sabbatha (Note: or Sabratha), and the inland towns are Nascus, Cardava, Carnus, and Thomala to which they bring their perfumes for export. One division of them are the Atramitae, whose chief place is Sabota, a walled town containing sixty temples; the royal capital of all these, however, is Mareliabata. They occupy a bay measuring ninety-four miles round, studded with islands that produce perfumes. Adjoining the Atramitae in the interior are the Minaei; beside the sea are also the Aelamitae with a town of the same name, and adjoining them are the Chaculatae, with the town of Sibis, the Greek name of which is Apate. . . ."[5]

A noticeable feature of this passage is that there is no mention of Ocelis, Qana (Cana) or Muza, the ports referred to by Pliny in talking of the journey to India. The source (or sources) appear to have known only the western coast of Arabia and even then not the southern parts of it, gathering information about other areas by enquiries at ports of call. Although the division into the peoples of Saba, Ma'īn, Qatabān and Ḥaḍramawt is not stated, these people appear in the list of tribes: Catapani (Qatabān), Chatramotitae (Ḥaḍramawt), Minaei and Sabaei, the latter still being "the best known of all the Arabian tribes because of their frankincense". The Chatramotitae, whom we infer as the people of what is now Ḥaḍramawt, are listed as a separate tribe from the Atramitae "whose chief place is Sabota (Shabwah)." Yet at the time of Eratosthenes Sabota was the capital of the Chatramotitae. The anomaly probably results from Pliny's use of two sources without realising that Chatramotitae and Atramitae were variations of the same name. Thomna, which Eratosthenes called Tamna, is not shown as the capital of the Catapani (or Qatabanians), as Eratosthenes gave it, but as one of the towns of a people called the Gebbanitae. The puzzle of the Gebbanitae, whose role in the incense trade was a significant one, will be considered in a later chapter.

The last reference to the south Arabian incense lands in Book 6 of Pliny is a short catalogue of facts obtained by the Roman expedition which are additional to those listed by Strabo. It is unnecessary to quote these in detail. The expedition had noted that the Homeritae were "the most numerous tribe," an indication of the growing power of these people who, originating in a wild mountain area north-east of Aden, set up their own "Himyarite" dynasty at Ẓafār and were eventually to take over control of most of south-western Arabia. But the Sabaei were still "the most wealthy, owing to the fertility of their forests in producing scent, their gold mines, their irrigated agricultural land and their production of honey and wax," while the Chatramotitae excelled as warriors. Pliny ended this part with the comment: "And strange to say, of these innumerable tribes an equal part are engaged in trade or live by brigandage; taken as a whole, they are the richest race in the world, because the vast wealth from Rome and Parthia accumulates in their hands, as they sell the produce they obtain from the sea or their forests and buy nothing in return."[6]

Identification of the tribes listed by Pliny in these passages with modern counterparts is almost impossible. The ebb and flow of population caused by war, drought and other political, economic and social pressures has been considerable in these harsh regions, particularly away from the high mountain areas, and any similarity of the tribal names of pre-Islamic times with those of today is likely to be fortuitous, although a few do survive. Place-names are more durable and many present-day names are testified in inscriptions or the works of the early authors, but in the latter there are corruptions too, resulting from misunderstandings, language difficulties, the problems of transliterating oriental sounds into Greek and Roman letters, the ignorance of guides, especially when talking about distant areas they had not actually been to, editorial mistakes and errors by the scribes who copied the manuscripts—inversions, misreadings of letters or words, omissions not only of words but even of whole lines. If Pliny's place-names are sometimes confusing, this is an inevitable result of the process through which the accumulation and recording of his information had to go rather than any reflection on his integrity.

In Book 12 of the *Natural History* Pliny deals not only with frankincense and myrrh but also with other products of Arabia which were derived from trees and shrubs. Here we learn of *tabaschir*, grown also in India, where the quality was superior, "a kind of honey that collects in reeds, white like a gum, and brittle to the teeth. . . . It is employed only as a medicine."[7] We also hear once again of *ladanum*, which Herodotus had been told was collected off the beards of he-goats:

"A considerable number of writers have stated that this becomes aromatic entirely by accident and owing to an injury; goats, they say, an animal very destructive of foliage in general, but especially fond of scented shrubs, as if understanding the prices they fetch, crop the stalks of the shoots, which swell with an extremely sweet fluid, and wipe off with the nasty shaggy hair of their beards the juice dripping from the stalks in a random mixture, and this forms lumps in the dust and is baked by the sun; and that is the reason why goats' hairs are found in *ladanum*; though they say that this does not take place anywhere else but in the territory of the Nabataei, a people from Arabia who border on Syria. The more recent of the authorities call this substance *storbon*, and say that the trees in the Arabs' forests are broken by the goats when browsing, and so the juice sticks to their hairs; but that the true *ladanum* belongs to the island of Cyprus."[8]

It is now thought that *ladanum* was the product of the rock-rose, known as *cistus*.[9]

Cinnamon and cassia are also discussed by Pliny at length in Book 12. The strange circumstances surrounding the cultivation and collection of these products, which Herodotus and others had recounted, he regarded as tales "invented by the natives to raise the price of their commodities" and being false "inasmuch as cinnamon grows in Ethiopia, which is linked by intermarriage with the Troglodytai" (i.e. the inhabitants of Somalia). "The latter buy it from their neighbours and convey it over the wide seas in ships . . . to the harbour of the Gebbanitae called Ocilia."[10] "Cassia," Pliny added, building on information first provided by Theophrastus, "grows close to the plains of cinnamon but on the mountains." Cassia shoots were cut into two-inch lengths and sewn up into "newly flayed hides of animals slaughtered for the purpose, so that as they rot maggots grow among the wood and hollow out the whole of the bark, which is protected from them by its bitter taste. The bark is valued most highly when fresh, when it has a very pleasant smell and is hardly at all hot to the taste, and rather gives a slight nip with its moderate warmth." But another kind of cassia "has a scent like that of balsam, but it has a bitter taste and consequently is more useful for medicinal purposes just as the black kind is more used for unguents."[11]

The position of cinnamon and cassia in the ancient Arabian spice trade is perplexing. These were highly valued commodities. In modern times cassia is recognized as coming from the bark of a forest tree *Cinnamomum cassia*, while cinnamon, also a bark, comes from *Cinnamomum macrophyllum* and a number of related species found in Assam, Vietnam and south-east Asia. None of these species exists in Somalia, which the classical authors traditionally regarded as the cinnamon-producing area. Innes Miller has proposed that from the very earliest times cinnamon and cassia were brought direct from south-east Asia to Madagascar and the neighbouring African coast by Indonesians in outrigger canoes and conveyed from there to Somalia.[12] But the arguments advanced for this are not convincing. They ignore, for instance, the descriptions of the plants which Theophrastus and, in greater detail, Pliny were able to give and the naming in the *Periplus* of different varieties of cinnamon found in different areas of Somalia (see page 139 below).

Furthermore, a regular, direct trading voyage of 4,500 miles over open sea in these early days is extremely improbable. It would seem most likely that the cinnamon and cassia of earlier times came from other plants which grew in Somalia or east Africa, until the similar but superior products of the Far East reached Europe through normal trading channels and replaced them.

Some three generations after Pliny, when the Roman Empire had reached its greatest extent, Claudius Ptolemaeus, otherwise known as Ptolemy, produced his famous *Geography*. Although, as mathematician, astronomer and geographer, he was one of the greatest of the classical savants, little is recorded about Ptolemy's life. He is known to have made astronomical observations in Alexandria in AD 139 and to have been alive in AD 161 and his dates are now generally put at *c.*AD 90–168.[13] The *Geography* consisted of a catalogue of place-names, with estimated latitudes and longitudes, and a few other brief details, designed as a descriptive supplement for a series of twenty-six maps in which he attempted to portray the whole of the known world.

Ptolemy made use of the works of earlier geographers, including Eratosthenes and Hipparchus, but his *Geography*, which was produced between AD 150 and 160, comprises in the main an improved, up-dated, completed and more scientifically prepared version of a work commenced by Marinus the Tyrian (*c.* AD 70–130). It was to remain an authoritative book until the advance of exploration and learning in the fifteenth century.

More than forty manuscript copies of the *Geography* are known at the present day, the oldest dating from the eleventh century; many are incomplete and they contain the usual textual variations; but, while these have preserved the eight books of text, Ptolemy's maps have not survived. Reconstruction of their detail from the texts presents considerable difficulties: the precise line of the coasts, mountain ranges, watercourses and other such features mentioned in the text cannot be defined; locations were often determined on understandable inexactitudes in the recording of distances; the calculations of longitude, under Ptolemy's newly evolved system of map projection, were considerably in error. Even in better attested areas, which can be satisfactorily checked,

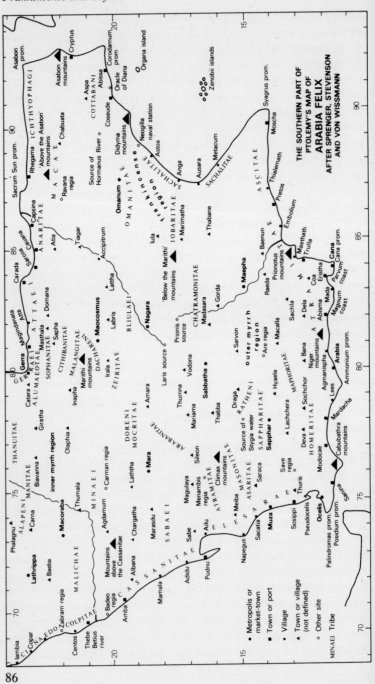

THE SOUTHERN PART OF
PTOLEMY'S MAP OF
ARABIA FELIX
AFTER SPRENGER, STEVENSON
AND VON WISSMANN

- ● Metropolis or market-town
- ■ Town or port
- • Village
- ▲ Town or village (not defined)
- ○ Other site

MINAEI Tribe

errors reveal themselves—coasts set down as rivers, names of mountains ascribed to tribes, place-names repeated or quoted with additional letters. While none of this detracts from Ptolemy's achievements, it means that he needs to be interpreted very carefully.

Various reconstructions of Ptolemy's maps have been undertaken since mediaeval times and in 1875 a European scholar, Aloys Sprenger, assembled the basic data approximately as they must have appeared in Ptolemy's original map of Arabia, publishing the result in his *Ancient Geography of Arabia* (*Alte Geographie*). This book is still a principal source in the difficult process of trying to identify the sites of Ptolemy's Arabian place-names.

Chapter 7 of Book 6 of Ptolemy's *Geography* contains over two hundred place-names of towns, villages, areas, mountains, capes, etc. in Arabia Felix, using that term in its broad classical sense to cover the larger part of the Arabian peninsula which lay south of Arabia Petra and Arabia Deserta. For the most part these data seem to have derived from the itineraries of traders travelling with overland caravans or coasting round the shores. The information from the caravaneers, perhaps more readily obtainable after Roman legions had moved into Arabia to annexe the kingdom of the Nabataeans, provided the first knowledge of many of the places in the interior, revealing the stations on some of the main caravan routes with an accuracy which makes it possible to equate many of them with existing oases. This is of course of particular value in trying to determine the incense road, as we shall see in a later chapter.

A reconstruction of Ptolemy's map of the southern part of Arabia can be seen opposite (page 86). Comparison with the detail provided by Pliny shows a new name, Arabia Emporium, or the "market town of Arabia", at the site of what is now Aden, and a large number of other new places. Of the tribal names, the Minaei, Sabaei, Homeritae and Chatramonitae (the different spelling will be noticed) are all familiar. One of the more noticeable topographical features is the river Prion (Prionis), which flows southwards to reach the sea a little east of Qana. It used to be supposed that this represented Wadi Masīlah, the name for the lower part of Wādī Ḥaḍramawt, but it may well have been Wādī Ḥagr, which lies a little further west and which, at the point where it reaches the sea, is that great rarity of Arabia, a perennial stream. The importance of this will become apparent in discussing the frankincense-growing region in a later chapter.

Ptolemy specifically referred to both the myrrh-growing and frankincense-growing regions, but what he had to say left the location of these regions very uncertain. He noted two myrrh-growing regions: firstly "below the Manitae is the *Smyrnofera interior region*; then the Minaei, a numerous tribe, below whom are the Doreni and the Mocritae, then the Sabaei . . .;" secondly, ". . . near Homerita (are) the Sappharitae and the Ratheni, above whom are the Maphotitae, thence to the beginning near the Chatramonitae is the *Smynofera exterior region*." This suggests that the "interior" region lay north of Wādī Gawf, the heartland of the Minaeans, while the "exterior" region is assumed, from this and the clues provided by Pliny, to have lain to the west of Ḥaḍramawt (the land of the Chatramonitae). The frankincense-growing region was even more obscurely described. It was "below the Cottabani", who apparently bordered the Omanitae, and was to be found between a river source and the "Asabon mountains". As the Asabon mountains were firmly placed near the entrance to the Arabian Gulf, this was originally held to mean that the region must have been in Omān. In reconstructing Ptolemy's map, Sprenger showed it in the area corresponding to modern Ẓufār (Dhofar) because that was where frankincense mainly grew in modern times, but it cannot be suggested that Ptolemy's data provides evidence for this location.

The next and chronologically the last of the main sources of information about the incense trade is a "periplus", or the narrative of a coasting voyage, the standard way by which the early Greek sea captains and traders recorded geographical knowledge as they expanded the boundaries of the known world. The "periplus" was more than a navigational log book, because it also contained information about the goods imported and exported at ports of call and brief details about the inhabitants of the lands visited.

The *Periplus of the Erythraean Sea* is an account by an unknown merchant or ship's master of the trading journey between Egypt and India written at a time when incense was the major export of south Arabia. A tenth-century copy of this manuscript, probably written in Constantinople, survives in Heidelberg and is known as *Codex Palatinus*, while the British Museum holds another much later copy, probably taken from the Heidelberg manuscript, which it acquired from a monastery on Mount Athos in 1853.[14]

The *Periplus* was translated into English and published in 1912 by an American scholar, W. H. Schoff, together with a comprehensive critical analysis which included an attempt to date it by the information it contained. Scholars had always held widely differing views about when it was written and Schoff's conclusion that it could be dated to about AD 60, or shortly before Pliny compiled his *Natural History*, left many unconvinced. In 1961 the Belgian orientalist, Dr Jacqueline Pirenne, published a study of certain south Arabian chronological problems which included a thorough re-examination of this matter.[15] A key point in Schoff's argument was a reference to "Malichas, King of the Nabataeans", which he held must refer to Malichas II (reigned between AD 40 and 71 or 77) and hence indicate a composition date preceding the Roman annexation of Nabataea in AD 106. Pirenne observed that there were conjectural mediaeval corrections in the Heidelberg manuscript and the mention of the Nabataeans was one of them. Her argument showed that the *Periplus* could have been written at some undefined date after AD 106. A reference in a papyrus discovered subsequently has shown that there was a King Malichas who can be dated on palaeographic grounds to at least a century later—a king reigning, like Herod, under Roman auspices. In subsequent years the rapid strides made in Indian archaeology have led to more positive opinions about the date of the passages referring to India, and it is now widely held, although still debated, that it was composed in the second or early in the third century AD.

A considerable portion of the *Periplus* concerns south Arabia and Somalia. So important are these passages as a source of information about the incense trade that they are appended below in full, using Schoff's translation with a few corrections (in italics) proposed by Professor Beeston:

"19. Now to the left of Berenice, sailing for two or three days from Mussel Harbour[16] eastward across the adjacent gulf, there is another harbour and fortified place, which is called White Village,[17] from which *there is a way up to Petra to the court of King Malichas*. It holds the position of a market town for the small vessels sent there from Arabia; and so a centurion is stationed there as a collector of one-fourth of the merchandise imported, with an armed force, as a garrison.

20. Directly below this place is the adjoining country of Arabia, in its length bordering a great distance on the Erythraean Sea. Different tribes inhabit the country, differing in their speech, some partially and some altogether. The land next to the sea is similarly dotted here and there with caves of the Fish-Eaters, but the country inland is populated by rascally men speaking two languages, who live in villages and nomadic camps, by whom those sailing off the middle course are plundered, and those surviving shipwrecks are taken for slaves. And so they too are continually taken prisoners by the chiefs and kings of Arabia; and they are called Carnaites. Navigation is dangerous along this whole coast of Arabia, which is without harbours, with bad anchorages, foul, inaccessible because of breakers and rocks, and terrible in every way. Therefore we hold our course down the middle of the gulf and pass on as fast as possible by the country of Arabia until we come to the Burnt Island;[18] directly below which there are regions of peaceful people, nomadic, pasturers of cattle, sheep and camels.

21. Beyond these places, in a bay at the foot of the left side of this gulf, there is a place by the shore called Muza, a market-town established by law, distant altogether from Berenice for those sailing southward, about twelve thousand stadia. And the whole place is crowded with Arab ship-owners and seafaring men, and is busy with the affairs of commerce; for they carry on a trade with the far-side coast and with Barygaza, sending their own ships there.

22. Three days inland from this port there is a city called Saua,[19] in the midst of the region called Mapharitis; and there is a local chieftain named Cholaebus who lives in that city.

23. And after nine days more there is Saphar, the metropolis, in which lives Charibael, lawful king of two tribes, the Homeritae and those living next to them, called the Sabaites; through continual embassies and gifts, he is a friend of the Emperors.[20]

24. The market town of Muza is without a harbour, but has a good roadstead and anchorage because of the sandy bottom thereabouts, where the anchors hold safely. The merchandise imported there consists of purple cloths, both fine and coarse;

clothing in the Arabian style, with sleeves; plain, ordinary, embroidered, or interwoven with gold; saffron, sweet rush, muslins, cloaks, blankets (not many), some plain and others made in the local fashion; sashes of different colours, fragrant ointments in moderate quantity, wine and wheat, not much. For the country produces grain in moderate amount, and a great deal of wine. And to the King and the Chief are given horses and sumpter-mules, vessels of gold and polished silver, finely woven clothing and copper vessels. There are exported from the same place the things produced in the country: selected myrrh, and the Gebanite-Minaean stacte,[21] alabaster and all the things already mentioned from Avalites and the far-side coast.[22] The voyage to this place is made best about the month of September, that is Thoth; but there is nothing to prevent it even earlier.

25. After sailing beyond this place about three hundred stadia, the coast of Arabia and the Berber country about the Avalitic gulf now coming close together, there is a channel, not long in extent, which forces the sea together and shuts it into a narrow strait, the passage through which, sixty stadia in length, the island Diodorus[23] divides. Therefore the course through it is beset with rushing currents and with strong winds blowing down from the adjacent ridge of mountains. Directly on this strait by the shore there is a village of Arabs, subject to the same chief, called Ocelis; which is not so much a market-town as it is an anchorage and watering-place and the first landing for those sailing into the gulf.

26. Beyond Ocelis, the sea widening towards the east, and soon giving a view of the open ocean, after about twelve hundred stadia there is Eudaemon Arabia,[24] a village by the shore, also of the kingdom of Charibael, and having convenient anchorages, and water places, sweeter and better than those at Ocelis; it lies at the entrance of a bay, and the land recedes from it. It was called Eudaemon, because in the early days of the city when the voyage was not yet made from India to Egypt, and when they did not dare to sail from Egypt to the ports across this ocean, but all came together at this place, it received the cargoes from both countries, just as Alexandria now receives the things brought both from abroad and from Egypt. But not long before our time Charibael destroyed the place.[25]

27. After Eudaemon Arabia there is a continuous length of coast extending two thousand stadia or more, along which there are Nomads and Fish-Eaters living in villages; just beyond the cape projecting from this bay there is another market town by the shore, Cana, of the Kingdom of Eleazus, the Frankincense Country; and facing it there are two desert islands, one called Island of Birds, the other Dome Island, one hundred and twenty

stadia from Cana. Inland from this place lies the metropolis Sabbatha, in which the King lives. All the frankincense produced in the country is brought by camels to that place to be stored, and to Cana on rafts held up by inflated skins after the manner of the country, and in boats. And this place has a trade also with the far-side ports, with Barygaza[26] and Scythia and Ommana and the neighbouring coast of Persia.

28. There are imported into this place from Egypt a little wheat and wine, as at Muza; clothing in the Arabian style, plain and common but the 'spurious' is more unusual; and copper and tin and coral and storax and other things such as go to Muza; and for the King usually wrought gold and silver plate, also horses, images, and thin clothing of fine quality. And there are exported from this place, native produce, frankincense and aloes, and the rest of the things that enter into the trade of the other ports. The voyage to this place is best made at the same time as that to Muza, or rather earlier.

29. Beyond Cana, the land receding greatly, there follows a very deep bay stretching a great way across, which is called Sachalites; and the Frankincense Country, mountainous and forbidding, wrapped in thick clouds and fog, and yielding frankincense from the trees. These incense-bearing trees are not of great height or thickness; they bear the frankincense sticking in drops on the bark, just as the trees among us in Egypt weep their gum. The frankincense is gathered by the King's slaves and those who are sent to this service for punishment. For these places are very unhealthy, and pestilential even to those sailing along the coast; but almost always fatal to those working there, who also perish often from want of food.

30. On this bay there is a very great promontory facing the east, called Syagrus,[27] on which is a fort for the defence of the country, and a harbour and storehouse for the frankincense that is collected; and opposite this cape, well out at sea, there is an island, lying between it and the Cape of Spices opposite, but nearer Syagrus: it is called Dioscorida,[28] and is very large but desert and marshy, having rivers in it and crocodiles and many snakes and great lizards, of which the flesh is eaten and the fat melted and used instead of olive oil. The island yields no fruit, neither vine nor grain. The inhabitants are few and they live on the coast toward the north, which from this side faces the continent. They are foreigners, a mixture of Arabs and Indians and Greeks, who have emigrated to carry on trade there. The island produces the true sea-tortoise, and the land-tortoise, and the white tortoise which is very numerous and preferred for its large shells; and the mountain-tortoise, which is largest of all and has the thickest shell;

of which the worthless specimens cannot be cut apart on the underside, because they are even too hard; but those of value are cut apart and the shells made whole into caskets and small plates and cake-dishes and that sort of ware. There is also produced in this island cinnabar, that called Indian, which is collected in drops from the trees.

31. It happens that just as Azania[29] is subject to Charibael and the Chief of the Mapharitis, this island is subject to the King of the Frankincense Country. Trade is also carried on there by some people from Muza and by those who chance to call there on the voyage from Damirica[30] and Barygaza; they bring in rice and wheat and Indian cloth, and a few female slaves; and they take for their exchange cargoes, a great quantity of tortoise-shell. Now the island is farmed out under the Kings and is garrisoned.

32. Immediately beyond Syagrus the bay of Omana cuts deep into the coast-line, the width of it being six hundred stadia; and beyond this there are mountains, high and rocky and steep, inhabited by cave-dwellers for five hundred stadia more; and beyond this is a port established for receiving the Sachalite frankincense; the harbour is called Moscha, and ships from Cana call there regularly; and ships returning from Damirica and Barygaza, if the season is late, winter there, and trade with the King's officers, exchanging their cloth and wheat and sesame oil for frankincense, which lies in heaps all over the Sachalitic country, open and unguarded, as if the place were under the protection of the gods; for neither openly nor by stealth can it be loaded on board ship without the King's permission; if a single grain were loaded without this, the ship could not clear from the harbour.

33. Beyond the harbour of Moscha for about fifteen hundred stadia as far as Asich, a mountain range runs along the shore; at the end of which, in a row, lie seven islands, called Zenobian.[31] Beyond these there is a barbarous region which is no longer of the same kingdom, but now belongs to Persia. Sailing along this coast well out to sea for two thousand stadia from the Zenobian Islands, there meets you an island called Sarapis,[32] about one hundred and twenty stadia from the mainland. It is about two hundred stadia wide and six hundred long, inhabited by three settlements of Fish-Eaters, a villainous lot, who use the Arabian language and wear girdles of palm-leaves. The island produces considerable tortoise-shell of fine quality, and small sailing boats and cargo-ships are sent there regularly from Cana.

34. Sailing along the coast, which trends northwards toward the entrance of the Persian Sea, there are many islands known as Calaei, after about two thousand stadia, extending along the

shore. The inhabitants are a treacherous lot, very little civilized. 35. At the upper end of these Calaei islands is a range of mountains called Calon, and there follows not far beyond, the mouth of the Persian Gulf, where there is much diving for the pearl mussel. To the left of the straits are great mountains called Asabon, and to the right there rises in full view another round and high mountain called Semiramis; between them and the passage across the strait is about six hundred stadia; beyond which that very great and broad sea, the Persian Gulf, reaches far into the interior. At the upper end of this Gulf there is a market-town designated by law, called Apologus,[33] situated near Charax Spasini and the River Euphrates.
36. Sailing through the mouth of the Gulf, after a six days' course there is another market town of Persia called Ommana.[34] To both these market-towns large vessels are regularly sent from Barygaza, loaded with copper and sandalwood and timbers of teakwood and logs of blackwood and ebony. To Ommana frankincense is also brought from Cana, and from Ommana to Arabia boats sewed together after the fashion of the place; these are known as 'madarata'. From each of these market-towns there are exported to Barygaza and also to Arabia, many pearls, but inferior to those of India; purple clothing after the fashion of the place, wine, a great quantity of dates, gold and slaves."

In its detail of the south Arabian coast, the *Periplus* correctly describes the frankincense port of Moscha, the site of which is believed to be Khor Rori in Ẓufār,[35] as lying well east of the promontory of Syagrus (Rās Fartak). It might be thought that Ptolemy would not have made the error of locating it to the west of Syagrus had the *Periplus* been available to him, and this is one argument for dating the *Periplus* after AD 150. We know from his own statement that Ptolemy corrected an error by Marinus when placing the Bay of Sachalitas to the west of Syagrus,[36] but he may have failed to realise that Marinus had located Moscha in relation to its position in that bay. However, the *Periplus* repeats the error of Marinus in indicating that the Bay of Sachalitas lay west of Syagrus, with the bay east of it, where Moscha was to be found, being called the Bay of Omana. No very confident deductions can therefore be made by comparing these passages as to whether the *Periplus* was written before or after Ptolemy produced his map.

The same difficulties arise in any attempt to see whether one of these sources shows a greater knowledge about the furthest known limits of exploration than the other, which could be a good pointer to which came first. In the *Periplus* the limit of exploration down the eastern coast of Africa was placed at Rhapta (probably near Dar es Salaam) "the very last market town of Azania". Thereafter "the unexplored ocean curves around toward the west, and running along by the regions to the south of Ethiopia and Libya and Africa, it mingles with the western sea." Ptolemy too recognized Rhapta as the most southerly known port and was also aware of Cape Prasum (possibly Cape Delgado), lying south of Rhapta, which was the most southerly limit known. But thereafter, in a confused passage, Ptolemy implied that the land mass continued by curving round to the east, becoming a part of the great southern continent which he called "the unknown land". The passage from the *Periplus*, with its apparent awareness that the African coastline curved round to join the Atlantic Ocean, has been held to demonstrate a more advanced geographical knowledge and hence to indicate a later date for the *Periplus*, but here again the matter is debatable. In the descriptions of the eastern coast of India, Ptolemy appears to have more detail than the *Periplus*.[37]

Scholars continue to work on these problems and archaeological discoveries may throw new light on them and provide a firmer dating for the *Periplus*. In the meantime it can only be concluded that, with so much in both Ptolemy and the *Periplus* which is remarkably similar, their respective dates cannot be very far apart.

Chapter 6
The Trees and Where They Grew

The earliest recorded descriptions of incense trees are found in Theophrastus and appear mainly to derive from the exploratory journey of Anaxicrates on behalf of Alexander the Great (page 62 above):

> "The trees of frankincense and myrrh grow partly in the mountains, partly on private estates at the foot of the mountains; wherefore some are under cultivation, others not; the mountains, they say, are lofty, forest-covered and subject to snow, and rivers from them flow down into the plain. The frankincense tree, it is said, is not tall, about five cubits high, and it is much branched; it has a leaf like that of the pear, but much smaller and very grassy in colour, like rue; the bark is altogether smooth like that of a bay. The myrrh tree is said to be still smaller in stature and more bushy; it is said to have a tough stem, which is contorted near the ground, and is stouter than a man's legs; and to have a smooth bark like that of the andrachne. Others who say that they have seen it agree pretty closely about the size; neither of these trees, they say, is large, but that which bears myrrh is smaller and of lower growth; however they say that, while the frankincense tree has a leaf like that of bay and smooth bark, that which bears myrrh is spinous and not smooth, and has a leaf like that of the elm, except that it is curly and spinous at the tip like that of kermes oak." [1]

This was a fairly accurate description, but of that Theophrastus could not be sure. There were other persons too who claimed to have seen the incense trees and Theophrastus felt obliged to record their accounts:

> "Others report that the tree which produces the frankincense is like mastich, and its fruit is like the fruit of that tree, but the leaf is

reddish: also that the frankincense derived from young trees is whiter and less fragrant; also that the tree which produces myrrh is like the terebinth but rougher and more thorny; that the leaf is somewhat rounder, and that, if one chews it, it resembles that of the terebinth in taste; also that of myrrh trees too those that are past their prime give more fragrant myrrh. Both trees, it is said, grow in the same region; the soil is clayey and caked and spring waters are scarce. Now these reports are contradictory to that which says that the country is subject to snow and rain and sends forth rivers. However, others make the statement that the tree is like the terebinth; in fact some say that it is the same tree; for logs of it were brought to Antigonus by the Arabs who brought the frankincense down to the sea, and that these did not differ at all from logs of terebinth. However these informants were guilty of a further more important piece of ignorance; for they believed that the frankincense and the myrrh were produced by the same tree. Wherefore the account derived from those who sailed from the city of Heroes is more to be believed; in fact the frankincense tree which grows above Sardes in a certain sacred precinct has a leaf like that of bay, if we may judge at all by this; and the frankincense derived both from its stem and its branches is like in appearance and smell, when it is burnt as incense, to other frankincense. This is the only tree which can never be cultivated."[2]

Some three hundred and fifty years later Pliny had more precise information about the appearance of the myrrh tree and realized that there were different varieties, although his description was still by no means very definite:

"Some authorities have stated that myrrh is the product of a tree growing in the same forests among the frankincense trees, but the majority say that it grows separately; and in fact it occurs in many places in Arabia, as will appear when we deal with its varieties. A kind highly spoken of is also imported from islands, and the Sabaei even cross the sea to the Cave Dwellers' Country to procure it. Also a cultivated variety is produced which is much preferred to the wild kind. The plant enjoys being raked and having the soil round it loosened, as it is the better for having its roots cool.

The tree grows to a height of nearly eight feet; it has thorns on it, and the trunk is hard and twisted, and thicker than that of the frankincense tree, and even thicker at the root than in the remaining part of it. Authorities state that the bark is smooth and resembles that of the strawberry-tree, and others that it is rough and prickly; and they say that the leaf is that of the olive, but more wrinkled and with sharp points—though Juba says it is like that of the alexanders. Some say that it resembles the juniper, only that it is rougher and bristling with thorns, and that the leaf is rounder but tastes like juniper. Also there have been writers who have falsely asserted that the frankincense-tree produces myrrh as well as frankincense."[3]

Despite the great increase in Graeco-Roman trade with south Arabia and the growing number of ships which called at the incense ports, Pliny was unable to resolve the uncertainties regarding the appearance of the frankincense tree which had been expressed by Theophrastus. The frankincense groves were inaccessible and the South Arabians did not encourage visitors. All Pliny could say was as follows:

"No Latin author so far as I know has described the appearance of this tree. The descriptions given by the Greeks vary; some have stated that it has the leaf of a pear tree, only smaller and of a grass-green colour; others that it resembles the mastich and has a reddish leaf; some that it is a kind of terebinth, and that this was the view of King Antigonus, to whom a plant was brought. King Juba . . . states that the tree has a twisted stem and branches closely resembling those of the Pontic maple and that it gives a juice like that of the almond. . . . It is well known that it has the

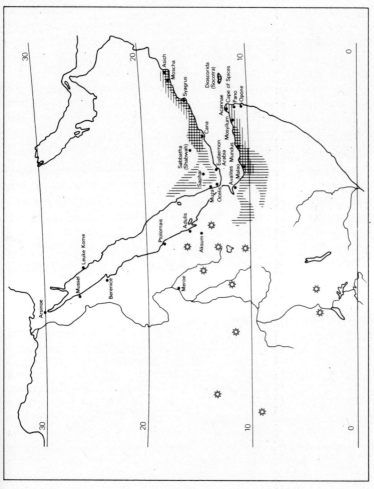

THE ANCIENT MYRRH
AND FRANKINCENSE
REGIONS

PLACE-NAMES IN THIS MAP
ARE THOSE RECORDED IN
THE 'PERIPLUS'

0 100   300   500 miles

0 200 400 600 800 kms

▦ Myrrh

▥ Frankincense

☀ Area where Boswellia
papyrifera attested in
modern times (after
Hepper)

bark of a bay tree and some have said that the leaf is also like that of the bay. . . . The ambassadors who have come to Rome from Arabia in my time have made all these matters still more uncertain, which may well surprise us, seeing that even some sprigs of the incense tree find their way to Rome, on the evidence of which we may believe that the parent tree is also smooth and tapering and that it puts out its shoots from a trunk that is free from knots."[4]

As the frankincense trees were in distant lands and, at least for the greater part, well inland, so that even the Greek traders who braved their way to Qana were still far from getting a sight of them, the uncertainty of the classical authors about their appearance is understandable. More surprising is the considerable inconsistency of information about the species quoted by modern writers and authorities.

Botanically, both frankincense and myrrh belong to the same family, the *Burseraceae* or Balsam family, which is distinguished by the presence of resin ducts in the bark. Within this family, frankincense comes from certain trees of the genus *Boswellia* and myrrh from trees of the genus *Commiphora*, formerly also known as *Balsamodendron*. Both are found fairly widely throughout tropical Africa and Asia and over twenty-five different species of *Boswellia* and two hundred and fifty of *Commiphora* have been recorded. Myrrh derives only from certain species of *Commiphora*, other species of that genus producing bdelliums (see page 123). Few species of either *Boswellia* or *Commiphora* have been found in

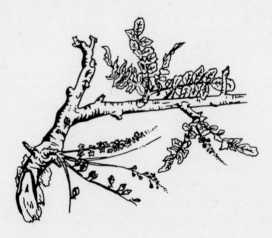

Arabia, but this may partly be attributable to the limited botanical field work which has as yet been undertaken there.

The first detailed description of Arabian frankincense to be provided in modern times came from Assistant Surgeon H. J. Carter, who landed at Rakhyūt from *H.M.S. Palinurus*, then engaged on survey work for the Government of Bombay, in 1844 and was given a branch in full flower. He did not see the tree from which this came. The specimen was sent to Bombay, where it was at first thought to be identical with the Indian species of frankincense, *Boswellia serrata*, and it was not until after Carter had presented his paper on the subject in 1847 that differences were noticed.[5] Carter made a detailed drawing of the branch presented to him, although he could not of course describe the tree from which it came.

In 1869 a further study of the subject was undertaken by Dr George Birdwood.[6] Birdwood noted three species of frankincense trees from specimens obtained from Somaliland or planted in botanical gardens in Bombay and Aden. The Somali names for these were *Mohr madow*, *Mohr add* and *Yegaar*. He found *Mohr madow* to be similar to the Arabian species described by Carter and named it *Boswellia carteri*. *Mohr add* he called *Boswellia bhau-dajiana* (after a prominent citizen of Bombay) and to *Yegaar* he gave the name *Boswellia frereana*. But the identification of *Mohr madow* with the plant found in Arabia by Carter was an uncertain one, because by that time the specimens provided by Carter had disappeared, while a rooted sample planted in Bombay had grown but failed to flower. Later Birdwood discovered that a rooted sample collected by Carter from near Rās Fartak in Mahrah country, where the tree was known locally as *Maghrayt d'sheehaz*,[7] was a smaller plant than the Somali variety, with smaller, more crumpled leaves and with other botanical differences. He was also able to discover two very distinct varieties of leaf in the specimens of *Mohr madow* from Somaliland: "one crenate, undulate, and pubescent on both sides; the other undulate and obscurely serrulate or almost entire, and velvety and paler below and glabrous above." The leaves of Carter's plant from Mahrah were of the former variety. Whether the differences represented two species of *Boswellia* or two varieties of the same species was not certain.

While identifying the three new species of frankincense tree, Birdwood was also able to clear up some confusion over the other known species of incense-producing *Boswellia*. *Boswellia serrata* was equated both with *Boswellia thurifera* and *B. glabra* as a tree of several varieties found in different parts of India and formerly thought by some to be the ancient source of frankincense.[8] It produces a gum-resin with a smell similar to, though more "turpentiny" than, true frankincense; this gum is extremely soft and will not harden into tears like true frankincense and after a while it melts into a glutinous liquid.

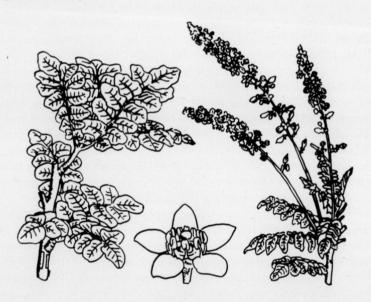

Boswellia papyrifera, evidently larger than the other frankincense-producing *Boswellias*, is claimed by the Ethiopians as the source of the frankincense of antiquity. It has been found not only in Ethiopia (where it is called the *mäqär* tree) and east Africa but also in several parts of the Sudan and further west.[9] In east Africa it is known as the Elephant Tree, since elephants feed on its leaves.[10] It produces an odoriferous gum-resin similar in smell to that from *Boswellia serrata* but not of the quality of Arabian and Somali commercial frankincense. The Arabian specimen sent to Bombay by Carter and planted had at first been regarded, once found different from *Boswellia serrata*, as a variety of this species; in consequence of that mistake the German botanist Flückiger had proposed that the name *Boswellia sacra* be used to embrace both the Abyssinian (Ethiopian) and the Arabian varieties.[11]

Despite Birdwood's clarifications, uncertainty about the species of frankincense persisted. Thus Hunter, basing his information on details provided by Miles, reported in 1877[12] that frankincense was derived from five different species of trees "so far as is known". These included Birdwood's three names, but with "*Mogharah shihaz* of Mahari country" listed as *Boswellia thurifera* and with "*Mohr madow* of Somal" shown as both *B. carteri* and *B. papyrifera* (the latter with reservations). Hunter's list also included a new species, the "*Boido* tree of Somal", described as "a somewhat taller species of tree, and its gum runs down in long tears, hence the name"; the botanical name for this tree was not known to Hunter. This report drew on specific information from Miles, following a visit to the Mijertain area, that in Somaliland there were four species of frankincense tree producing two types of gum, the first type coming from the *Mohr add*, *Mohr madow* and *Boido* trees, and the second coming from the *Yegaar* tree.[13] It is therefore odd that the *Boido* tree has not been reported subsequently; possibly it is identical with *Boswellia papyrifera*, which it is not unreasonable to expect might grow in Somalia.[14]

In his book published in 1912, which included a detailed study of gums and resins produced in Somalia, R. E. Drake-Brockman noted only two types of frankincense tree, the *Mohor* tree (*Boswellia carteri*) and the *Yehar* (*B. frereana*).[15] Drake-Brockman stated that the *Mohr* tree "was first described by Speke as 'a tree with rugged bark, smooth epidermis of reddish tinge, pleasant aromatic odour and strong astringent flavour'." Although mentioning that both trees could grow to a height of twenty feet, he gave no other description of either, apparently not having seen them growing. He made no mention of either the *Mohr add* tree or the *Boido* tree, even though he discussed in some botanical detail a number of other resin-producing trees.

Although Carter had seen frankincense trees growing at two points on the south Arabian coast, Marbaṭ and Rās Fartak, no description by him of their general appearance has survived. Nor have more than a handful of Arabian travellers described either frankincense or myrrh trees in any detail since, while few drawings or photographs of them have been published.

One of the earliest of travellers after classical times to mention frankincense trees in Arabia was Marco Polo, who recorded that they grew both in Shiḥr and in Ẓufār (Dhofar), although he never visited south Arabia himself. He observed that the Shiḥr district (which in mediaeval times signified a very much wider region of south Arabia than it does today) produced "a large quantity of white frankincense of the best quality, which distils, drop by drop, from a certain small tree that resembles the fir".[16] A century later Ibn Battuta, after leaving Ẓufār (in regard to which, oddly enough, he made no comment about frankincense) continued east to the port of Hāsik, where he reported: "Here they have a great quantity of frankincense trees. They have thin leaves out of which drips, when they are slashed, sap like milk. This turns into a gum which is frankincense."[17]

Theodore and Mabel Bent, who travelled widely in south Arabia towards the end of the nineteenth century, found frankincense both on the mainland and on the island of Socotra. In Ẓufār:

> "we passed through one of the districts where frankincense is still collected, in a narrow valley running down from the mountains into the plain of Dhofar. The valley was covered for miles with this shrub. . . . We did not see any very large trees, such as we did in Sokotra. . . . The shrub itself is a picturesque one, with a leaf not unlike an ash, only stiffer; it has a tiny green flower, not red like the Sokotra flowers, and a scaly bark. . . . Myrrh too grows in large quantities in the Qara range and we obtained specimens of it in close proximity to the frankincense tree." [18]

In Socotra the Bents had come across "valleys entirely full of incense trees with rich red leaves, like autumn tints, and clusters of blood-red flowers".[19] The same scene was found by the Oxford University Expedition to Socotra in 1956, as described by Douglas Botting:

"In parts of the mountains and in particular in the valley which leads down to Qalansiya, these [frankincense and myrrh] trees grow in abundance and fill the entire valley with magnificent scent. The myrrh tree (of which there are six specimens in Socotra) is like a low-spreading cedar. The frankincense tree (of which there are three or four specimens on the island) looks like a decomposing animal. It has stiff low branches. The leaves are scanty, curled and indented. A thick bark (which the local beduin sometimes make into buckets) and a tiny whitish peel cling closely round the trunk of a peculiarly blotchy colour. The woody fibre of the tree, distended with sap, looks like rotten animal flesh, and the clear yellowish-white resin oozes from incisions with a strong aroma. The fruit is a berry the size of a marble and the flowers are few, red and geranium-like on the end of short spikes."[20]

In 1930, during his exploration of northern Ẓufār, Bertram Thomas noted: "hidden in these desolate wadi beds which drain north across the steppe, flourishes the wild 'mughur', frankincense tree. In appearance it is like a young sapling, having almost no central trunk, but from near to the ground there springs out a clump of branches which grow to a camel's height and more, with ash coloured bark and tiny crumpled leaves". From incisions in the branches "a gum exudes . . . and hardens into large lozenge shaped tears of resinous substance which is known as frankincense (liban)".[21]

The American traveller Wendell Phillips, whose expedition visited Zufār in 1958, wrote: "The scraggy, picturesque frankincense tree shrub or tree . . . grows wild and appears as a mass of ash coloured branches with tiny leaves close to the ground and with little central trunk."[22] His colleague, the archaeologist Gus W. Van Beek, described the tree as one "which lacks a central trunk; its branches spring from near the ground, giving it the appearance of a shrub. Normally it attains a height of only seven or eight feet, but under very favourable conditions it sometimes reaches a height of about fifteen feet."[23] Thomas, Phillips and Van Beek all published photographs to support their descriptions.

The *Yegaar* tree of Somalia, *Boswellia frereana*, was described by Birdwood. Quoting contemporary travellers who had seen it growing, he noted that this tree grew up to forty feet high (elsewhere twenty feet is mentioned) with a central stem about two feet in circumference and branches springing out rather scantily from the top; but the remarkable feature of this species was the way the trees grew outwards and upwards from the side of smooth limestone rocks, to which they clung by growing what Miles described as "a large white bulbous mass".[24]

In an important article published in 1969, Nigel Hepper of the Royal Botanic Gardens, Kew, attempted to rationalize some of the uncertainties over the identification and distribution of the different species. By that time other botanists had undertaken further field work in Somalia, on the results of which he was able to draw, while he was also able to secure more information about the Arabian trees from recent visitors to Zufār.[25] His major conclusion was that the species identified by Birdwood from a Somali specimen as *Boswellia carteri* was a distinctly different species from any of the frankincense trees found growing in Arabia. The name *Boswellia carteri*, although intended to commemorate Carter's Arabian discovery, could therefore apply only to the Somali species and a different species name would have to be found for the Arabian plant. He proposed to take over for the purpose the name *Boswellia sacra*, which Flückiger had earlier devised in his mistaken belief that the Arabian and Abyssinian species were identical.

The Somali tree now labelled *Boswellia carteri* is the *Mohr madow* tree. It has a "normal" central trunk and, according to Hepper, shares the habit of *Boswellia frereana* (the *Yegaar*) in sometimes clinging to rocks and boulders by growing a bulbous base. A specimen in a photograph published by Hepper appears to be twenty to twenty-five feet high. The German scholar Grohmann, who assembled a mass of detail about the incense trees including information picked up in the Yemen by the nineteenth-century scholar Glaser, recorded it as four to five, occasionally six, metres high with a smooth, pale brown-yellow bark which peels in strips like pieces of paper, and noted that its new growth is covered with short yellow hairs.[26]

The *Boswellia sacra* tree as now designated by Hepper is however still a little indeterminate. It is the *Mogharah shihaz* (also called *Mghār*, the plural form) of Mahrah, the *Mughur* of Ẓufār, a small tree with almost no central trunk, as described by Bertram Thomas and others in the extracts quoted above. But insufficient samples have been available

for proper botanical examination to determine whether there are botanical distinctions between the trees of different areas, as photographs might suggest. Certainly the quality of the gum varies considerably in different regions, but this may be due purely to environmental circumstances.[27]

A puzzling problem remains over the *Mohr add* tree of Somalia, classified by Birdwood as *Boswellia bhau-dajiana*. Birdwood's identification was based both on dried specimens and on live cuttings which had been planted in Bombay and had flowered, so that he was able to make proper comparisons between the three species he identified. It is therefore surprising that the tree has never been reported by any traveller since, so that its size and appearance in its natural surroundings are still unknown. Particularly odd is the fact that it did not even come to the notice of Drake-Brockman during his careful and detailed study of the Somali incense trees. In the circumstances there would seem to be reason for some doubt as to whether this tree exists as a major producer of frankincense, although one supposes it may be found growing in some very restricted area of Somalia.

One informant of Glaser spoke of a tree in Somalia called *Ḥaqar*, of which there were two types, the *Ḥaqar madow* (black) and the *Ḥaqar add* (white). Separately Glaser was told that the *Ḥaqar* tree produced *lubān*, which means frankincense.[28] *Ḥaqar* may equate with *Yagār* (i.e. *Boswellia frereana*). While there could therefore have been a distinction in Somalia during the nineteenth century between two varieties of *Yagār*, the "black" and the "white", and similarly between two varieties of *Mohr*, another possibility is that the word *mohr*, derived from the Arabic *mughur*, was an alternative name for *yagār* (or *ḥaqar*); in such case there may never have been more than two species of frankincense tree recognized in the Somali language, the *Mohr* (or *Ḥaqar*) *madow* and the *Mohr* (or *Ḥaqar*) *add*, the "white" tree (*add*) producing the paler gum. We shall revert to the question of gums in the next chapter.

In his compilation of available information about incense trees, Grohmann gave the local names of certain other trees growing in Somalia and thought to be *Boswellia*. These included the *Muqla*, which he incorrectly identified as *Boswellia neglecta*, stating that it also grew in Arabia under the name of *Huri* (there is clearly a likelihood here of confusion with the bdellium *mukul*, discussed on page 124). Also listed were the *Niyal* or *Nijale* from Maḥir; the *Gunre* (alternatives *Qunre*, *Gurra* and *Qarran*), which it would seem may be an acacia noted by Drake-Brockman called *Gurha* or *Jirin*[29]; the *Kabrārro*, said to yield inferior frankincense and possibly identical with the balsam tree (*bashām*) (see page 126 et seq.); the *Ṭabaq*, which may perhaps be an incorrect rendering of *habbak* (see pages 123–124); and the *Moḥr lebēb*. (The spellings here are Grohmann's).

In Socotra botanical knowledge of the frankincense trees is fairly complete. This island has received considerable attention from organized expeditions and six species of *Boswellia* have been found there: *Boswellia ameero*, *B. elongata*, *B. javanica*, *B. socotrana*, *B. nana* and *B. popoviana*. But the last word on the species and varieties of frankincense tree in both Arabia and Somalia has clearly still to be written. Frankincense trees have indeed retained into the present day something of the mystery which clung to them in ancient times.

A problem almost as vexing as that of resolving the different species of frankincense-producing trees is the question of the area in south Arabia which produced frankincense in classical times. That area was clearly much more limited than the myrrh-producing areas. One might find myrrh anywhere where there was frankincense, but myrrh also grew in more westerly regions of both south Arabia and the Horn of Africa. We have already noted the scribal inversion in the extract from Eratosthenes quoted by Strabo: "Cattabania produces frankincense and Chatramotitis produces myrrh" (page 65 above). In general, Arabian frankincense came from the considerable area of southern Arabia dominated at one time or another by the people of Ḥaḍramawt (Chatramotitis), while Arabian myrrh was the main incense crop of the south-western regions which were controlled, during the time dealt with by Eratosthenes (*c.*200 BC), by the Qatabanians and Sabaeans.

While we can indicate a general area for the frankincense region, defining the limits precisely is more difficult, although the matter has an important bearing on south Arabian pre-Islamic history. We have already noted (page 88 above) that Ptolemy spoke of the frankincense region in very vague terms, as a result of which scholars had originally located it in Omān. This confusion is the greater because of the incorrect placing, by Ptolemy, of the frankincense port of Moscha and, by the *Periplus*, of the Bay of Sachalita to the west instead of to the east of the "promontory of Syagrus" (Rās Fartak). The identification of ancient Sachalita with modern Zufār (Dhofar) has now been confirmed by the discovery of inscriptions at Khor Rori, on the Zufār coast, referring to the region as "Sa'kalan" (not to be confused with the Arabic word *saḥil*, meaning a coastal plain, which is the present name of that coastal area). These inscriptions name the king of Ḥadramawt and so confirm the overlordship of the Chatramotitae in the area. They show that the king had sent a party to found a settlement, then named "Smhrm", in the first century BC or a little later.[30] It is likely that this is the site of Moscha, with the harbour and town bearing that name while the citadel, where the inscriptions were found, was called Smhrm, although this identification has not yet been positively established.

According to the *Periplus*, Moscha handled the "Sachalitic frankincense". It seems likely the town was founded for that purpose. It traded frankincense directly with ships calling there in addition to sending it, as the *Periplus* noted, "to Cana on rafts held up by inflated skins after the manner of the country and in boats" for transport by camel overland to Shabwah. Qana in addition received frankincense from other south Arabian ports (such as Syagrus) and also the "Far-Side frankincense" from the Somali ports. In Pliny's account of the journey to India (page 79 above) he described Qana as being "in the frankincense producing district".

In another passage Pliny gave a picture of the frankincense region in the following terms:

> "The chief products of Arabia, then, are frankincense and myrrh; the latter it shares also with the Cave Dwellers' country, but no country beside Arabia produces frankincense, and not even the whole of Arabia. About in the middle of the country are the Astramitae, a district of the Sabaei, the capital of their realm being Sabota, situated *in a region of high mountains*; and eight days' journey from Sabota is a frankincense-producing district called Sariba—according to the Greeks the name means 'secret'. The region faces north-east, and is surrounded by impenetrable

rocks, and on the right hand side bordered by a sea coast with inaccessible cliffs. The soil is reported to be of a milky white colour with a tinge of red. The forests measure 20 schoeni in length and half that distance in breadth—by the calculation of Eratosthenes a schoenus measures 40 furlongs, that is five miles, but some authorities have made the schoenus 32 furlongs. There are hills rising to a great height, with natural forests on them running right down to the level ground. It is generally agreed that the soil is clay, and that there are few springs and those charged with alkali."[31]

The production of frankincense was not of course confined to Arabia as Pliny here states, an error which emphasizes the caution one must exercise in taking him literally. But in general terms Pliny's description of this frankincense-producing region could apply to the neighbourhood of the present Wādī Ḥagr, south-east of Wādī Ḥadramawt, as well as to the Qarā region of Ẓufār. Pliny firmly described the region as "eight days' journey from Sabota". The direct distance from Ẓufār to Shabwah is about 400 miles, but any overland route would have occasioned a significantly longer journey, requiring, for a camel caravan moving twenty to twenty-five miles a day, up to thirty days of travel, as is attested by early Arab writers.[32] We shall have more to say about this overland journey in a later chapter when we come to the matter of the trade routes, but the key point here is that it is vastly more than the eight days' journey mentioned by Pliny, whereas eight days is a correct journey time between Shabwah and the Wādī Ḥagr region. Bearing in mind the manner in which many place-names have endured until modern times, it may be relevant to Pliny's naming of his region as "Sariba" that there is a settlement on the watershed of the mountains feeding Wādī Ḥagr which now bears the name "Sarab". If the reference to the name as meaning "secret" provides a clue, however, then it may be significant that the Arabic for "secret" is *sarīrah* and Wādī Ḥadramawt is today known as as-Sarīr in this sense.[33] But the journey from Qana to Shabwah would also have taken about eight days and that may be where Pliny's figure derived.

When he first discovered frankincense growing in Arabia, Carter noted that in modern times the main frankincense-producing region of Arabia was the inland "Nejd" area of Ẓufār, lying between longitudes 52°47′ East and 55°23′ East and that the largest quantities were exported from towns on the coast between these longitudes; at the same time frankincense was grown in lesser quantities on the coastal plain of Ẓufār, the "Sahil", principally between Rās Naws and Rās Sagar (and particularly near Marbat and Raysūt). The eastward limit of the frankincense region was clearly defined by geographical features, but its westward extent was not readily apparent. Carter sought to determine this "by carefully enquiring at each town along the coast in that direction, what quantity of frankincense is annually brought to it from the interior, until arriving at that place where the produce of the Arabian tree is never seen." This enquiry showed "the quantity of frankincense exported from the different towns gradually diminishing after the bay of Al Kammar until we arrive at Mukalla, from whence none is exported from the interior of Arabia and but little used except what is brought from the African coast opposite that town."[34] Unfortunately Carter did not list the towns covered in this exercise, but an officially sponsored report published in 1949 lists eleven ports from which frankincense was then being exported, lying between Hadhbaram in the east and Qishn in the west,[35] while Sayḥut, some 40 miles west of Qishn, has also been quoted as a frankincense port.[36]

The explorer Bertram Thomas stated that frankincense "is found growing, as a commercial crop, only in central South Arabia between two thousand and two thousand five hundred feet in a region which happens to be identical with the territorial limits of the Qara tribe, from long. 53°00′ E to long. 55°21′. Its occurrence on the edge of the unique summer rain belt of Dhufar suggests that climatic conditions favourable to its growth exist nowhere else in the peninsula".[37] Paradoxically, however, he then added a footnote referring to the varieties of Dhufari (Ẓufāri) frankincense, one of which, known as *sha'abi*, he described as "a poor quality of the plain around Risut".

These passages by Carter and Thomas show that in modern times the best and commercially most profitable frankincense grows in the highlands of Ẓufār. This was probably the case in classical times as well. But Carter's researches indicated an extension of the frankincense-growing region westwards at least as far as al-Mukallā, and this is supported by the observations of other travellers and authorities. For example, Van der Meulen and Von Wissmann photographed "incense bushes" growing near Ghayl-bā-Wazīr "on the coastal terrace between Mukalla and esh-Shihr".[38] Freya Stark observed: "Incense still grows in the Hadhramaut valleys; I found it used all over the country . . . both in small earthenware braziers or floating on drinking water 'to make it pure' and always locally grown. . . . The incense was probably in the gullies of the Jol as it is today."[39] On his journey along the ancient transmontane route to Shabwah from Qana, Harold Ingrams saw incense trees growing near Sidārah and noted that "in many of the little dry valleys of [the Wādī Ḥagr] the incense trees still flourish and the incense is collected by Somali gatherers."[40] More recently R. B. Serjeant learned that frankincense on sale in al-Mukallā had been brought down from the mountain area to the north of the town by Somali collectors.[41] Other reports have even suggested that frankincense (*lubān*) was collected from as far west as Ḥabbān. Some uncertainty existed over these reports because South Arabians have tended to use the word *lubān* to designate any form of incense, including gum from myrrh and balsam trees, rather than frankincense specifically. But the evidence they provide that frankincense is produced in this western region to this day has now been confirmed by the discovery by Professor Théodore Monod, of the French National Museum of Natural History, of frankincense trees (*Boswellia sacra*) growing at a number of places in the region—north of al-Mukallā, in Wādī Ḥagr and Wādī Du'ān, further west in Wādī 'Amāqīn, even in the side valleys of Wādī Ḥaḍramawt itself.[42]

Sufficient has already been stated to disprove the contention by Bertram Thomas that frankincense would grow only at an elevation of 2000 to 2500 feet, although it may be correct that the best quality of Arabian frankincense comes from trees growing at that altitude. *Boswellia sacra* grows on the coastal plain of Ẓufār and Carter saw it at Rās Fartak growing "within a few feet of the sea". Not far from Salālah Wendell Phillips described "the four hundred flourishing frankincense trees which the Sultan had transplanted from the Dhofar steppe",[43] while Hepper published a photograph of a tree growing within a mile of the coast.[44] Nor was it impossible to grow the plant in completely different locales. Birdwood described *Boswellia* plants from Somalia growing in the botanical gardens of both Aden and Bombay, while Theophrastus, in the passage quoted on page 97 above, referred to a tree apparently successfully transplanted to a sacred precinct at Sardes, the Lydian capital in western Asia-Minor.

We can safely assume that anywhere where frankincense trees are found growing today produced frankincense in ancient times. The reference in the *Periplus* to frankincense being stored at Syagrus shows quite clearly that in ancient times the area producing commercial frankincense extended well to the west of Ẓufār and the available evidence of its present extent suggests that frankincense of one quality or another was in fact produced in those days along the coast and in the hinterland of the whole five hundred mile stretch lying between Qana to the west and modern Hadhbarah to the east. The contention of Van Beek and others,[45] which has tended to be generally accepted, that the ancient frankincense region was in Ẓufār and Ẓufār alone would seem to be incorrect.

Factors of geography, geology, altitude and climate do not seem to affect the ability of the frankincense trees to survive so much as they determine the quality of their produce—although they appear to require a limestone soil—while the observation by Miles in 1872 that the prolonged drought of that time had killed so many trees in Somalia that little frankincense was being produced any more[46] may be another reason why the species do not flourish over a wider area. The quality of the coastal frankincense growing wild may never be as good as that of inland frankincense growing wild, so that the tendency has been for only the inland produce to be commercially profitable in modern times; but the coastal variety can be improved by careful husbandry until it is also a viable commercial crop in favourable marketing conditions. In ancient days the vast demand will have encouraged commercial exploitation of all frankincense trees wherever they grew; even the poorer qualities of produce from the coastal plains would probably have been profitable if the trees were carefully tended. This brings us right back to Theophrastus and the very first recorded descriptions of the incense trees with which this chapter commenced: "The trees . . .

grow partly in the mountains, partly on private estates at the foot of the mountains; wherefore some are under cultivation, others not."

As already stated, myrrh was gathered over a very much wider area than frankincense. Pliny, in a passage we will come to, described a number of different types of myrrh from south Arabia, evidently derived from different areas of that country, while in the paragraph quoted at the beginning of this chapter (page 98 above) he noted not only that it grew in many places in Arabia but also that it was imported from islands and from the Cave Dwellers' Country—i.e. that part of Somalia now known as the Horn of Africa. Strabo too mentioned incense from the African mainland; quoting Artemidorus and describing what one found as one moved south from Egypt he referred to myrrh from "the next country after Deire", which would be the region of what is now Djibouti. Strabo continued:

". . . after these one comes to the country that bears frankincense; and here is a promontory and a temple that has a grove of poplars. In the interior lie the river-land of Isis, as it is called, and another river-land called Neilus, both of which produce both myrrh and frankincense along their banks. . . . And one comes to several river-lands in succession that produce frankincense . . . then to the Daphnus Harbour and to the river-land of Apollo . . . which produces, in addition to frankincense, both myrrh and cinnamon . . . then to the last promontory of this coast—Notu Ceras." [47]

Strabo also reported that myrrh trees had been found by Alexander's troops in a different part of the orient altogether, in Gedrosia—modern Baluchistan. "Gedrosia, a country less torrid than India, . . . produces spices, in particular nard plants and myrrh trees, so that Alexander's army on their march used these for tent coverings and bedding, at the same time thereby enjoying sweet odours and a more salubrious atmosphere." [48] Aristobulos, who took part in Alexander's campaigns, reported, according to Arrian, that there were many myrrh trees in the Gedrosian desert which were "a good deal taller than the ordinary myrrh", adding that "the Phoenicians who followed the army as traders collected the gum of the myrrh, for it was abundant, coming from such large trunks and never having been gathered before and loaded up their pack mules with it." (Aristobulos added that the Phoenicians also collected a spikenard root from this desert which grew plentifully there and was very fragrant).[49] It seems most likely that the myrrh found in Gedrosia was not a true myrrh but a bdellium called *muqul* derived from an Indian species of *Commiphora* (see page 124 below).[50]

In modern times myrrh has been found growing all over south and west Arabia. The plant was rediscovered in 1826 by Professor Ehrenberg on a scientific expedition to Arabia; he found myrrh growing in the extreme south of what is now Saudi Arabia, near Qīzān and on the Shahrah and Karah mountains nearby.[51] It has since been found further north still, in 'Asīr, particularly in Wādī Tandahah. Glaser learned of its existence in a number of places, including the Wadis Gār and Zabīd (where the trees were called *buḥt*), in the Tihāmah and in Gawf, on the western slopes of Sirāt, in Dathīnah, in Habbān and in the area between Ta'izz and Qa'ṭabah.[52] In the high mountains of Yemen it has been discovered at Hajja, Habūr and Sūda (some 25 to 50 miles north-west of San'ā'). The French botanist Deflers, who visited Yemen in 1887, reported that the gum was collected in the north of Wādī Surdūd and, in greater quantity, in the Sūda area.[53] In 1920 it was being cultivated commercially in the vicinity of Qa'ṭabah, which lies at about 5000 feet at the foot of the main Yemeni massif some 100 miles north of Aden. Until the end of the nineteenth century myrrh was collected from the low hills of the Fadhli and Lower Yafi' areas, a little west of Aden. Further east it has been reported from several parts of 'Awlaqī and, recently, near Shabwah. The Bents found it growing in the area of Wādī Ḥagr as well as in Zufār and on the island of Socotra. Myrrh is also found on the African continent. It grows widely in Somalia, both on the coast and on the inland plateau, and also in Ethiopia,[54] while along the same latitude the African myrrh tree, producing an inferior but usable gum, is found as far west as Chad and northern Nigeria.

Ptolemy referred to a "Smyrnofera" (i.e. myrrh-growing) "interior region" in Arabia which would appear to have been just to the north of the Minaean tribal area. This probably encompassed present-day north Yemen and 'Asīr. In addition he described the "Smyrnofera exterior region" which lay between the "Sappharitae" and the "Chatramonitae" tribes. This "exterior region", lying in the area of hills and wadis south of a line between modern Bayḥān and Shabwah, was probably the principal myrrh-growing area in Arabia, comprising the modern tribal area of Yāfiʿ, Dathīnah, ʿAwdhalī, Raṣṣāṣī, ʿAwlaqī and Wahidī. This division into an "interior" and "exterior" region suggests a description deriving from one of the Minaean merchants who controlled the incense trade, for their homeland lay between these two regions.

Modern authorities are for the most part quiet about the different species of myrrh trees, and the various forms of gum produced from them have never been fully described or correlated with the trees. By the nineteenth century the Aden myrrh trade, though fairly substantial, involved a high proportion of myrrh collected in Somaliland. This trade was handled in Aden by Indian merchants who tended to use their own or Somali terms for the different types of tree and gum concerned. Moreover, the collection of gums from both frankincense and myrrh trees in south Arabia outside of Ẓufār seems to have been almost entirely in the hands of Somali traders, who paid the local tribesmen for the right. What little information was recorded about the trade therefore tended to have a Somali character.

In 1877 Hunter recorded: "But little is accurately known to botanists regarding the tree from which this gum (myrrh) is grown. It has been classified as 'Balsamodendron Myrrha' and 'Balsamodendron Ehrenbergianum'. It is brought to Aden from the Somali and Arabian coasts. Two trees produce myrrh, viz *didthin* and *habaghadi* of the Somal. The first is common to Arabia and Africa, while the latter is found only on Agadain and in the districts round Hanar . . . [The *didthin* is] found in Arabia in the provinces of Yemen, Hadramaut, and probably the southern portions of Omān. In Africa it is found on the range of hills which run parallel to the Somali coast."[55]

In fact we can be more precise about the *Didthin* or *Didin* tree, which is identified as *Commiphora myrrha* Nees (also named *Balsamodendron myrrha*), for it is one of the trees which produces true myrrh, known to the Arabs as *murr*, "bitter", on account of its taste.[56]

In his study of Somaliland published in 1912, R. E. Drake-Brockman recorded two main types of true myrrh in that country, a superior quality coming from the high plateau

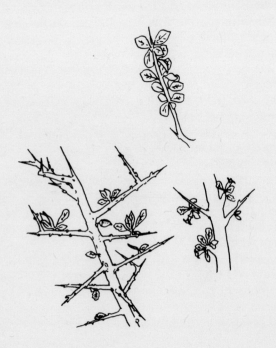

areas of the far interior, such as Ogadain, and known as *ogo-malmal*, and an inferior quality, fetching half the price, which was collected in the maritime hills and "the low-lying, sun-parched coast-region" and was known as *guban-malmal*. The *Didin* tree of the coastal region had by then been firmly identified as the species *Commiphora myrrha* Nees, but there was doubt whether the *Didin* tree producing the superior gum was the same species. It was not Hunter's *Habaghadi*. That, with the name corrected by Drake-Brockman to *Habbak haddi*, was a gum known as "false myrrh" which was collected from the *Haddi* tree, identified as *Commiphora erythraea* var. *glabrescens*. A further species, the *Hagar* tree, produced a gum very similar to *guban-malmal*.[57]

Botanically *Commiphora myrrha* is described as "spiny; 3 leaflets 0.8–2 cm. long; flowers few together shortly stalked; fruits 1 cm. ovoid with conspicuous beak". Other species vary in the size of the leaves, in being extremely prickly or without prickles, and in other ways.[58] Travellers have described the myrrh tree as looking like a low-spreading cedar[59] and like a common hawthorn.[60] Drake-Brockman noted that the *Didin* tree of the Somali coastlands seldom exceeded four or five feet in height, although that of the interior might reach fifteen feet, with a trunk more than a foot in diameter and with branches spreading outwards more than ten feet from the trunk. He described it as a thorny tree, with a gnarled trunk and ash-grey coloured branches and noted that its flowers appear before the leaves. The leaves grow in small tufts and the flowers are white to light green.[61] Wyman Bury described trees in the Lower 'Awlaqī area as followed: "It was on Munkaa that I first saw myrrh growing in any quantity. They are weird dwarf trees averaging some ten feet in height, and on that stony and somewhat sterile plateau convey the impression of a Beardsley landscape. Trunk, branches and twigs all zig-zag at abrupt angles, without a vestige of curved outline, which is rendered all the more conspicuous by the small sparse foliage."[62]

The myrrh trees which grew in the Fadhli/Lower Yafi' area, east of Aden, have been identified as *Commiphora simplicifolia*; the tree was known there as *Qafal* and that name was found by Glaser for myrrh growing in north Yemen, Gawf, Qa'tabah and Dathīnah. *Qafal* wood was exported to

Egypt and sold in the Cairo bazaars for burning as an incense.[63] Glaser also listed a species known locally as *Hadash*, which grew in the southern hills of Yemen and which Grohmann has suggested was *Commiphora abyssinica* Engl. and might equate with a Somali species called *Qāran* (not mentioned by Drake-Brockman; it may possibly be confused with an acacia called *Jirin*, see page 109 above). These species would in fact seem to be the same and can be described under the botanical equation "*Commiphora habessinica* (= *C. abyssinica* var. *simplicifolia*)".

A further myrrh-producing species growing in the intermediate altitudes of the south-western highlands of Arabia is called locally *Qataf* and has been classified as *Commiphora kataf*. This was first reported by Fôrskal, the botanist with the ill-fated eighteenth-century Danish expedition. Philby found it near the coast in the Yemeni–Saudi-Arabian boundary area.[64] A non-prickly species found in Zufār is called *Commiphora foliacea*. In Mahrah the German traveller Hirsch found myrrh, not identified botanically, called locally *Dik'ik*.[65] Also unidentified botanically is the *Buht* tree, which Glaser, as already noted, reported as a myrrh-producing tree in the Wādī Zabīd area of the Yemeni Tihāmah; possibly it is this tree which produces the myrrh called *hudaydah jebeli*, coming, as the name implies, from the mountains inland from the Red Sea port of Ḥudaydah. There appear to be other species—F. N. Hepper recently collected two in north Yemen which are not yet identified, as well as *Commiphora myrrha*.[66] But a problem arises from the difficulty of distinguishing between the myrrh-producing trees and those of the genus *Commiphora* which produce bdelliums, a point enlarged on in the next chapter. *Commiphora mukul* and *Commiphora schimperi* both appear to be bdellium-producing species which have been found in Arabia.[67]

Chapter 7

Incense: Ancient and Modern and "Far-Side"

In modern times the commercial centre for trading in incense gums has been Aden, which also handled many other spices. In 1875, in a vast list of imports and exports, Aden's commercial statistics included ten kinds of spices in a list which reads much like those of classical times: betel-nut from India; cinnamon and cassia from India and China; cloves from Zanzibar; cardamom and ginger from India; pepper from India and Singapore; turmeric and chillies from India; and aloe wood (used as an incense by the Arabs to perfume their garments) from Singapore and China.[1]

The same statistics detailed Aden's trade in gums and resins: gum-arabic, frankincense, myrrh, gum-mastic, copal, benjamin, Socotra aloe and dragons'-blood. The trade was not a simple one, for there were many varieties of these products. Gum-arabic, for example, which derives from four different species of acacia, is divided into two kinds and seven different qualities, while some indication has already been given of the many varieties of frankincense and myrrh. When they reached Aden these gums and resins were cleaned and sorted, mainly by Somali women, before being exported to distant markets—at that time principally to the United Kingdom, India, Egypt and Trieste. In 1875 over 600 tons of gums and resins were handled by the Aden merchants, including 300 tons of frankincense and 70 tons of myrrh. Just before the first World War the exports of myrrh from Aden had reached over 1000 tons annually and, although this decreased subsequently with a decline in the amount brought over from Somaliland, the trade in Arabian-grown myrrh actually increased, from 140 tons in 1913 to over 250 tons in

1920.[2] Since then the quantity of myrrh handled has dwindled considerably, but gums and resins are still imported and exported from Aden (in 1946, for example, 2800 tons of them) just as they were two thousand years ago.[3]

Available statistics provide no differentiation of the various types of myrrh handled by the Aden traders, although it is only to be expected that the variations not only of species but also of environment would result in different kinds and qualities of resin. In fact the differences appear to be very marked, although information determining from which species of myrrh tree each variety of gum derives is by no means complete. In 1877, Hunter could only say that the true myrrh "comes in dark red-coloured round lumps about two inches and upwards in diameter" and was sold in Aden "in a leather package called *jild* weighing from 40 to 50 lbs".[4]

From *Commiphora myrrha*, the Somali *Didin* tree, came, as we have said, true myrrh, the myrrh of pharmacy, *murr* to the Arabs, *malmal* to the Somalis and *hirabol* to the Indians. It is said to be almost without scent and is the species from which "oil of myrrh", or stacte, was distilled.[5] "Myrrh is either 'fluid' or 'solid'," Theophrastus observed, adding: "That of better quality is tested by its taste and of this they select that which is uniform in colour."[6] In a separate work about the making of perfume, Theophrastus stated: "From the myrrh when it is bruised flows an oil: it is in fact called 'stakte' (in drops) because it comes in drops slowly . . . others declare that the manufacture of 'stakte' is as follows: having bruised the myrrh and dissolved it in oil of 'balanos' over a gentle fire, they pour hot water on it; and the myrrh and oil sink to the bottom like a deposit; and as soon as this has occurred, they strain off the water and squeeze the sediment in a press."[7]

In discussing the myrrh trees, we have already noted Drake-Brockman's information that the Somalis recognized two qualities of myrrh—*guban malmal*, gathered from trees on the coastal plain, and *ogo malmal*, drawn from the inland plateaux—and that the *ogo* variety was superior and fetched double the price of the *guban*. It was not hard to tell one from the other. "The Ogo malmal is more friable, has a powdery surface, has a slightly different smell, has a more bitter taste and is darker in colour; and if the freshly cut surface is scraped with a knife it is found to be somewhat brittle, while the tiny

fractured fragments have a pale reddish-yellow appearance
. . . Guban malmal . . . has a more oily appearance when
freshly cut and if the surface is scraped the scrapings are
white."[8] Glaser recorded three varieties of myrrh coming
from Somaliland, their names being derived from the names
of their places of origin: Nuqali (from the interior); Dabiri
(from Dabir, near Berbera) and Maḥiri (from the eastern
region between Bandar Jadīd, Bandar Ziāda and Maḥir, near
Rās Hāfūn).[9]

Only certain species of Commiphora produce myrrh, while
other species produce bdellium, a somewhat similar substance often regarded as myrrh. It is not certain which
bdelliums were distinguished from myrrh in ancient days.
Pliny recognized bdellium as a separate product from myrrh,
but he also mentioned "scented myrrh" as one of the varieties
of true myrrh whereas it seems to have been a bdellium. In
western parts of Somalia the *Habbak haddi* tree (Hunter's
Habaghadi tree), identified botanically as *Commiphora erythraea* var. *glabrescens*, produces "sweet myrrh", also known
as "false myrrh", "coarse myrrh", "sweet bdellium" or
"perfumed bdellium" and called *bissabol* by the Indians. This
would appear to have been the "scented myrrh" of Pliny. It
has a much stronger smell than true myrrh, with a suspicion
of turpentine in it; its appearance is more oily than true myrrh
and its taste, although less bitter than the *ogo malmal*, is
slightly aromatic, while some of the older pieces are nearly
black in colour. It has been exported to India and China for
making perfume and scenting joss-sticks and was used by the
Egyptians for embalming. In Chapter 2 above it is suggested
that this was the substance known as '*ntyw* which the ancient
Egyptians collected from the Land of Punt (page 27).

Another variety of Somali bdellium comes from *Commiphora hildebrandti* and is known locally as *habbak hagar*. In
colour and appearance it is very similar to *guban* myrrh,
though more brittle, less oily and weaker in both taste and
smell. Drake-Brockman noted that while it had no market
value it was sometimes used to adulterate true myrrh. An
opaque bdellium called in Somalia *habbak hodai* comes from
the tree *Commiphora playfairi*. It is used in Somalia as a
liniment for washing hair and as a purgative for horses and in
earlier days it was used for whitening shields.[10] Its appear-

ance varies from white to reddish-brown. Other opaque bdelliums derive from other species of Commiphora found in Somalia, including varieties known as *Habbak dunkal, Habbak malo wa harod* and *Habbak daseino*, which is discussed below.

Drake-Brockman's information is not complemented by any similar study of Arabian myrrh and we know little more about the varieties of the Arabian produce than has already emerged in the previous chapter in discussing the trees. Most of the available information was compiled in the nineteenth century by Glaser and has been summarized by Grohmann.[11] The myrrh known as *qafal* was reported by Fôrskal to be used in the Yemen as a purgative. That known as *qataf* (or *kataf*) is used by Yemeni women for shampooing their hair. The *hudaydah jebeli* variety of myrrh, which is a dark red-brown in colour, is said to be strongly aromatic and very bitter; it has been suggested (page 120 above) that this may derive from a species of tree named by Glaser as *Buht* and in such case could be the variety of myrrh named by Glaser as *baht*. Glaser also listed another myrrh found in Yemen called *habashi*, which came from the Habayshi (?Habashi) country around Ta'izz and which he equated with "hirabol myrrh" (overlooking the fact that *hirabol* is simply the Indian name for myrrh in general).

Nairne, in his book on Indian plants,[12] referred to a related species *Balsamodendron mukul*, which grows in parts of India and which is also classified as *B. wighti*, *B. roxburghi* and *Commiphora mukul*. *Mukul* is quoted elsewhere as a type of myrrh produced in Zufār.[13] Carter mentioned finding, growing "side by side with frankincense trees and . . . equally plentiful . . . a tree called by the bedouins *akor*, which yields *moql*, a gum slightly resembling myrrh in appearance and taste, but not in its perfume, which is disagreeable, and which the Persians and Arabs use as a fumigation in the cure of Haemorrhoids."[14] Elsewhere it is said to be used in Persia to treat rheumatism and stomach complaints.[15] The early Arab geographer al-Maqdīsi referred to a bdellium called *muql* which grew in the area of al-Marwah, in the Hijaz north of al-Madīnah,[16] while according to al-Nuwayri a bdellium called *muql azraq* grew in the Yemen.[17]

It is apparent that the different varieties of myrrh were distinguished with much greater precision during the period of the ancient incense trade than they are in our time, and the number of them, as is evident from Pliny, must have been considerable. Pliny described myrrh in the following passage:

"The myrrh-producing tree is also tapped twice a year at the same seasons as the frankincense tree, but in its case the incisions are made all the way up from the root to those of the branches that are strong enough to bear it. But before it is tapped the root exudes of its own accord a juice called 'stacte', which is the most highly valued of all myrrh. Next after this comes the cultivated kind, and also the better variety of the wild kind, the one tapped in summer. No tithes are given to a god from myrrh, as it also grows in other countries; however, the growers have to pay a quarter of the yield to the king of the Gebbanitae. For the rest it is bought up all over the district from the common people and packed into leather bags; and our perfumiers have no difficulty in distinguishing the different sorts by the evidence of the scent and consistency.

There are a great many varieties, the first among the wild kinds being the Cave-dweller myrrh, next the Minaean, which includes the Astramitic, the Gebbanitic and Ausaritic from the kingdom of the Gebbanitae; the third quality is the Dianite, the fourth a mixture from various sources, the fifth the Sambracene from a sea-board state in the kingdom of the Sabaei, and the sixth the one called Dusirite. There is also a white kind found in one place only, which is brought into the town of Mesalum for sale. The Cave-dweller kind is distinguished by its thickness and because it is rather dry and dusty and foreign in appearance, but it has a stronger scent than the other sorts. The Sambracene variety is advertised as surpassing other kinds in its agreeable quality, but it has not a strong scent.

Broadly speaking, however, the proof of goodness is given by its being in small pieces of irregular shape, forming in the solidifying of the juice as it turns white and dries up, and in its showing white marks like fingernails when it is broken, and having a slightly bitter taste. The second best is mottled inside, and the worst is the one that is black inside; and if it is black outside as well it is of a still inferior quality.

The prices vary with the supply of buyers; that of stacte ranges from 3 to 50 denarii a pound, whereas the top price for cultivated myrrh is 11 denarii and for the Erythraean 16—this kind is passed off as Arabian—and for the kernel of Cave-dweller $16\frac{1}{2}$, but for the variety called scented myrrh 12.

Myrrh is adulterated with lumps of lentisk and with gum, and also with cucumber juice to give it a bitter taste, as it is with litharge of silver to increase its weight. The rest of the impurities can be detected by taste, and gum by its sticking to the teeth. But the adulteration most difficult to detect is that practised in the case of Indian myrrh, which is collected in India from a certain thorn-bush; this is the only commodity imported from India that is of worse quality than that of other countries—indeed it is easily distinguished because it is so very inferior.''[18]

As already suggested, Pliny's "scented myrrh" may have been the modern "sweet myrrh" (*Commiphora erythraea* var. *glabrescens*). It is difficult to propose other correlations between the myrrhs described by Pliny and those known in modern commerce. The town of Mesalum (or Mesala), where the unique white myrrh was sold, appears to be a ruin site now called am-'Aṣalah, in the area a little east of Aden which in modern times produced *qafal* myrrh. However, since *qafal* has also been found in other areas this does not provide grounds for deducing it may have been the white myrrh of Pliny's time. But the Indian myrrh so scathingly described by Pliny seems very likely to have been *mukul*.

As with the bdelliums, a problem exists over how balsam was classified in classical times. There is a possibility that the Arabian variety of this may also have been regarded as one of the myrrhs. All derive from species of Commiphora. To understand the matter, information about the balsam tree needs to be looked at in some detail.

The Arabian balsam tree, Balsam of Makkah, more correctly a shrub, is now classified botanically as *Commiphora gileadensis*. Uncertainties in the past have given it other botanical names, all of which are now equated (i.e *Commiphora opobalsamum; Balsamodendron gileadensis; Balsamodendron ehrenbergianum*; and *Balsamea meccanensis*).[19] Its botanical name derives from a confusion in the past with "Balm of Gilead" mentioned in Genesis 37. 25; that was almost certainly a totally different product, possibly resin from the terebinth.[20]

The Arabic for a balsam tree is *Bashām* and it is known by this word in south Arabia. In Ḥaḍramawt it is sometimes termed "Ḥaḍramawt myrrh" and its gum, said to be oily and to taste like a lemon, is used as a chewing-gum and is called *meetiya*.[21] It is the *Daseino* tree of Somalia, where its gum, *habbak daseino*, comes in large, hard, irregular lumps with air spaces inside, some of which contain a gummy aromatic substance not unlike the gum-resin exuded from pine-trees; this gum has a pine-like smell when freshly picked which soon disappears. The Somalis both chew it and burn it as an incense, although the smell when it is burnt is said to be suggestive of burning india-rubber.[22]

Harris called the tree, which he appears to have seen near Aden, "a dwarf shrub" and recorded that when incisions were made in its stem the balm flowed freely but the volatile oil quickly evaporated, leaving an insipid gum.[23] Grohmann, however, stated on Glaser's information that the tree had a trunk about 30 centimetres thick which branched out from close to the ground[24] and Drake-Brockman noted that it was of "straggly" appearance and, unlike the Somali myrrhs, thornless. The tree (or shrub) grows widely in south-west Arabia as in Somalia and has been reported, for example, in Gawf, in the Red Sea coastal plain near 'Abū 'Arīsh[25] and on the Yemen/Saudi border,[26] as well as in the southern mountains of Qa'tabah and Ta'izz. Fôrskal, the botanist with the ill-fated Danish expedition of 1763, discovered the first specimen, a tree in full bloom, in the mountains north-west of Ta'izz, thus fulfilling one of the primary botanical objectives of that expedition. He noted that the local people did not know how to collect balsam from it.[27]

Lane's *Lexicon*, quoting an Arab botanical work, described *bashām* as an "odoriferous kind of tree of sweet taste, the leaves of which, pounded and mixed with henna, blacken the hair"; the tree had a stem, branches and small leaves, with no fruit but only a blackish seed; "when the stem is cut it pours forth a white milk and its twigs are used for cleaning the teeth."[28] However, under the alternative Arabic word *balasān* (really a Greek word from which the English word "balsam" derives) and curiously not cross-referenced, Lane quoted other mention of the Balsam of Makkah tree, derived principally from the great Arabic lexicon, the *Tāj al-'Arūs*, published in Cairo in AD 1767. Here it is described as "a kind of tree or shrub resembling the *henna*, having many leaves inclining to white, in odour resembling the rue, the berry of which has an unguent which is hot and its unguent is in great request. . . . Its unguent (*opobalsamum*) is more potent than its berry (*carpobalsamum*) and its berry is more so than its wood (*xylobalsamum*)—the best of its wood is the smooth, tawny-coloured, pungent and sweet in odour." Ailments said to be benefited by burning the wood as a fumigant included stoppages of the nose, sciatica, vertigo, headache, cloudiness of the eye, flaccidity of the womb and barrenness, while it was also an antidote to "poisons and the bites of vipers".

In mediaeval times the main centre for the production of balsam from the Balsam of Makkah tree, that product then enjoying a vogue, was in the Ḥijāz, particularly at al-Arg, about half-way between Makkah and al-Madīnah.[29] Lane noted that attempts to grow it near Cairo in mediaeval times failed and that it was mostly found in the Ḥijāz "between Ḥarameyn and El-Yembo', whence it is conveyed to all countries."

Pliny wrote of the balsam tree: "But every scent ranks below the balsam. The only country to which this plant is vouchsafed is Judaea, where formerly it grew only in two gardens, both belonging to the king." Josephus pin-pointed the location of these gardens, noting that, after Anthony had given parts of Judaea to Cleopatra, King Herod made an arrangement with her to farm "those revenues that came to

her from the region about Jericho. This country bears that balsam which is the most precious drug that is there, and grows there alone."[30] Pliny noted that balsam was held in such esteem that, since the time of Pompey the Great, balsam trees had been carried among the captives in triumphal processions and the tree "is now a subject of Rome, and pays tribute together with the race to which it belongs."[31] Pliny went into considerable detail about the three types of balsam tree cultivated in Judaea, the methods of harvesting it and the uses made of it, noting that it was being cultivated like a vine. He stated that it did not grow more than three feet in height. Its product, *opobalsamum*, was extremely sweet in taste (cf. the gum of the Arabian tree, said to taste like a lemon, and Drake-Brockman's statement that the Somali gum has "a suspicion of a bitter taste") and exuded in tiny drops and only in minute quantities, being collected in a shell as a liquid which did not harden for some time. The rarity of opobalsamum, together with its quality as a perfume, gave it an extraordinarily high price of as much as 1000 denarii a pint, which may be compared with 6 denarii a pound for the best quality of frankincense. Theophrastus, one of Pliny's sources, noted that the pure gum of balsam sold for twice its weight in silver and recognized it, as do other classical authors, as coming from Syria rather than from Arabia.[32] But the main trade, according to Pliny, was by his time in balsam-wood, the branches and shoots being cut off and boiled down so that "in (perfume) manufacture they have taken the place of the actual juice of the shrub." The price of balsam-wood was, like the best frankincense, 6 denarii a pound.

From Pliny's information it looks distinctly as if the Judaean balsam of classical times was a product very different from the product of the Arabian balsam tree, the Balsam of Makkah, having quite different qualities. Hepper has suggested it may have been *Pistacia lentiscus*, which yields a widely used resin, but has noted other possibilities.[33] This differentiation may be indicated in the account of the scholar-scientist al-Baghdādi (AD 1162–1231), who noted the existence in Egypt of one small plantation of balsam bushes (*balsān*), which grew "a cubit or more in height" with leaves resembling rue. He observed that this plant used to grow in Palestine but no longer did, and described how the sap was collected with the finger into a shell and then processed to extract a small amount of oil. He appears to distinguish this tree from the "wild, male balsam . . . known as *bashām*", which was found in "the Naḡd, the Tihāmah, the Arabian deserts and the maritime regions of Yemen and Persia" and which he understood yielded no oil.[34] But whether the trees were distinctive species or not, the problem arises of where to identify the gum of the Arabian tree among the products of Arabia listed by the classical authors, which did not include balsam.

In 1975 Dr Jacqueline Pirenne, while working on excavations at Shabwah, was taken to see incense (*lubān*) trees said to grow nearby. She was shown myrrh trees (*Murr*) and her guides told her of the *Bishāmah* trees which grew in the area (in Somalia too the *Daseino* tree is always found growing in the same locality as myrrh);[35] the product of both trees appears to have been referred to locally as "*lubān*", which we would normally expect to mean "frankincense".[36] In the nineteenth century Glaser received various reports confusing the product of the balsam tree with frankincense and at one point noted that "the *bashām* produces a type of frankincense which resembles the genuine product well enough to deceive persons with expert knowledge of Arabian incense."[37] Drake-Brockman too has commented on the similarity of the balsam gum with frankincense: "*Habbak daseino* is more like frankincense in its properties than myrrh and it is owing to this fact that the Somalis . . . frequently call it by the same name, '*hanjibeyo*'." He also observed that the gum was rare and therefore not collected for export, even though the tree was common enough.[38]

We have already commented on the looseness of terminology under which the word "incense" is used to mean frankincense *per se* as well as other types of gum or compounds which smell pleasantly when burnt. The same difficulty arises in German with the word "Weihrauch" and confuses understanding of statements by Glaser and Grohmann. It is evident that in Arabic this problem exists too and that the word *lubān* may at times signify any sort of incense gum rather than frankincense alone, even though an Arabic word, *bakhūr*, exists which describes any incense used as a fumigatory. We cannot therefore infer that a reference to the product of the *Bashām* tree as *lubān* necessarily connotes any confusion with frankincense, although at times confusion has clearly existed. The possibility that in ancient times the product of the *Bashām* was regarded as a frankincense is in any case belied by the fact that frankincense was clearly found only in the kingdom of Ḥadramawt, whereas *Bashām* is now and must then have been widespread.

Possibly the Arabs of classical times did not regard the balsam tree as worth exploiting at all. We do not at present know enough about its gum to say whether it would have been practical to trade with it as a luxury product—perhaps it deteriorated during transit, or the small amount produced by each tree was regarded as not worth the collecting. Hence it may be that Pliny did not know of Arabian balsam simply because none was sent from there in classical times. It is certainly improbable that the ancients regarded it as frankincense. In the nineteenth and twentieth century Aden trade statistics, balsam gum, although technically a bdellium, appears to have been accounted for as a myrrh.[39] As another product of *Commiphora*, it would seem most likely that in classical times too it was among the many types of myrrh that the gum of the Arabian and Somali balsam tree was to be found.

More information is available about the varieties and grades of frankincense in modern times than exists about myrrh, but the detail provided by different sources is confused and conflicting, as is our knowledge of frankincense trees, so that much uncertainty still remains. The following paragraphs attempt to summarize what has been recorded.

The normal word in Arabic for frankincense gum is *lubān* and this word is used in Somalia (pronounced *loban* or *lobān*) as an alternative to the Somali word *beyo*. The word *kundūr* is also found in Arabic, being of Indo-Iranian derivation and the term used in India.[40] As already noted, the word *lubān* may also be used sometimes in south Arabia to signify other sorts of incense gums. Early in the nineteenth century an apparent distinction was noticed, by travellers enquiring about the incense trade, between *lubān* and another frankincense gum found only in Somalia called *mayti* (also spelt *maidi*, *meytee* and in other variations) which came from the *Yegaar* (alternatives *Yehar* and probably, *Haqar*) tree (see page 108 above). However, in 1843 *maiti* was listed as one of the kinds of *lubān* on sale in the Aden bazaar,[41] while Drake-Brockman has recorded the gum as *loban maidi*, so this distinction evidently does not imply that *mayti* was regarded as an alternative to frankincense. The name derives from Bandar Mayt, the main area of its collection.

According to Hunter in 1877, the Aden merchants divided the *mayti* frankincense into two qualities—*amshot* and *duka*. "It arrives," he said, "in large milky white flakes or coagulated lumps."[42] Drake-Brockman described it as a pale topaz-yellow or sometimes deep orange substance; its "tears" were sometimes large, irregular lumps up to six inches long and four inches wide; it was said to be less fragrant than *lubān* but preferred for chewing.[43] In Somalia it is regarded as superior to *lubān*, but its quality in comparison with the *lubān* of Zufār is uncertain, some sources claiming that the one is superior, some supporting the other. Hunter noted that in 1876 *mayti* commanded a price of $2 per 28 lbs (the Indian maund being used in Aden) compared with $1¾ per maund for the top quality *lubān*.

The categories of *lubān* are more complicated than of *mayti*

and have probably become particularly confused as a result of
the wrong identification of the Arabian frankincense tree with
the *Mohr madow* of Somalia. Different terms seem to have
been used at different periods and at different stages of the
trading, and these may be based either on the area of origin or
on the appearance or quality of the gum itself. Thus Hunter's
report of 1877 gave names used in the Aden market as *luban
dthafāri* for frankincense from Ẓufār; *luban barajami* for that
from the Somali coast (the usual name for which was
Barr'Ajam); *luban bedawi* for, apparently, gum from inland
areas of Somalia (brought in by bedouin), although this term
seems also to be used for gum brought from inland areas of
Arabia; *luban shehri* for that brought in from ash-Shiḥr (this
name was said to distinguish the product of the Somali tree
Mohr add, which was imported into ash-Shiḥr and thence
conveyed to Aden),[44] although other authorities have suggested that it included Arabian frankincense.[45] But the use
of these names in the Aden market, the main trading centre
for gums, does not appear to have been long-standing, for in
1843 the kinds of *lubān* on sale there had been classified rather
differently as four from Somalia and one from Arabia, the
former being *maitee, makur, nankur* or *aungare* (from the
Bandar Angare (Ankar) region) and *berbera* or *muslika* (which
has "dark, vitreous tears"), and the latter being *marbat* or
saharee (i.e. *shiḥri*); the Arabian kind was the highest priced.[46]
While each of these kinds came from a different geographical
area, the names *makur* (on which see below) and *muslika* do
not seem to have a geographical origin.[47]

In Somalia, according to both Cruttenden in 1838 and
Drake-Brockman in 1912, only two varieties of frankincense
gum are recognized: *loban dakar* from the *Mohor* tree and
loban maidi from the *Yehar*. The former, known to Indian
traders as *isas*, was inferior, darker in colour and came from
the maritime hills.[48] Drake-Brockman did not record the
Mohr add tree. He did however deal in some detail with the
opaque bdelliums coming from various species of Commiphora found in Somaliland, as we have already noted in
discussing myrrh. These gums are known as *habbak*, a term
which in fact embraces all gums, including frankincense and
myrrh, although these latter are more usually known by their
own distinctive names.[49]

The term *loban dakar* in Somali (and *lubān dhakar* in Arabic) means "male frankincense". Grohmann listed a variety called *iskughir*, which he noted as meaning "female frankincense" and coming from the area of Anqor and Ruquda.[50] The derivation of this name is not apparent and he does not identify the tree from which this gum was obtained. It seems likely to be an alternative name for *mayti*, which Drake-Brockman described as "female frankincense".[51]

The *makur* frankincense found on sale in Aden in 1843 may possibly correlate in name with *mäqär* (spelt *makker* by Birdwood), the Abyssinian name for the tree *Boswellia papyrifera*, which it is suggested might be the Somali *Boido* tree mentioned by Miles (see page 103 above). Miles included its gum among that known as *bedwi* or *sheheri*.

The local categorisation of frankincense produced in Zufār (i.e. gum from *Boswellia sacra*—the *Mughur* tree of Zufār and *Magharah shihaz* of Mahrah) was recorded by Bertram Thomas as, firstly, *negedi* or *nejdi* (the best; "the silver variety which is the product of the intra-montane uplands of the Samhan and Qara mountains"—*nejd*, or *nagd*, means "plateau") secondly, *shazari* (from the Shazari region of mountains); and thirdly, *sha'abi* ("a poor quality from the plain around Risut"—more correctly this must refer to the product of the valleys running up into the hills from the coastal plain, to conform with the meaning of *sha'ab*).[52] But earlier on the Bents had noted only two varieties of frankincense in Zufār, called *leban lakt* (from the *Nagd*) and *leban resimi* (from the area of Raysut and Rakhyūt, i.e. the coastal plain).[53] No breakdown is available of the names of varieties of frankincense gum produced in Mahrah (where the general name for the gum is *shihaz*) or Hadramawt.[54] J. R. L. Carter has noted recently that in Omān frankincense gum burnt on its own is called *Awd* and that it is sometimes mixed with sugar and sandal-wood into a cake, also burnt as incense, called *Samagh* or *Ghabūr*, or powdered and liquified, sometimes with powdered sandal-wood, for use as a cosmetic.[55]

Other terms define the quality of the gum. In Somalia *luban bedwi* was stated by Miles to be divided into three qualities: *fusoos* (the best), *safee* and *mujamdal*. This terminology was evidently used in Aden as well, where Hunter quoted three qualities as *fusus*, *safi* and *jandal*.[56] According to Miles, however, *mayti* was all of one quality, *safai*, whereas Hunter stated that two qualities were recognized in Aden (*amshot* and *duka*, as already noted above). Miles also recorded that the Somalis defined the quality of Arabian frankincense, which they considered inferior to their own, as *asli* (meaning "sweet").

Of the appearance of *lubān* we have Hunter's description that it arrived in Aden in "semi-transparent, tear-shaped drops or tears less than one inch long and of a yellow or palish brown colour. The finer descriptions consist of nearly colourless tears." Drake-Brockman stated of the Somali *lubān* that it was "like false amber with a pinkish tinge", being darker and more amber-like than the *mayti*.[57] Miles noted that the *Boido* tree "is so named from the gum running down in long tears."[58] The Bents mentioned that the frankincense tears of Zufāri trees were sometimes "larger than an egg".[59] Unlike the *mayti*, which, because of its gummy consistency, tends to conglomerate into large masses when packed, the Somali *lubān* remains in separate pieces, being drier and more friable.[60]

In Hunter's time the trade in frankincense was substantially greater than that of myrrh and so it has since remained. His figures for 1875 quote an export from Aden of some 210 tons of "olibanum" and 105 tons of "maieti" frankincense, nearly one third going to Bombay, with other large quantities being sent to the United Kingdom, Trieste, Egypt, the Yemen and Saudi-Arabia. Roughly two-thirds of this had arrived from Somali ports and the rest from ports on the south Arabian coast. About forty years earlier it was estimated that 732 tons of frankincense were exported from Somaliland annually,[61] while twenty years later the Bents reported that 450 tons of frankincense were being exported annually from Zufār alone direct to Bombay.[62] Over the five-year period 1929–1933 a total of 1547 tons was conveyed from south Arabian ports into Aden, with rather less coming from Somaliland.[63] In 1939 400 tons and in 1940 about 290 tons were imported into Aden from south Arabian ports.[64]

Hunter noted that frankincense was usually brought packed in wooden cases or baskets formed like cages and covered with matting, called by the Somalis *hori*, although sometimes mat bags were used. This contrasts with the skins used for packaging myrrh. The difference was presumably conditioned by the nature of the merchandise, for myrrh is an oily substance, whereas frankincense is drier and more brittle and care needs to be taken in packing to prevent the tears conglomerating when compressed. Hence myrrh required a packaging which would retain the oil, whereas the cage-like basket used for frankincense prevented it from becoming crushed and broken during the journey. One can visualize the camels of the ancient incense caravans with frankincense baskets bulging on either side of their saddles or swinging to the weight of myrrh in more compact, tightly closed goat-skins.

Pliny provided a very full account of the growing and collection of frankincense in ancient times, although he did not include any information about the different varieties of frankincense recognized in his time, other than in reference to the different qualities:

"It used to be the custom, when there were fewer opportunities of selling frankincense, to gather it only once a year, but at the present day trade introduces a second harvesting. The earlier and natural gathering takes place at about the rising of the Dog-star, when the summer heat is most intense. They make an incision where the bark appears to be fullest of juice and distended to its thinnest; and the bark is loosened with a blow but not removed. From the incision a greasy foam spurts out, which coagulates and thickens, being received on a mat of palm leaves where the nature of the ground requires this, but in other places on a space round the tree that has been rammed hard. The frankincense collected in the latter way is in a purer state, but the former method produces a heavier weight; while the residue adhering to the tree is scraped off with an iron tool, and consequently contains fragments of bark.[65]

The forest is divided up into definite portions, and owing to the mutual honesty of the owners is free from trespassing, and though nobody keeps guard over the trees after an incision has been made, nobody steals from his neighbour. At Alexandria, on the other hand, where the frankincense is worked up for sale, good heavens! no vigilance is sufficient to guard the factories. A seal is put upon the workmen's aprons, they have to wear a mask or a net with a close mesh on their heads, and before they are allowed to leave the premises they have to take off all their clothes; so much less honesty is displayed with regard to the produce with them than as to the forests with the growers.

The frankincense from the summer crop is collected in autumn; this is the purest kind, bright white in colour. The second crop is harvested in the spring, cuts having been made in the bark during the winter in preparation for it; the juice that comes out on this occasion is reddish, and not to be compared with the former taking, the name for which is '*carfiathum*', the other being '*dathiathum*'. Also the juice produced by a sapling is believed to be whiter, but that from an older tree has more scent. Some people also think that a better kind is produced on islands, but Juba says that no incense grows on islands at all.[66]

Frankincense that hangs suspended in a globular drop we call male frankincense, although in other connections the term 'male' is not usually employed where there is no female; but it is said to have been due to religious scruple that the name of the other sex was not employed in this case. Some people think that the male frankincense is so called from its resemblance to the testes. The frankincense most esteemed, however, is the breast-shaped, formed when, while a previous drop is still hanging suspended, another one following unites with it. I find it recorded that one of these lumps used to be a whole handful, in the days when men's eagerness to pluck them was less greedy and they were allowed to form more slowly.[67]

The Greek name for frankincense formed in this manner is 'drop-incense' or 'solid incense', and for the smaller kind 'chick-pea incense'; the fragments knocked off by striking the tree we call manna. Even at the present day, however, drops are found that weigh as much as a third of a 'mina', that is 28 denarii. . . .[68]

[Frankincense] is tested by its whiteness and stickiness, its fragility and its readiness to catch fire from a hot coal; and also it should not give to pressure of the teeth, and should rather crumble into grains. Among us it is adulterated with drops of white resin, which closely resemble it, but the fraud can be detected by the means specified."[69]

Elsewhere, as we shall see (page 154 below), Pliny spoke of three qualities of frankincense on sale in Rome, of which the price of the best quality was double the price of the worst. The *Periplus* made no distinction at all between the different grades of frankincense, although in relation to that obtained from the "Far-Side" ports, now Somalia, it mentioned other forms of incense which may possibly have been varieties of gum now regarded as frankincense. To understand the proper significance of these references, it is necessary to see the geographical setting in which they occur and this can best be done by quoting the relevant passages in full. They show the trade with imperial Rome, in Greek ships from Egypt, at probably its fullest expansion:

"7. From this place the Arabian coast trends towards the east and becomes narrowest just before the Gulf of Avalites. After about four thousand stadia, for those sailing eastward along the same coast, there are other Berber market towns, known as the 'far-side' ports; lying at intervals one after the other, without harbours but having roadsteads where ships can anchor and lie in good weather. The first is called Avalites; to this place the voyage from Arabia to the far-side coast is the shortest. Here there is a small market town called Avalites, which must be reached by boats and rafts. There are imported into this place, flint glass, assorted; juice of sour grapes from Diospolis; dressed cloth, assorted, made for the Berbers; wheat, wine and a little tin. There are exported from the same place, and sometimes by the Berbers themselves crossing on rafts to Ocelia and Muza on the opposite shore, spices, a little ivory, tortoise-shell, and a very little myrrh, but better than the rest. And the Berbers who live in the place are very unruly.

8. After Avalites there is another market-town, better than this, called Malao, distant a sail of about eight hundred stadia. The anchorage is an open roadstead sheltered by a spit running out from the east. Here the natives are more peaceable. There are imported into this place the things already mentioned, and many tunics, cloaks from Arsinoe, dressed and dyed; drinking-cups, sheets of copper in small quantity, iron, and gold and silver coin, not much. There are exported from these places myrrh, a little frankincense (that known as far-side), the harder cinnamon, *duaca*, Indian copal and *macir*, which are imported into Arabia; and slaves, but rarely.

9. Two days' sail beyond Malao is the market-town of Mundus, where the ships lie at anchor more safely behind a projecting

island close to the shore. There are imported into this place the things previously set forth, and from it likewise are exported the merchandise already stated, and the incense called *mocrotu*. And the traders living here are more quarrelsome.

10. Beyond Mundus, sailing toward the east, after another two days' sail, or three, you reach Mosyllum, on a beach, with a bad anchorage. There are imported here the same things already mentioned, also silver plate, a very little iron, and glass. There are shipped from the place a great quantity of cinnamon, (so that this market town requires ships of larger size), and fragrant gums, spices, a little tortoiseshell, and *mocrotu*, (poorer than that of Mundus), frankincense (the far-side), ivory and myrrh in small quantities.

11. Sailing along the coast beyond Mosyllum, after a two days' course you come to the so-called Little Nile River, and a fine spring, and a small laurel-grove, and Cape Elephant. Then the shore recedes into a bay, and has a river called Elephant, and a large laurel-grove called Acannae; where alone is produced the far-side frankincense, in great quantity and of the best grade.

12. Beyond this place, the coast trending toward the south, there is the Market and Cape of Spices, an abrupt promontory, at the very end of the Berber coast toward the east. The anchorage is dangerous at times from the ground-swell, because the place is exposed to the north. A sign of an approaching storm which is peculiar to the place, is that the deep water becomes more turbid and changes its colour. When this happens they all run to a large promontory called Tabae, which offers safe shelter. There are imported into this market town the things already mentioned; and there are produced in it cinnamon (and its different varieties, *gizir, asypha, arebo, magla* and *moto*) and frankincense.

13. Beyond Tabae, after four hundred stadia, there is the village of Pano. And then, after sailing four hundred stadia along a promontory, toward which place the current also draws you, there is another market-town called Opone, into which the same things are imported as those already mentioned, and in it the greatest quantity of cinnamon is produced, (the *arebo* and '*moto*'), and slaves of the better sort, which are brought to Egypt in increasing numbers; and a great quantity of tortoise-shell, better than that found elsewhere.

14. The voyage to all these far-side market towns is made from Egypt about the month of July, that is Epiphi. And ships are also customarily fitted out from the places across this sea, from Ariaca and Barygaza, bringing to these far-side market-towns the products of their own places; wheat, rice, clarified butter, sesame oil, cotton cloth, (the *monache* and the *sagmatogene*), and girdles,

and honey from the reed called *sacchari*. Some make the voyage especially to these market towns, and others exchange their cargoes while sailing along the coast. This country is not subject to a King, but each market-town is ruled by its separate chief." [70]

Identification of the place-names in these passages from the *Periplus* describing the Horn of Africa is not easy and authorities differ. In succession from the west the ports listed are Avalites (immediately beyond the straits of Bāb al-Mandab), Malao, Mundus, Mosyllum, the "laurel grove" called Acannae, the Market and Cape of Spices, Pano (a village) and Opone. Ptolemy provided a very similar list, commencing after the straits with Dire town and followed by Avalites, Malao, Mondu, Mosyllum (promontory and market-town), Cobe, Acanna, Aromata (promontory and market-town), Pano (a village) and Opone. Ptolemy's longitudes for this stretch of coast were considerably fore-shortened, but there is no doubt that his promontory and market-town of Aromata are identical with the "Market and Cape of Spices" of the *Periplus* and with the modern Cape Gardafui. This was also Strabo's "Notu-Ceras" (see page 115 above). It is now generally accepted that Avalites is modern Zeila and Malao is modern Berbera, while Mundus is probably modern Heis (or Bandar Hais), Mosyllum is thought to be near modern Rās Koreh (or perhaps further to the west) and Acannae is modern Alula. Just before Cape Gardafui, a village now known as Olok has been suggested as the site of the market-town by that cape testified by both Ptolemy and the *Periplus*, while beyond it to the south Pano is thought to lie at modern Rās Binnah and Opone at modern Rās Ḥāfūn. [71]

The writer of the *Periplus* repeatedly used the term "far side" to describe the frankincense collected from these ports, although this was quite unnecessary in terms of geographical origin and was not used in describing the Somali myrrh. The probable explanation for this would seem to be that the Somali frankincense was recognized as a different variety to the Arabian produce, which is borne out by the fact now established that the Somali and Arabian varieties came from different species of *Boswellia*. The same distinction is apparent in the modern names for the gums already discussed.

The Graeco-Roman ships first encountered Somali "far-side" frankincense at Malao, where the supply was small, and Mundus. It was found in larger quantities at Mosyllum and "in great quantity and of the best grade" at Acannae and the Market of Spices. This conforms with modern evidence that frankincense trees are found in greatest abundance in the north-eastern areas of Somalia, especially the Mijjertain.

At Mundus and Mosyllum was also found "the incense called *mocrotu*", the best quality of which came from Mundus. Schoff has interpreted this as "probably a high grade frankincense", assuming a correlation with the modern Somali *mohr* and Arabic *mughur*. But in the *Periplus* this product is clearly regarded as something quite different from the ordinary "far-side" frankincense, whether of good quality or not. The supposed site of Mundus is close to the modern Mait, which has given its name to the *lubān mayti* of modern times, the product of the *Yegaar* tree and nowadays regarded as a high grade of frankincense. It seems possible that the *mocratu* of the *Periplus* may have been *mayti* frankincense, the term "far-side" frankincense referring only to the product of the *Mohr madow* tree (*Boswellia carteri*).

From Malao and Mundus, but not from the ports further to the east, was exported, according to the *Periplus*, a product called *macir*. Pliny referred to *macir* as "a substance imported from India . . . the red bark of the large root of a tree of the same name, which I have been unable to identify. This bark boiled with honey is considered in medicine to be a valuable specific for dysentery."[72] Celsus makes no mention of *macir* in his list of medicaments. It seems rather improbable that the *Periplus* was here referring to a product brought from India, particularly because in that case one would have expected to find it available in the Somali ports lying closer to India and not just in the most westerly Somali ports. Miles, in his description of Somaliland, mentioned that "besides the frankincense gum, the black and white Mohr trees yield a beautiful red dye, which is extracted from the thin papery bark."[73] Certainly frankincense had a medicinal value in classical times for curbing haemorrhages among other purposes. One might therefore look to the possibility that *macir* was a product of the bark of a frankincense tree. But the tree from which it came would be a species found more in the west than in the east of the country. It is tempting to suggest that the name *macir* may equate with *makur*, the type of frankincense from Somalia which we have suggested may have derived from *Boswellia papyrifera*, the Ethiopian *makker* (or *mäqär*) frankincense tree, and that this could be the origin of the medicament.

Epigraphic evidence about early Arabian incenses is scarce but seems to indicate that the gods of ancient South Arabia were propitiated with many different varieties of aromatics. Several small incense altars have been found in the region, usually cubes of stone some five to ten centimetres high, with the name of an incense inscribed on each of their four sides. These have provided the local names of a dozen different incenses. *Qlm*, *Qst*, *Kmkm* and *Ldn* are recognisable respectively as Calamus, Costus, Cancamum and Ladanum, all mentioned by Pliny. *Lbny*, which would seem to be frankincense (Lubany), occurs less frequently. Most common are *Rnd* and *Drw*, which latter name still exists in Yemen in the form *Daru* as the name of a tree (possibly *Pistacia lentiscus*), the gum of which is still called *Kamkām*. It seems most probable that the offerings made on these little altars were all locally-grown incense materials.[74]

Plate No. 1

Plate No. 2

Plate No. 3

Plate No. 4

Plate No. 5

Plate No. 6

Plate No. 7

Plate No. 8

Plate No. 9

Plate No. 10

Plate No. 11

Plate No. 12

Plate No. 13

Plate No. 14

Plate No. 15

Plate No. 16

Plate No. 17

Plate No. 18

Plate No. 19

Plate No. 20

Plate No. 21

Plate No. 22

Plate No. 23

Plate No. 24

Plate No. 25

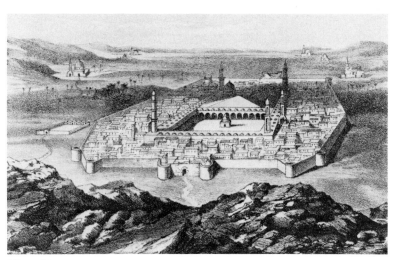

Plate No. 26

Plate No. 27

Plate No. 28

Plate No. 29

Plate No. 30

Chapter 8

The Harvest and
the Trade

We have already discussed the nature and location of the
incense trees and the varieties of frankincense and myrrh
which they produced. It now falls to examine what is known
about the manner of collecting and handling the crop. Some
of the excerpts from classical sources quoted in previous
chapters have already touched on this subject.

It will be recollected that Theophrastus was able to quote
the evidence of a Greek expedition which had set out from
Suez (the Bay of Heroes) on a coasting voyage, probably
under the command of Anaxicrates, had landed on the
southern shore of Arabia to look for water "and so saw the
trees and the manner of collecting their gums" (page 62
above). The relevant part of his account read as follows:

"They reported that with both [frankincense and myrrh] trees
incisions had been made both in the stems and in the branches,
but that, while the stems looked as if they had been cut with an
axe, in the branches the incisions were slighter; also that in some
cases the gum was dropping, but that in others it remained
sticking to the tree; and that in some places mats woven of palm-
leaves were put underneath, while in some the ground underneath was merely made level and clean; and that the frankincense
on the mats was clear and transparent, that collected on the
ground less so; and that which remained sticking to the trees they
scraped off with iron tools, wherefore sometimes pieces of bark
remained in it. . . .[1]

They also reported another thing which they said they had
been told, that the myrrh and frankincense are collected from all
parts into the temple of the sun; and that this temple is the most
sacred thing which the Sabaeans of that region possess, and it is
guarded by certain Arabians in arms. And that when they have

143

brought it, each man piles up his own contribution of frankincense and the myrrh in like manner, and leaves it with those on guard; and on the pile he puts a tablet on which is stated the number of measures which it contains, and the price for which each measure should be sold; and that, when the merchants come, they look at the tablets, and whichsoever pile pleases them, they measure and put down the price on the spot whence they have taken the wares, and then the priest comes and, having taken the third part of the price for the god, leaves the rest of it where it was, and this remains safe for the owners until they come and claim it." [2]

Pliny's account of the harvesting, already cited on pages 136 to 137 above, reveals that by his time the demand for frankincense had increased so much that two harvests were being extracted each year, the main one "at about the rising of the Dogstar, when the summer heat is most intense" and the second in the spring, for which incisions were made during the winter. Myrrh was also being harvested twice. The rising of the Dogstar was in Roman reckoning the beginning of July, when the "dog days", the six to eight hottest weeks of summer, commenced in Rome (it was believed that when Sirius, the brightest star, rose at the same time as the sun, this added to the heat of the day). Pliny appears to have used the phrase here to stress that it was at the hottest period of the summer, rather than as a specific indication of a calendar date. In south Arabia this fell a little earlier than in the Mediterranean, in May and June, before the summer rains commenced. Pliny's statement that frankincense from the summer crop was collected in the autumn also requires explanation; the original Latin ("autumno legitur ab aestivo partu") is compatible with the probable meaning that the summer crop was not taken away to the coast until autumn, a point we shall return to.

We have two modern descriptions of frankincense harvesting in Ẓufār which it is interesting to relate to Pliny's account. In the first the Bents wrote:

"The Bedouin choose the hot season, when the gum flows most freely, to do this puncturing. During the rains of July and August, and during the cool season, the trees are left alone. The first step is to make an incision in the trunk, then they strip off a narrow bit of bark below the hole, so as to make a receptacle in which the milky juice . . . can lodge and harden. Then the incision is deepened, and after seven days they return to collect what are, by that time, quite big tears of frankincense, larger than an egg. . . . It is only collected in the hot weather, before the rains begin and when the gum flows freely, in the months of March, April and May, for during the rains the tracks on the Qara mountains are impassable. The trees belong to the various families of the Cara tribe; each tree is marked and known to its owner, and the product is sold wholesale to Banyan merchants, who come to Dhufar just before the monsoon to take it away."[3]

In the second the account is by Bertram Thomas:

"The tree begins to bear in its third or fourth year. The collectors, women as well as men, come to make slight incisions here and there in the low and stout branches with a special knife. A gum exudes at these points and hardens into large lozenge-shaped tears of resinous substance which is known as frankincense (liban). After ten days the drops are large enough for collection, and the tree will continue to yield from these old incisions deepened as necessary at intervals of ten days for a further period of five months. After this the tree dries up and is left to recover, the period varying from six months to two years according to its condition. Collection of the 'liban' is made chiefly during the summer months. It is stored in the mountain caves until the winter, when it is sent down to the ports for export, for no country craft put to sea during the gales of the summer south-west monsoon. This delay enables the product to dry well, though normally it is ready for export in from ten to twenty days after collection."[4]

The process was more or less similar for harvesting frankincense from the different species of *Boswellia* found in Somalia. Miles wrote:

"The season for collecting the gum lasts for four months—from May to September; the trees may be gashed any number of times without injury, but unless rain falls soon after, the tree withers and dies. The gum is gathered fifteen days after the tree is cut, as it has then ceased to exude, and the bark, which heals rapidly, is again gashed. The knife with which the tree is cut is called *mingāf*."[5]

These descriptions by the classical and modern writers are fairly consistent. They reveal a significant feature of the incense trade and that is its seasonal nature. This arose not only from the obvious restriction of the tapping process to certain times of the year but also from another important factor, that the movement of the produce could not take place during the monsoon.

Farmers in southern Arabia today generally divide the year into four seasons: the *rabi'* (spring) from January to March; the *sayf* (summer), which is roughly March to June; the *kharīf* (autumn), which is approximately July to September; and the *shitā* (winter), which is from October to the end of December.[6] The major climatic factors for agricultural purposes are the timing and strength of the rain-bringing south-west and north-east monsoons and these can vary considerably from year to year. The main rains of southern Arabia come with the south-west monsoon, which blows between June and September, though not necessarily for the whole of that time, bringing heavy thunderstorms to the mountains. Arab seamen of the south Arabian coast nowadays recognize this as a ninety-day period, known as the "closing" or "locking" of the sea, when the movement of shipping ceases and fishing is reduced to a minimum.[7] The north-east monsoon blows for a part of the period between November and April and usually brings a much lighter rainfall. The timing of the monsoons varies not only from year to year but also by a week or two between the western and eastern parts of the region, the western part receiving the south-west monsoon first and the north-east monsoon last. Pliny's reference to the autumn frankincense crop as *carfia-thum* (page 137 above) relates to the Arabic word *kharīf*. Both *carfiathum* and *dathiathum* (Pliny's spring harvest) are recognizable in their non-Latin form in pre-Islamic south Arabian inscriptions as meaning respectively "autumn" and "spring".[8]

When one correlates the available details about the frankincense harvest with the seasonal factors the pattern of the ancient incense trade begins to emerge. Incisions were made in the frankincense trees between April and June, once the hot weather had commenced. After a week or ten days the trees were re-visited and the frankincense tears collected and probably stored away locally, further incisions being made or new crops being gathered at intervals of ten days to a fortnight over the next few weeks. In July and August, with the arrival of the monsoon rains, collection off the trees ceased. In the

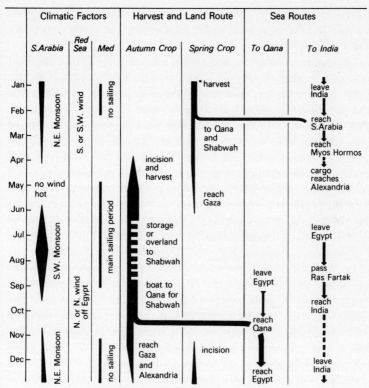

*The Frankincense Harvest and Trading Cycle –
1st to 3rd centuries AD*

period September/November, once the south-west monsoon had blown out, the incense started on its long journey, that from Ẓufār being taken down to the coast for conveyance to Qana on boats and rafts buoyed up by inflated skins; before this time the tracks were difficult or impassable and the flotillas of small craft could not in any case set out to sea. Produce from the African coast would start arriving in Qana at the same time. For the spring crop incisions seem likely to have been made in the winter period November/December, with the collection of the tears, which at this season take very much longer to ooze out and coagulate, taking place in about

147

February; that crop would then be shipped to Qana as soon as the north-east monsoon had died down sufficiently to allow a safe passage.

Although in modern times the harvesting of frankincense in Zufār is carried out by groups of Arabs on behalf of the Qarā tribe, who own the trees,[9] elsewhere both frankincense and myrrh have almost invariably been collected by Somalis who travelled over from Somalia for the purpose and paid rent to the Arab owners of the trees.[10] This has been the trading pattern since early in the nineteenth century and possibly much earlier. A century ago Hunter recorded: "In the country of the Yaffai and other districts in the south of Arabia, Somalis gather incense . . . but further eastward, in the vicinity of Ras Morbut, Dhufar, Ras Fartak, etc., it is collected by the inhabitants of the district."[11]

The Bents observed that the demand for frankincense was so limited when they were in Zufār that no care whatsoever was taken of the trees, only the most promising ones being tapped at all.[12] This local indifference may have existed for centuries, but for the millennium over which the incense trade flourished we can be sure that the trees were very differently regarded and their value must have been considerable. In that period it would not be surprising to find ritualistic measures incorporated into the harvesting process to safeguard the yield from any divine ill-will. Pliny has been assumed to give account of this in the following passage:

"Adjacent to the Astramitae is another district, the Minaei, through whose territory the transit for the export of frankincense is along one narrow track. It was these people who originated the trade and who chiefly practise it, and from them the perfume takes the name of 'Minaean'; none of the Arabs beside these have ever seen an incense tree, and not even all of these, and it is said that there are not more than 3000 families who retain the right of trading in it as a hereditary property, and that consequently the members of these families are called sacred, and are not allowed to be polluted by ever meeting women or funeral processions when they are engaged in making incisions in the trees in order to obtain the frankincense, and that in this way *the trade is increasingly subject to* the scruples of religion. Some persons report that the frankincense in the forests belongs to all these people in common, but others state that it is shared out among them in yearly turns."[13]

We shall return to the Minaean interest in the frankincense trade when we look at the problem of the Gebbanitae, referred to so frequently by Pliny. Here the Gebbanitae are not mentioned, which suggests, particularly in view of its separate position in Pliny's text, that this passage derives from a different source.[14] While we can accept that the Minaeans controlled the conveyance of the frankincense northwards, it seems very unlikely that they undertook the actual harvesting, as Pliny here infers. There is no other evidence at all, either inscriptional, or in the classical sources, or in surviving traces or traditions, testifying to the existence in any of the frankincense-producing areas of a settled Minaean population of the size suggested (3000 families should perhaps be reckoned at about 15,000 persons). Possibly the Minaean traders visited the frankincense groves at the appropriate seasons to make the incisions under ritualistic conditions, leaving local persons to collect the tears; possibly the whole passage refers to the carriers rather than the growers; or possibly Pliny has incorrectly amalgamated two separate items of information, firstly that the Minaeans had the monopoly of the transit trade and secondly that the tribe which farmed the trees accepted certain ritual prohibitions during the harvesting. Whatever the answer, it is quite clear that the value and ultimate use of frankincense led to it being handled in a very different way from myrrh. Rules and regulations governed its collection and conveyance which did not apply to myrrh and it was conveyed along designated routes. Even when it entered the Roman Empire its special character was recognized, for the Roman customs admitted it free of duty, whereas myrrh, like most other commodities, was subject to an import tax of 25 per cent.

Once collected, the frankincense crop seems to have been stored away until the south-west monsoon had died down during August. The crop from the eastern areas was then, on the evidence of the *Periplus*, carried down to the coast and conveyed by small craft to Qana, which also received the "Far-side" produce. From here the frankincense was transported to Shabwah – the "Sabota" of Pliny and the "Sabbatha" of the *Periplus*. But Pliny referred only to frankincense being taken from the area where it grew to Shabwah and made no mention of a sea voyage (see page 110 above). His sole reference to Qana was in a separate passage describing "Cane in the frankincense-producing district" as a possible port of call on the way to India (page 79 above), while he made no reference at all to Moscha, in Ẓufār, which by the time of the *Periplus* had become a significant frankincense port. We have seen that most of Pliny's sources date back to about 50–25 BC (although his reference to Qana was probably from a contemporary one), giving a gap of two or three hundred years between his information and that of the *Periplus*. Is it possible that over that period there was a significant change in the trading pattern?

It can be argued that, when Pliny's sources were reporting, knowledge of south Arabia was much less precise than it had become by the time of the *Periplus*, while at the same time Pliny's information about the incense trade derived in the main from somebody familiar with the land route but not acquainted with Qana. But by Pliny's time the journey to India was being made fairly frequently and it is difficult to accept that information about the role of Qana as a frankincense port would not have filtered through to Pliny from one of the sea captains with experience of the Arabian ports.

In Chapter 5 mention was made of the discovery by Hippalus, probably a little before 100 BC, of how the monsoon winds could be used to assist the journey to India (page 79 above). The development of this discovery was a gradual affair, at first just a matter of making a coasting voyage at the correct time of year in order to take advantage of the wind direction; by about the time of Tiberius (AD 14–37) ships had begun to coast past Aden and Qana as far as the great headland of Rās Fartak and then head across the ocean to Patala, on the Indus; finally and shortly afterwards, probably during the reign of Claudius (AD 41–54), the ships' captains began to brave a more south-easterly course after Rās Fartak in order to sail directly to the Malabar coast for pepper, the most sought after of all the Indian produce.[15] This journey to India commenced from Egypt at about the time of "the rising of the Dog-star" (see page 79 above), which was the beginning of July (page 144 above), and the ships would then pass Rās Fartak around mid-August; this was of course before the frankincense crop began to reach Qana, so that the ships bound for India which put in at Qana would not necessarily have become aware of that trade.

But there was another highly significant development over this period which affected the incense trade. This was the expansion and consolidation of the Roman Empire's south-eastern reaches through the campaigns of Julius Caesar and the administration of Augustus, culminating in the annexation of the Nabataean kingdom in AD 106 and the subsequent establishment by Trajan of a Roman fleet in the Red Sea to protect shipping from piracy. In the first two centuries AD, and particularly from the time of Trajan up to the death of Marcus Aurelius in AD 180, the *Pax Romana* enabled the Mediterranean communities to realize an unprecedented wealth, and there was a vast increase in their demand for luxury commodities, including spices and incense. The consequent upsurge in trade may have increased the price of frankincense and would certainly have induced the Arabians to draw on frankincense supplies from ever more remote areas, while making the harvesting even of low quality frankincense from the nearer regions profitable. Pliny's remarks about the huge amount of frankincense used in Rome

in his day do not describe the incense trade at its maximum expansion; undoubtedly it increased considerably more in the century which followed his death.[16]

It is possible that in earliest times the bulk of the frankincense brought northwards overland from Shabwah was harvested in the groves of Ḥaḍramawt and that, as the trade expanded, these supplies were supplemented with produce from further afield, from Mahrah, Ẓufār, Somalia and Socotra; hence Moscha and Qana may not have become well known as frankincense ports until a much later period. By the time of Ptolemy and the *Periplus*, however, the quantities of frankincense brought in to Qana from Ẓufār and Somalia would seem to have greatly exceeded the production from the regions nearer to Shabwah, while, despite efforts to keep the overland trade running, increasing quantities were being exported both west and east from Qana, and even directly from Moscha, by foreign trading vessels.

This apparent late expansion of the incense trade seems to be borne out by what is so far known about the ruins of Shabwah and Moscha. The former city appears to have reached the peak of its prosperity in the second or third century AD. In Ẓufār archaeological investigation has so far revealed very few pre-Islamic sites, leading to the conclusion that, to quote Wendell Phillips, "sedentary occupation of any importance came late to this part of Arabia." Phillips noted that the ancient town of Khor Rori, believed to be the site of Moscha, was "built by outsiders as a colony, probably not long before the Christian era".[17] Inscriptions commemorating the foundation of the town by the King of Ḥaḍramawt have since been found which are thought to originate from some time between the first century BC and the second century AD.[18]

The heightened demand for frankincense and the high prices obtainable may have led to overcropping. Even in Pliny's time an artificial second crop of frankincense was being gathered. Bertram Thomas observed that after being tapped for some while, the frankincense tree needs to be left alone for a period of six months to two years to recover (see page 145 above). If, because of the easy profits, the trees were not given this respite, they may eventually have withered. Moreover, there appears to be some risk to the trees in the very procedure of tapping it, for Miles noted, presumably of the species *Boswellia carteri*, that "the trees may be gashed any number of times without injury, but unless the rain falls soon after, the tree withers and dies."[19] While there was an ample supply of trees this would not matter, except that it would have had the effect of compelling the gatherers to go increasingly further afield for their supplies, but it could mean that during the height of the incense trade the available supply of frankincense trees was being run down.

While there are uncertainties about the date of Qana's development as the main frankincense port arising from divergencies in the information provided by Pliny and the *Periplus*, both these sources are agreed that the inland trading centre for frankincense was Shabwah, the Ḥadramawt capital, and it is apparent that all frankincense, excepting that traded by special permission with ships calling at Moscha or Qana, was conveyed there. By insisting on the use of Shabwah as the marketing centre, the King of Ḥadramawt was able to exercise a complete control over the trade, an arrangement which must have suited the Minaean merchants as well, for they held a monopoly over the carriage of the commodity along the inland trading route to the north and must have been reluctant to see too much of it being collected by ship. That a considerable amount was eventually conveyed by sea is evident from the *Periplus*; the desire to trade with the goods brought by the Greek and Roman vessels must have been irresistible; but it is equally clear from the *Periplus* that Shabwah remained the frankincense capital until the incense trade itself came to an end.

Pliny described the role of Shabwah in a well-known passage as follows:

"Frankincense after being collected is conveyed to Sabota on camels, one of the gates of the city being opened for its admission; the kings have made it a capital offence for camels so laden to turn aside from the high road. At Sabota a tithe estimated by measure and not by weight is taken by the priests for the god they call Sabin, and the incense is not allowed to be put on the market until this has been done; this tithe is drawn on to defray what is a public expenditure, for actually on a fixed number of days the god graciously entertains guests at a banquet. It can only be exported by the Gebbanitae, and accordingly a tax is paid on it to the king of that people as well.

Their capital is Thomna, which is $1487\frac{1}{2}$ miles distant from the town of Gaza in Judaea on the Mediterranean coast; the journey is divided into 65 stages with halts for camels.

Fixed portions of the frankincense are also given to the priests and the king's secretaries, but beside these the guards and their attendants and the gate-keepers and servants also have their pickings: indeed all along the route they keep on paying, at one place for water, at another for fodder, or the charges for lodging at the halts, and the various octrois; so that expenses mount up to 688 denarii per camel before the Mediterranean coast is reached; and then again payment is made to the customs officers of our empire. Consequently the price of the best frankincense is 6, of the second best 5, and third best 3 denarii a pound." [20]

Pliny took care, in the case of almost every one of the commodities which he discussed in his *Natural History*, to quote the prevailing prices, which we can assume represent the retail price in Rome. A tabulated list of these is of considerable interest in showing the relative values of these items at the time. The prices quoted by Pliny were as follows:

Commodity	Price in denarii per pound
Amomum	48–60
Balsam	1000 (per pint)
Balsam-wood	6
Bdellium	3
Cardamomum (best)	3
Casia	5–50
Casia Daphnis'	300
Cinnamon	1500
Cinnamon-wood	10
Frankincense (best)	6
Frankincense (2nd quality)	5
Frankincense (3rd quality)	3
Ginger	6
Ladanum	4 ("40 asses")
Mastich, white	10
Mastich, black	2
Myrrh, Stacte	3–50
Myrrh, Cave Dweller	$16\frac{1}{2}$
Myrrh, Erythraean	16
Myrrh, Scented	12
Myrrh, Cultivated	11
Nard	100

Commodity	Price in denarii per pound
Nard leaf	40–75
Nard, Gallic	3
Pepper, long	15
Pepper, white	7
Pepper, black	4

Two striking points to emerge from this list are, firstly, the relative cheapness, weight for weight, of frankincense and myrrh in comparison with many of the other luxury commodities and, secondly, the fact that frankincense is less than half the price of myrrh. But the real comparison lies, of course, in the amounts of the different luxuries which a household able to afford them at all might be prepared to purchase; there is no doubt that the quantity of frankincense used was comparatively substantial, so that more would be expended on it than on almost any other item. In later times, although not, judging from his statement in the extract just quoted, during the time of Pliny, frankincense was not taxed at the Roman border. The "Red Sea" or "Alexandrian" Tariff, first codified under Marcus Aurelius (AD 161) and incorporated in the Digest of Roman Law produced in Justinian's reign (AD 527), listed the spices and aromatics which were subject to the standard 25 per cent import duty on luxuries. This excluded both frankincense and black pepper, probably because both had become regarded as necessities, the former for use in religious ceremonials and the latter as a condiment.[21] Precisely when this exclusion was introduced is not however known.

It is clear from the evidence of all the classical writers that frankincense and myrrh formed the bulk of the trade from Arabia and it can be deduced from this price comparison and other evidence that the great demand for frankincense was met by a substantial supply. The yield of resin from the frankincense tree may be higher than that from the myrrh tree, while the specialist uses of myrrh made it a significantly different type of commodity. Myrrh was primarily purchased by apothecaries and tradesmen to be processed as an ingredient for medicines, cosmetics, unguents, etc., whereas frankincense was widely purchased for domestic as well as for religious purposes both by private citizens and by public and religious bodies. Myrrh, because of its oily content, wasted during travel, which frankincense, provided it was not crushed, did not. In volume frankincense would appear to have held a pre-eminent position of all the south Arabian exports.

Although frankincense emerges as one of the least costly of the spices and incenses, it was not by any measure inexpensive. Pliny reveals how the price was conditioned by, among other things, the enormous costs of the overland journey, with its multitude of tithes and customs taxes, aggregating 688 denarii for a camel-load by the time it reached the Mediterranean. In one of his articles on incense, Van Beek has noted that information relating to the cost of living in the second century AD shows that the basic necessities of life in Roman Syro-Palestine at that time required, on a mean figure, 120 denarii a year; on a comparative basis the cost of one pound weight of the best quality frankincense would represent two weeks' wages of a modern American factory worker.[22]

Unfortunately no details or statistics are available which provide an accurate account of the size of the frankincense trade, nor indeed of the volume of the incense and spice trade as a whole. Pliny has mentioned the expenses of a camel-load and the number of stages on the journey, but nowhere does he record, for example, the size of the camel caravans or the quantities of incense which they carried. However, two figures quoted by Pliny do enable very tentative calculations about the volume of the incense trade to be made.

In Book 12 Pliny stated: "And by the lowest reckoning India, China and the Arabian peninsula take from our empire 100 million sesterces every year – that is the sum which our luxuries and our women cost us; for what fraction of these imports, I ask you, now goes to the gods or to the powers of the lower world?"[23] In Book 6 he observed that: "In no year does India absorb less than fifty million sesterces of our empire's wealth, sending back merchandise to be sold with us at a hundred times its prime cost."[24] The Chinese trade included the trade in silk, but this did not become of major significance until after Pliny's time; whether it was included with India in the latter quotation is uncertain, but if it was then the total Roman trade with Arabia Felix in Pliny's estimate would seem to have cost the Roman economy of his time some 50 million sesterces a year – or roughly 13,500,000 denarii.[25] Coming from a senior official with an interest in public finances and some access to the Treasury statistics, Pliny's figures should at very least be intelligent guesses.[26]

There has been substantial debate over whether Pliny was assessing the cost of the luxury imports in terms of both the quantity obtained by barter and that purchased by bullion or whether he was referring to the damaging waste of bullion alone. It is acknowledged that the Roman Empire was unable to export anything like sufficient produce to pay for its imports and that the resultant draining away of bullion was one cause of the currency debasement which significantly contributed to the Empire's eventual economic collapse. The oil and wine with which Rome paid for most of its imports from north-west Europe were not wanted in India and Arabia and could not in any case be conveyed there along overland routes. Rome was not a manufacturing country. The list of exports from Rome is small compared with that of its imports. Ships from Puteoli often loaded with ballast when leaving to collect goods from Alexandria. If there was an industrial centre in the Empire it was in Alexandria and not in Italy.[27] Whereas we know, both from the clear statements in the *Periplus* and from the many discoveries in India of hoards of Roman coins, that bullion was sent to India in large amounts, we can only assume this was the case with Arabia of Pliny's time, but that would seem most probable. Scholars now generally conclude that Pliny was here drawing attention to the wastage of bullion, in the sense of precious metal whether coined or not, to pay for the excess of imported over exported goods. For a long time this "wastage" did not matter, because the receipts from tribute, the spoils of war and the output of newly captured gold and silver mines covered the excess. One hundred million sesterces was the equivalent of 22,000 Roman pounds' weight in gold (or about 571,000 of our gold sovereigns).[28] On Roman national standards this was not an exceptional sum. There were individuals whose private fortunes were far greater (Seneca was said to be worth 300 million sesterces). A century earlier, Julius Caesar had received only slightly less than this weight of coronary gold in tribute at his triumph,[29] while the reserve funds of the state when he took power in Rome consisted of 15,000 gold and 30,000 silver bars, together with 30 million sesterces. Trajan's campaign in Dacia in AD 106 alone is reputed to have resulted in the capture of treasure worth five million pounds' weight of gold. But the situation changed dramatically once the Empire began to shrink and the mining areas were lost, leading to serious debasement of the coinage and to such disastrous inflation that the price of Egyptian wheat rose from 7 or 8 drachmae a measure in the 1st and 2nd centuries AD to between 12 and 20 drachmae early in the 3rd century and to 120,000 drachmae by the beginning of the 4th century.[30]

The exports to south Arabia listed by the *Periplus* are: to Muza – "purple cloths, fine and coarse"; clothing in Arabian styles; saffron; sweet-rush; muslins; cloaks; blankets; sashes; fragrant ointments; wine and wheat ("not much, the country producing both"); and also, as presents to the King and Chief, "horses, sumpter-mules, vessels of gold and polished silver, finely woven clothing, copper vessels": to Qana—all the above items plus copper, tin, coral and storax and, for the King, "wrought gold and silver plate, horses, images, thin clothing of fine quality". This is the list of exports after the trade had become highly developed and after considerable effort had been made by later Roman emperors to develop a barter trade. Coin is not specifically mentioned, although the *Periplus* lists it among the exports to both Somalia and, in considerable quantity, India, but valuable metals in the form of copper and tin went to Qana to buy the frankincense and the "gold plate" mentioned may in fact be a mistranslation for "coin".[31]

The *Periplus* of course lists only goods conveyed by sea. In Pliny's time, when the incense trade was still almost wholly overland, some of these items, such as wine, could not have been transported. It is clear that the major portion of the exports to Arabia noted by the *Periplus* consisted of various types of clothing and blankets. Such items may have reached south Arabia down the overland route, but the value of each camel-load of these bulky goods would have been so much less than that of the similar weight of frankincense carried north that most of the payment for the incense seems likely to have been made in coin and precious metals. It is improbable that many more camels would have been used to carry bulky goods south than conveyed the incense north. If the portion of incense bartered rather than paid for in cash amounted to one fifth of the total (and it is difficult to see that it could have been much more), then Pliny's figure of 50 million sesterces represents the remaining four-fifths paid for in bullion and metals. On this basis the total value of goods brought into Rome from Arabia in Pliny's time would have been $62\frac{1}{2}$ million sesterces, or roughly $16\frac{1}{2}$ million denarii.

This is a crude estimate but worth considering further. To take the calculation forward an assessment is needed of the division of the Arabian exports as between frankincense, myrrh and other commodities. Available figures which suggest this proportion are fairly consistent. In 243 BC Seleuces II sent to the Council and people of Miletus ten talents of frankincense, one of myrrh and two minae each of cassia, cinnamon and costum; the Gerrhaean tribute to Antiochus III in 205 BC included one thousand talents of frankincense and two hundred of "stacte" myrrh; [32] the gift Alexander sent to his old tutor after the capture of Gaza consisted of five hundred talents of frankincense and one hundred of myrrh (see page 204 below). Bearing in mind the higher price fetched by myrrh, a reasonable rough estimate of the division of expenditure to produce this proportion in quantity would be 60 per cent on frankincense, 30 per cent on myrrh and 10 per cent on other commodities. On this basis the total of $16\frac{1}{2}$ million denarii divides into 9,900,000 denarii expended on frankincense, 4,950,000 on myrrh and 1,650,000 on other commodities.

While the price of frankincense quoted by Pliny was presumably the retail price in Rome, the expenditure out of the Roman economy would have been the price paid to the Arab trader at the Mediterranean terminal, perhaps Gaza, by a Roman merchant who thereafter transported it either direct to Rome or to Alexandria for processing. The camel-load had borne 688 denarii of expenses and taxes on the journey and had thereafter to pay another tax to the Roman customs. But on what weight were these charges paid? How much was a camel-load?

With his usual meticulousness, Hunter listed the weights carried by each of the six species of camel found in Aden in his time (i.e. 1875), which ranged from 450 pounds to 1000 pounds.[33] But the desert camel of south-west Arabia is a lighter breed than the coastal and mountain camels generally found in Aden; the normal weight carried in recent times by Bal Ḥārith camels engaged in the Bayḥān salt trade, for example, is 300 to 400 pounds.[34] Elsewhere the average load of a desert camel has been assessed as 330 pounds.[35] While it cannot be confirmed that the camels found in the interior desert in ancient times were of the same breed as today, a lighter breed is better favoured for desert conditions, a lighter load would be carried on a long haul, while the weight-carrying ability of camels has probably increased over the centuries under controlled breeding. In AD 301 an edict on prices issued by Diocletian specified 8 denarii as the charge for carrying a camel-load of 600 Roman pounds (i.e. 430 pounds avoirdupois) over one mile, but this charge was clearly for a short haul.[36] A load of 400 pounds (= 533 Roman pounds) for the incense camels therefore seems a reasonable assessment and is the basis used in the calculations which follow.

If the mean price paid for frankincense by the Roman merchant at Gaza was $2\frac{1}{2}$ denarii a Roman pound (or half the retail price for medium grade frankincense in Rome) then a camel-load would have fetched 1333 denarii, of which the Arab merchant would receive 645 denarii after deducting the expenses of the journey. Pliny's figure of 688 denarii may not have included the original purchase price from the grower, so the 645 denarii was not necessarily all profit, but a terminal profit of this order, perhaps divided among a number of merchants handling the commodity along the route, would not seem out of keeping with the circumstances of the trading.

At 1333 denarii a camel-load, the figure of 9,900,000 denarii represents 7427 camel-loads and a total weight of approximately 1326 tons of frankincense. Were the mean price at Gaza 2 denarii a Roman pound, then the volume traded works out at about 9381 camel-loads weighing 1675 tons, while if the camels carried only 330 pounds each, then that tonnage would have required 11,370 camels to transport it. In broad terms this suggests that in Pliny's time a minimum of around 1300 to 1700 tons of frankincense was carried into the Roman Empire in some 7000 to 10,000 camel-loads annually.

These figures do not represent the total Arabian production of frankincense, because additional quantities were exported for Mesopotamia through the Arabian Gulf town of Gerrha along an overland route, while further amounts went to India by sea and much was undoubtedly consumed in south Arabia itself. The total production at the time might thus be assessed at a minimum of between 2500 and 3000 tons a year, a figure which would have substantially increased by the time of the *Periplus*, with much of the increase being carried by ships.

On the basis that myrrh might account for 30 per cent of the total value of the Arabian trade, the minimum quantity of myrrh entering the Roman Empire annually during Pliny's time can be roughly assessed under the same calculation at about 211 tons, or 1184 camel-loads, assuming a mean terminal price at Gaza of 8 denarii a pound. At a lower price of 6 denarii a pound these figures would read 276 tons or about 1548 camel-loads. Taking into consideration the myrrh exported to Gerrha, India and elsewhere and that used locally, it may then be inferred that the minimum annual production of myrrh in Pliny's time would have been about 450 to 600 tons.

These calculations are of course extremely conjectural, but they produce figures which fit into Pliny's original estimate of the trade costing the Roman economy 50 million sesterces a year at a minimum and which conform with the ratio of 4 or 5:1 for the production of frankincense and myrrh. That same ratio is also reflected in the modern Aden trading figures quoted on page 121 above of 300 tons of frankincense and 70 tons of myrrh handled in 1875. A higher tonnage of myrrh would have to be matched by a very much greater decrease in the comparatively much cheaper frankincense, significantly altering this ratio.[37] Unless Pliny's estimate was substantially too low, or the figures in his text are corrupt, the total volume of the incense trade in his time therefore seems likely to have been near the figures suggested.

Quite how much the trade expanded after Pliny's days it is impossible even to speculate with any confidence, but it would not seem unreasonable to suggest a two-fold or even a three-fold expansion at least, perhaps much more, with most of the increase being carried by sea. The overland route for frankincense was still enforced at the time of the *Periplus* and special permission from the King was needed to export frankincense from Moscha by ship, but such export was evidently commonplace and would clearly have been attractive to both Romans and South Arabians alike in view of the wider variety of desirable goods which the ships could bring for exchange. But this period of peak prosperity for south Arabia was short-lived. From early in the fourth century AD the incense market began to collapse.

The most specific cause of the collapse was the spread of Christianity, marked in particular by the conversion of the Emperor: until about the middle of the fourth century no incense was used at all in the ceremonies of the Church and by the end of the century Theodosius had forbidden the pagan practice of making offerings, including incense, to the household gods. But at the same time internal crisis and severe inflation were beginning to paralyse the Roman economy, while the weakening of Roman power and influence led to internal strife and insecurity not only along the incense route but also in south Arabia itself. It is doubtful whether the overland aromatics trade survived the fourth century, while the sea-borne trade continued only on a very much smaller scale.

The revival of the overland trading route by the Quraysh merchants of Makkah in the sixth century AD, when there was little sea commerce, introduced a new trading pattern. The Quraysh organized two great co-operative trading caravans, one setting out in the winter for the Yemen, the other in summer for Syria, which are mentioned in the Qur'ān (Sura 106). These huge convoys, with a thousand or even two thousand camels escorted by up to three hundred men, brought oriental and African goods and slaves imported through south Arabia, together with some frankincense. The visits of these caravans became conveniently linked to the traditional pilgrimages to local shrines, setting the pattern in many parts of Arabia for great trading fairs held annually around the shrines, at which local people would stock up with their requirements for the year.[38]

At this time Constantinople took over as the main centre of perfumery. A sixth-century description of the cathedral of Saint Sophia refers to its hundreds of perfumed lamps. The continuation of the export of aromatics from south Arabia into the early Middle Ages is revealed in the detailed commercial laws drawn up by Leo VI in AD 895, where perfume ingredients permitted to be sold include both myrrh and frankincense, but this trade was a mere shadow of what it had been seven hundred years before.[39]

It may be postulated that the over-cropping of the incense trees during the period of boom conditions may have continued, once the market began to decline, in the more central incense-producing areas as the growers tried to maintain their income in the face of falling prices; at the same time trees in the more remote areas may no longer have been tapped. Over-cropping may have led to the withering of many more trees. In the following centuries the disappearance of the incense trees from much of south Arabia has proceeded apace. Severe droughts, such as occurred in the region in the fifth and sixth centuries AD, have added their toll to the depredations of that continual process of desiccation brought about by over-grazing, gradual climatic change and other factors which has afflicted Arabia over the past two millennia. Such desiccation may have shrunk the frankincense habitat, which would seem to require a minimal but regular rainfall. It is a significant factor that the frankincense tree makes an excellent fodder for camels and goats, so that after it had become valueless as an incense producer many trees may have been destroyed by grazing. Significant too is the fact that it also makes an excellent fuel: the denudation of the Arabian landscape for miles around the population centres to meet the need for firewood and charcoal is characteristic of the Arabian scene. Nor is this use for incense wood anything very new, for it is testified by Pliny before the trees lost their value. Pliny recorded:

> "For the rest, no other kinds of wood are in use among the [south Arabians] except those that are scented; and the Sabaei even cook their food with incense-wood and other tribes with that of the myrrh tree, so that the smoke and vapour of their towns and districts is just like that which rises from altars. In order therefore to remedy this smell they obtain styrax in goat-skins and fumigate their houses with it: so true it is that there is no pleasure the continual enjoyment of which does not engender disgust."[40]

In the light of all these factors the scarcity of frankincense trees in the Wādī Ḥagr region and the valleys of Ḥaḍramawt and the present-day rarity of myrrh trees, which once grew almost everywhere in south-west Arabia, are not difficult to understand.

Chapter 9

The Road through the Incense Lands

In discussing the problem of Pliny's frankincense-growing area in Chapter 6 (page 111 above *et seq.*), it was noted that the overland journey from Ẓufār to Shabwah, a direct distance of about 400 miles, would have taken a camel caravan at least twenty and more probably about thirty days. The point was then made that this was not compatible with Pliny's description of the frankincense growing area called "Sariba" as eight days' journey from Shabwah. Because of this statement by Pliny modern writers on the subject, assuming that "Sariba" was modern Ẓufār, have tended to accept that there was a direct overland route for frankincense from Ẓufār to Shabwah in addition to the sea route through Qana. Maps showing the ancient incense routes are consequently marked to indicate the existence of these routes as arteries of the incense trade. In fact it seems improbable that more than a trickle of frankincense ever reached Shabwah from Ẓufār by this means.

Two possible inland routes between Ẓufār and Ḥaḍramawt do exist—along the northern edge of the mountains past the wells at Sanau and Thamūd, or south of the main mountain range, from Ḥabarūt through Mahrah country. Thesiger, who covered both these routes, reported nothing which gives any indication of either ever having been used as a major trade route[1] and this is in keeping with the paucity of archaeological sites in Ẓufār as a whole and the absence of any site which could have been the point where caravans assembled before leaving Ẓufār.[2] The mediaeval Arab geographers say nothing to suggest that the routes were of any significance in their times and make it apparent that persons travelling on the pilgrimage may even have found it easier to take a coastal route at least as far as ash-Shiḥr.[3] Travel over these inland routes would have involved substantial distances over waterless terrain and have been extremely arduous; neither is practical as a major trade route and the northerly one is so barren and difficult that it can confidently be discounted.[4] Wendell Phillips was told whilst at Shisūr, the easterly point of departure for anyone taking the northern route, that "it is eight days to water in the Eastern Aden Protectorate."[5] The massive caravans needed to haul frankincense on a large scale to Shabwah could not have operated in such conditions, particularly since watering from deep wells is a very slow procedure, while desert wells and water-holes rapidly become empty if there is heavy water consumption. In general, Shabwah could be reached very much more easily, cheaply and quickly by sending the produce of Ẓufār to the coast and thence by sea to Qana. While small quantities of frankincense may have gone overland from Ẓufār for special reasons, such as tax avoidance, a temporary state of insecurity, or to fetch a high price at the start of the season, it seems clear that the major portion of Ẓufār's frankincense must always have come through Qana. If political circumstances made this route impossible, then the overland route could not have been used on any large scale as an alternative.

We have already seen that frankincense was produced in Arabia not from Ẓufār alone but from the whole stretch of country between Ẓufār and Qana. The little boats and the rafts made of inflated goatskins, as described in the *Periplus*, will have set out in small fleets from fishing villages all along the coast as soon as the high winds and heavy seas of the monsoon began to moderate in September and November. From points nearer to Qana there may have been some camel-borne traffic as well, bringing frankincense to the Qana warehouses along a coastal route. The produce of the region south of Ḥadramawt valley, including the Wādī Ḥagr area which may have been Pliny's "Sariba", would have been conveyed directly to Shabwah, while some may have been conveyed from the western areas of what is now Mahrah along pathways which file down into the lower reaches of Wādī Ḥadramawt (where it becomes known as Wādī al-Masīlah). But undoubtedly, once the trading pattern was

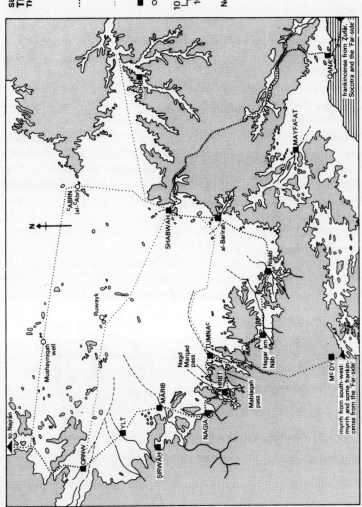

SUGGESTED ROUTES OF
THE INCENSE ROAD
THROUGH SOUTH ARABIA

.... Main route during
the hegemony of
Qatabān

.... Secondary and
alternative routes

■ Towns

○ Other sites

10 5 0   10   20   30   40 miles

10 0   20   40   60 kms

Note. ancient names are
shown in capital
letters

fully developed, the greatest quantity of frankincense was conveyed to Qana and thence to Shabwah.

From Qana there are two possible routes to Shabwah, the distance along either of them being about 160 to 170 miles. The first, circling round from the east, follows up the course of Wādī Mayfaʿah, crossing a narrow band of the mountain range at the head of its tributary, the Wādī ʿAmāqīn, to Wādī Girdān and then skirting round the northern edge of the mountains along sandy tracts to Shabwah. This route would have suited camel caravans, being mostly soft underfoot and over level ground, and it would have passed through some fertile, well watered and populous territory, as is testified by the number of significant ruin sites to be found in both the Mayfaʿah and Girdān areas. The second route headed due north from Qana through a pass in the mountains into Wādī Ḥagr and then, after following the wadi course for some fifty miles, climbed out of the valley on to the uplands, passed through the Kinafah pass and dropped down through the Futurah pass into the head of Wādī ʿIrmah, which watered Shabwah. This route, mountainous and comparatively difficult, still reveals many traces of its ancient use—graffiti and inscriptions, ruined buildings and miles of paved roadway.[6] It may be asked why this difficult route was brought into use, with a need for considerable road engineering to make it suitable for heavy caravan traffic, when the alternative route via Wādī Mayfaʿah, not very much longer, would seem to have offered an easier journey!

In fact the Wādī Mayfaʿah route would have been very difficult to control. Passing westwards from Qana, the caravans would come out into the wide plain of sand-dune desert which joins the dry delta area of that wadi, the country here being almost waterless. Various routes lead westwards off this plain and off the wadi valleys to the north; by slipping into one of these a caravan could have joined the main incense road at Tumnaʿ on a route much shorter than that going through Shabwah. Since, as Pliny testified, the caravan was required to pay a tax when it reached Shabwah, the temptation of a shorter journey which avoided the tax would have been considerable. In contrast the mountain route was narrow and confined and it would be almost impossible to diverge from it. To ensure that the Shabwah taxes were paid and to prevent a frankincense "black market" outside of their own monopoly, the kings of Ḥaḍramawt may have decided that the caravans must take the latter road, the high road off which, according to Pliny (see pages 153–154 above), it was a capital offence to deviate.

Moreover, Wādī Mayfaʿah roughly marks the boundary between the kingdoms of Qatabān and Ḥaḍramawt. This division is a marked one both geographically, because the geological formation of the terrain changes between east and west in this area quite suddenly, and linguistically, because the Hadrami dialect of the ancient South Arabian language was confined to the same boundary. Caravans taking the westerly route through Wādī Mayfaʿah could thus escape from Hadrami into Qatabanian territory. At a later stage the situation altered with the growing power of the Himyarites. A Himyarite population appears to have settled in the wide plain west of Qana and posed a considerable threat to that port (to this day the area is inhabited by a tribe called the Lesser Himyar). These people seem to have found the incense caravans a tempting prey, forcing the Hadrami authorities to fortify the mountain pass of Qalat, north of Qana, and other passes too, in order to prevent raiding parties infiltrating into the rich valley of Wādī Ḥagr through which the caravans passed.[7] At that time the fortified town of Mayfaʿat,[8] in the Wādī Mayfaʿah, remained in Hadrami hands, but the countryside around was probably quite unsafe for travellers, so that the trading caravans from Qana would seek the mountain road for their own security. Into that mountain road would also funnel all the frankincense grown in the region north of Qana. It is the existence of these sources of incense linked by overland routes to Shabwah which probably explains why Shabwah was the main taxation point; had Ẓufār and Somalia been the only production areas, as some writers have maintained, then frankincense could as easily have been taxed at Qana and then allowed to take a more direct route to Tumnaʻ. In so far as the raiding Himyars would allow, other materials imported into Qana may well have followed the more direct route through Niṣāb to Tumnaʻ, which would in any case have been used by the myrrh caravans, but all frankincense, other than that released exceptionally to foreign vessels calling at Qana, was taken to Shabwah to be taxed, sold, stored and prepared for the long journey north. Shabwah can therefore with accuracy be called the Frankincense City.

Shabwah's ruins lie in a remote and inaccessible area which must once have been irrigated and fertile but is now desert. Until very recently no archaeological excavations have been possible there and very few archaeologists or travellers had ever been allowed to visit it; some who tried were ejected at gun-point. In 1975 a French expedition under Dr Jacqueline Pirenne commenced the first season of a major programme of excavation and exploration of the site. Until the results of this expedition are published[9] the most complete description of the place remains that of Philby, to all intents and purposes the first foreign traveller to see it, who mapped it with his usual thoroughness during brief visits in 1936. Philby was disappointed with what he saw, describing the ruins as "poor and vicious and mean" and "disappointingly small and insignificant".[10] He calculated the total area of the site of the walled city at about twenty-seven acres (which is about half the area of the ruin-site of Tumna'), together with another eighteen acres for an unwalled "suburban" area on an adjacent ridge which appeared to include the royal palace. The French expedition now excavating Shabwah has found the site to cover a much larger area than this and it now appears that Shabwah, while smaller than Mārib, was probably larger than any other of the ancient south Arabian capitals.[11]

The location of Shabwah is rather surprising. It is built at the mouth of a wadi with only a small catchment area, inferring limited possibilities for irrigation from flash-floods in the traditional method, and it is sited on a salt dome, a feature of economic value but likely to cause considerable difficulties over the procurement of drinking water. Moreover it is too far from the desert entrance of the Ḥaḍramawt valley to have exercised any effective control over movement into that valley other than over traffic coming in from the south-west. It is also extremely isolated from the agricultural areas of the Ḥaḍramawt valley and can have exercised little administrative influence over the main areas of the state of which it was for so long the capital.

The French excavations have revealed that the city of Shabwah was sacked and burned, probably by the Himyarites, but under the debris substantial parts of many of the buildings still remain. The surface ruins are attributed to somewhere between the first century BC and the fourth century AD on the basis of the style of building and some inscriptional evidence. An important inscription seems to refer to rebuilding in the later part of this period, from which it becomes apparent that the city must have been a much less impressive place in Pliny's time, perhaps an indication of how the wealth from frankincense increased so greatly in the first and second centuries AD. Lankester Harding, an archaeologist who obtained a brief glimpse of the ruin site, noted stratification revealed by erosion in one place to a depth of seven or eight metres, which suggests extensive remains of an earlier date,[12] but Lord Belhaven, spending six weeks there on a local military operation not long after Philby's visit, found the single building he investigated to rest directly on the bed-rock of the salt dome.

Belhaven excavated one chamber to a depth of about nineteen feet, discovering "fragments of archaic Sabaean texts of not later than the fourth century BC". These had been incorporated into the building from an earlier one during a reconstruction. But he also found himself puzzled by what he saw:

> "I walked now with care among the ruins. I examined the tops of the large buildings in which the direction of the interior walls are visible. All are of a similar pattern: a passage runs through the length of them, orientated to the north-west. On either side of this passage are chambers, varying in size but averaging approximately ten feet by four, with no observable access to the passage and none to the outside air, from which they are guarded by the massive outside walls. We then noted that, wherever the surface permitted a view, the upper courses of similar chambers could be seen. The whole area of the ruin, indeed, with the exception of the few paths between the mounds, consisted of the large buildings, divided into small chambers, which extended in every direction, joining building to building. Where the ruin near the temple had fallen one could see chambers of similar size, superimposed one upon another. I am of the opinion that these chambers are graves. Nowhere within the walls could we find any building which resembled a human habitation."[13]

Preliminary investigations by the French expedition have confirmed Belhaven's description without yet solving what these tomb-like chambers were. They may be no more than the ground-floor design of buildings with their living quarters constructed on higher floors from mud-brick which has now eroded. Few houses in south-west Arabia today of traditional design have living quarters on the ground floor, which is kept for storage and stabling and is usually windowless. But the attractive possibility exists that these numerous chambers round the main temple were the storage rooms in which the wealth of Shabwah, its frankincense, was held when it arrived up the highway from the south in a huge annual flood.

There is little doubt that, at the time of Pliny's information, the frankincense was conveyed from Shabwah on a route which ran westwards towards, though not necessarily through, Tumna' (or "Thomna"), the capital of Qatabān. The ruins of this city lie at the northern end of what is now Wādī Bayḥān, where it debouches into the sands called the Ramlat Sab'atayn, or Ṣayhad, and are firmly identified by inscriptions found there.[14] Pliny's actual words are that frankincense "can only be exported by the Gebbanitae. . . . Their capital is Thomna, which is $1487\frac{1}{2}$ miles . . . from Gaza . . .; the journey is divided into 65 stages with halts for camels."[15]

While this statement of Pliny's may suggest that the journey from Tumna' to Gaza was $1487\frac{1}{2}$ miles and divided into 65 stages, it is important to note that it is not what Pliny says, and the sixty-five stages may well relate to the journey from Shabwah or elsewhere. The pace of a loaded camel is slightly less than $2\frac{1}{2}$ miles an hour over flat ground and an average day's travel in the course of a long journey by laden camels will rarely exceed 25 miles, which is ten hours of travelling, and will probably be less. At this rate Pliny's figures, working out at 23 Roman miles for each stage, would seem roughly correct for the distance of $1487\frac{1}{2}$ miles, but we have no idea how the figure for this distance was arrived at and in the surviving early manuscripts of Pliny's work many other wildly differing figures are quoted, editors having selected this one simply as that nearest to reality. Yet the distance would hardly have been quoted to the nearest half mile. Nor can we be sure that each stage represented one day's journey, for the staging posts seem likely to have been watering stations, which must in some areas have been further than one day's journey apart.

The ability of the camel to go long without water varies according to the season; in winter it may be able to last weeks without drinking provided it receives a continuous supply of green fodder, but in desert conditions in the heat of summer it needs water every two or three days.[16] The merchants conducting the frankincense caravans are unlikely to have strained their animals on the very first stage of their journey and, although the direct distance from Shabwah to Tumna' across the Ramlat Sab'atayn desert is only ninety miles, a journey by a heavily-laden camel caravan across that desert would have involved difficult detours and seems improbable. The sand-dunes of the Ramlat Sab'atayn are up to 300 feet high (in the Empty Quarter there are hills of sand as high as 700 feet); as a laden camel cannot traverse the steep slopes of such dunes a route has to be found round them, enormously lengthening the journey. On either side of the flood-bed of Wādī Bayḥān these dunes now reach about 200 feet and on the eastern side of that flood-bed they now pile directly on to the hills which edge the southern flank of the desert, blocking the approach. Here the dunes constantly change their shape, so that guides are necessary. Wyman Bury recorded a story about a merchant who preferred to take his baggage camels through the difficult Nisīyin hills rather than attempt this desert route.[17] Whether the sand had encroached so far south in this area in pre-Islamic times is uncertain, but it is unlikely that the sand obstacles were greatly different two thousand years ago and probable that movement through this stretch of desert faced the same difficulties then as it does now.

To this day there is in fact a recognized route between Bayḥān and Shabwah which avoids most of the sand-dunes. The flood-bed of Wādī Bayḥān extends far out into the desert, curling round towards the east; along it caravans can move without great difficulty and in modern times many Bayhanis use it, mainly to collect salt from the desert mine called Ayadīm which lies in the sand-dune area about a third of the way from Bayḥān to Shabwah. A few miles south of this mine the encroaching sand ends in a vast gravel plain which can be traversed northwards towards Shabwah, crossing the alluvial mouth of Wādī Girdān on the way. But there is still a long haul of three days without water between the last wells of Girdān and the first of Bayḥān, which makes it uncertain whether heavily laden frankincense caravans would have followed this route.

Alternative routes exist north of this Shabwah-Tumna' road which caravans could possibly have followed on their way to Gaza, although both would have cut out Tumna' and Mārib. The first crosses the Ramlat Sab'atayn north-west from Shabwah and then heads into Wādī Gawf; Philby covered it by car with a supporting caravan, but it is a difficult route, waterless for nearly 150 miles until the wells of Wādī Gawf are reached; there are no known traces of its use by the frankincense caravans and it seems unlikely that they would have turned to it except, perhaps, when other roads were blocked because of war. A second way heads due north of Shabwah, crossing the Ramlat Sab'atayn to al-'Abr, a place testified in a pre-Islamic inscription, and thence, finding a passage way along Wādī al-Aqābih through very rough, rocky country, proceeds to the distant well at Mushayniqah and so round the southern edge of the sands of the Empty Quarter to join the main route. This road does appear to have been used for trading, because there are numerous graffiti on the rocks in Wādī al-Aqābih, while the well at Mushayniqah is an ancient one bored through the rock.[18] But again this would be a very arduous journey and its use on any scale seems improbable unless hostilities made the westward route from Shabwah impassable. In neither case could traffic ever have been substantial because of the difficulties of watering large caravans.

At the time Pliny's sources provided their information, when the inland desert areas appear to have been strongly administered and peaceful, the King of Ḥadramawt had an agreement with the King of the Gebbanitae about the collection of taxes; this suggests that the main route moved through Bayḥān to Mārib and that other routes were discouraged. Under Pliny's description the whole journey was organised into clearly defined stages where lodging, water and fodder would be available. In such case we might expect the frankincense caravans to have taken the more roundabout but easiest of the possible roads to Bayḥān. That route lies through Wādī Markhah.

Caravans taking the Markhah route from Shabwah to Bayḥān travel in the first place to Wādī Girdān, as they do on the first stage of the desert route. The ruin sites of al-Barīrah and al-Binā testify to the importance of Wādī Girdān in pre-Islamic times. From there they head south-west across the gravel plain until they reach the flood-bed of Wādī Markhah, which they then follow. Alternatively they can head a little further south until they strike the flood-bed of Wādī Hammām, which leads them to Niṣāb. From Niṣāb there is open access into the wide valley of Markhah through a gap in the hills where lies the ruin site of an ancient town now called Ganadīnah. At the end of their second day's travelling up the Markhah valley the incense caravans, swollen at this stage by myrrh caravans, for this was the myrrh-growing area, would reach a major city, the ancient name of which has not yet been identified but the ruins of which are now called Hagar an-Nāb. In very early days this area was a separate kingdom called Awsān. The caravans then struck north through an easy pass in the mountains,[19] eventually reaching Wādī Bayḥān about one day's journey south of Tumna'. The staging posts of this journey are recognizable and the route is used to this day, although involving a crossing over the frontiers between South and North Yemen at the pass called Rahwat ar-Rib'ah. From Shabwah to Tumna' was a journey of eight or nine days in easy stages along this route; by the desert route it was five or six days, but the journey was a hard one.[20]

Of all the pre-Islamic ruin sites now lying within the borders of the Peoples' Democratic Republic of Yemen the largest after Shabwah is Tumna' (now known as Ḥayd Kohlan), once the capital of Qatabān. Pliny described it as a city of sixty-five temples, which may be compared with the sixty temples he reported in Shabwah, but the basis of that information is not understood since each city appears to have possessed but one main temple. Possibly the word "temple" is a corruption for a word indicating area, but other explanations are possible.

Parts of Tumna' were excavated in 1950 and 1951 by an expedition of the American Foundation for the Study of Man headed by the prominent biblical archaeologist Professor W. F. Albright. It was on a high mound covering an area of more than fifty acres, hidden for the most part beneath sand-dunes which had invaded it from the open desert to the north. On the south-east corner a bastion of enormous stones marked the main gateway and bore long inscriptions setting out some of the laws; it was from a visible part of these that the city had first been identified as Tumna'—or more accurately as TMN', since the vowelling is known only from the transliterations in the classical texts. Within the walls an open area marked the market place, in the centre of which a small obelisk, about five feet high, bore an inscribed text containing the market regulations. One clause of these states: "Any Qatabanian, Minaean or other inhabitant of Tumna' who leases his house or residence to a stall-holder shall pay the market tax in Tumna' to the King of Qatabān . . ." In commenting on these regulations, Professor Beeston has observed that: "there was evidently a colony of Minaeans and other non-Qatabanians resident in Tumna' and owning property there; and . . . the Minaean colony was of sufficient importance to be specifically mentioned." The use of certain words in the text also indicated that the Minaean population of Tumna' had a special status compared with that of other non-Qatabanian residents.[21]

Several references to the Minaeans have already been quoted from the works of classical authors. Ma'īn was referred to by Eratosthenes ("the Minaeans . . . whose largest city is Carna" (p. 64 above)). Agatharchides talked of frankincense and spices brought to Palestine by "the Gerrhaei and Minaei" (p. 68 above). Pliny mentions the Minaei as a tribe adjoining the Atramitae (p. 81 above) and they are also listed as a tribe by Ptolemy. But there are other significant references to them in Pliny. In a passage quoted in the previous chapter he described them as "the Minaei, through whose territory the transit for the export of frankincense is along one narrow track. It is these people who originated the trade and who chiefly practice it, and from them the perfume takes the name of 'Minaean'" (p. 148 above). In discussing myrrh he noted that there was a variety of myrrh called "the Minaean, which includes the Astramitic, Gebbanitic and Ausaritic from the kingdom of the Gebbanitae" (p. 125 above).

We know of the Minaeans as a people who lived in a small area of Wādī Gawf, north-west of Mārib. When Aelius Gallus invaded south Arabia their ancient capital of Qarnaw may already have been a ruin site, for it is not mentioned in the existing accounts of that campaign, although Pliny did record the report of those who took part that "the Minaei have land that is fertile in palm groves and timber and wealth in flocks." But despite their loss of independence to the Sabaeans, it is clear that the Minaeans were resilient and retained a strong position as controllers and carriers of the incense trade. Their important role in that trade is underlined by the discovery of Minaean inscriptions in north-west Arabia, indicating the existence of a Minaean colony at al-'Ula (Dedan) early in their history; this is discussed in the next chapter. It was, from the context, to the Minaeans of Dedan that Pliny was referring when he mentioned, in a rather confused list of tribal names, "the Minaei, who derive their origin, *as is believed*, from King Minos of Crete; part of them are the Carmei."[22]

In the territory adjacent to the Minaeans we would expect to find the Qatabanians. Their capital was Tumna', as is well attested not only by Eratosthenes (the Catabanians whose territory extends down to the straits and the passage across the Arabian Gulf and whose royal seat is called "Tamna"—see page 64 above) but also by very many inscriptions. It is probably safe to assume that the Qatabanian kingdom commenced before 400 BC (it could be considerably earlier), but there is much doubt about when it ended; even a layer of ash in the top strata of the site of Tumna', which marked its destruction by a conflagration, has not yet been dated; the date of 50 BC at first proposed for this event[23] has been challenged by other proposals putting it into the first or second centuries AD.[24] But the destruction of the capital does not seem to have marked the end of the kingdom. Sabaean inscriptions show the existence of kings of Qatabān at the end of the second or early in the third century AD. Ptolemy (AD 150) mentioned the Qatabanians only in the uncertain reference to a tribe called "Cottabani". Pliny also mentioned a tribe, the "Catapani", who apparently lived next to the Gebbanitae (see page 80 above). However, where we may expect to find Pliny referring to the Qatabanians he talks all the time about the Gebbanitae instead.

In Pliny's Book 6 it was the Gebbanitae who had "several towns, of which the largest are Nagia and Thomna" (see page 80 above), while in Book 12 frankincense could only be exported "by the Gebbanitae . . . their capital is Thomna" and a tax was collected for their king at Shabwah (see page 153 above). Their king also collected as tax one quarter of all the myrrh grown (see page 125 above). The name also occurs in the nomenclature of myrrh, for the best quality grown in Arabia, called Minaean, included "the Astramitic, Gebbanitic and Ausaritic from the kingdom of the Gebbanitae" (see page 125 above). In addition the Gebbanitae featured in Pliny's account of the trade in cinnamon, which was brought over from Somaliland on rafts "to the harbour of the Gebbanitae called Ocilia", while "the right of controlling the sale of cinnamon is vested solely in the king of the Gebbanitae, who opens the market by a public proclamation".[25]

It has been generally assumed that Pliny used the term "Gebbanitae" in error for "Qatabanian". One then sees the writ of the Qatabanian kings extending at one time as far as the straits of Bāb al-Mandab, at which time they also enjoyed a relationship with their eastern neighbours, the kings of Ḥaḍramawt, which enabled them to collect frankincense taxes directly from the Hadrami capital at Shabwah. In a paper read to the Seminar for Arabian Studies, in 1971, however, Professor Beeston proposed that this might not be the right interpretation.[26]

Pliny appears to have regarded the "Catapani" and the "Gebbanitae" as separate peoples, the latter being significant for their monopolistic control over the aromatics trade. But other evidence, including other parts of Pliny's text, shows that this latter feature also applied to the Minaeans. It so happens that there is considerable evidence in inscriptions from the site of ancient Maʿīn that the dominant group of people among the Minaeans was called by a name which can best be written in Roman script as "Geban". To other South Arabians the Minaeans would have been known as Minaeans, and this was the name used for them in the market regulations on the obelisk in Tumnaʿ. But if, as one might suspect, Pliny derived his information about the aromatics trade from a Minaean trader, then that person might have used the more specific "Geban" to identify the group of Minaeans who ran that trade. These people, with a trading headquarters in Tumnaʿ, would have established other colonies elsewhere in the main trading centres, to which other groups may in course of time have linked themselves in a commercial league. They could well have established a separate kingdom of their own in some part of south-west Arabia. But where would that kingdom have been? Their territory was next to Shabwah, from Pliny's information, and produced Ausaritic myrrh. The area of Niṣāb and Wādī Markhah is geographically well suited to this and there still lies south of Nisāb a place named Ḥuṣn al-Wusr, while an area called "Wusr" (which in its plural would have had the form "Awsar" to signify its people) is attested in inscriptions.

Beeston's suggestion remains no more than an idea which, like so much else in the ancient history of the incense kingdoms, awaits further discovery before it can be proved or disproved – another example of how scholars must conjecture until archaeologists have explored south Arabia more fully with their spades.

After Tumnaʿ the incense caravans set out for the city of Mārib. Lying west of Wādī Bayḥān is another major wādī called Ḥarīb and beyond it a complex of smaller wādī systems now known as Wādī Gūbah, from which, turning north, one reaches the great Wādī Adhanah, which fed water to Mārib and to the two "gardens", irrigated from the famous dam, which are described briefly in the Qur'ān.[27] The direct distance from Tumnaʿ to Mārib is about ninety miles, but once again the most direct road would have been a waterless one and the incense caravans are likely to have taken a more comfortable but longer route.

There is not much doubt about the way the caravans went when they left Tumna'. Skirting the northern edge of the mountains, with high sand-dunes on their right-hand side, they would reach, after about fifteen miles, a low gap in the hills which led into the valley of Wādī Harīb, where there were good wells. Beyond, on the desert side, the sand-dunes piled up against the mountains, making further progress extremely difficult. In this gap, known nowadays as Nagd Marqad, are the remains of a very strange construction, a paved roadway more than five hundred yards long, with stone walls on either side, which leads over the crest of the pass. The walls, some twenty yards apart where they begin, narrow inwards until the distance between them at the centre of the pass is about nine yards. The principal effect of this arrangement was to restrict the passage through which traffic could move. At one point near the entrance on the desert side there is a low ramp. The purpose of this construction must have been to funnel caravans through in file so that they could be counted and taxed. It would have been needed only if the volume of traffic passing through this gap in the hills was substantial.

At some time during the period of Qatabān's greatest prosperity, perhaps in the first or second century BC, another route was opened up from Wādī Bayhān into Wādī Harīb which literally cut through the mountain barrier dividing them. The pass now called Mablaqah, approached from Bayhān by a side wadi, is a skilfully built paved road about twelve feet wide which zig-zags up the steep mountain side on artificial embankments and passes at the top through a man-made cleft in the solid rock some fifty feet deep and over a hundred feet in length. On the western side, leading into Wādī Harīb, it twists down again until more open ground is reached. A finely lettered inscription on the western side states (with spelling simplified here for ease of reading): "Aws'am, son of Yasurr'am of the family of Madhim, servant of Yada'ab Dhubyan, son of Shahr, King of Qatabān, directed and carried out all the work and paving of the mountain road of Mablaqat and all the work and restoration of the house of Waddum and Atirat and the palace of the king at Qly, on the order of his lord Yad'ab."[28] The ancient name of Mablaqat has survived from then until today and the pass remains a testimony to the achievements of Qatabanian engineering.

The catchment area which feeds Wādī Ḥarīb is very much smaller than that of Bayḥān and does not as a result produce floods comparable to the huge "sayls" of Bayḥān, which sometimes flow through the length of the valley and far out into the desert for days on end. Most of the flood water of Wādī Ḥarīb is used in irrigating the valley area and it does not possess, like Wādī Bayḥān, a fertile delta extending into the Ramlat Sab'atayn; the mountains narrow at the wādī mouth and the sand-dunes close in, high and menacing. Passage for baggage camels across the desert mouth of Wādī Ḥarīb is consequently difficult and the incense caravans are unlikely to have attempted it; instead they would take a route which crossed the mountains on the western flank of Ḥarīb and led them to the next natural staging post on the way to Mārib, in the area known as Wādī Gūbah.

It seems probable that the Mablaqah pass may have been part of a more grandiose road construction scheme. There is evidence in an inscription in an ancient sanctuary on the hill-side in Wādī Ḥarīb of another such road over a pass, constructed by the same engineer "Aws'am, son of Yassurr'am", at a place called Zaram (more correctly ZRM, since we do not know the vowelling). This place has not been identified, but the most likely site would seem to be one of the three routes by which access to Wādī Gūbah can now be gained over the mountains from Wādī Ḥarīb.[29]

In Wādī Ḥarīb, not far from the side wadi down which the caravans came from Mablaqah, was a town the ruin-site of which is now known as Hagar Ḥennu az-Zurīr and the name of which is identified from inscriptions as HRBT. Again, since the written Early South Arabian language has no vowelling we cannot say how this was pronounced, but the name is not synonymous with the modern Ḥarīb, because the initial H is a different consonant in the two names, the one "soft" (which we write H) and the other "hard" (which is written Ḥ). An inscription reveals that the people of HRBT, which for ease of reading may be written "Haribat", had settled there from Sawwa in south-west Yemen, the "Saua in the midst of the region called Mapharitis" mentioned in the *Periplus* (see page 90 above).

Haribat was probably not a town in the modern sense. The culture of this time was based on agriculture organised communally by a group of clans known as "*sha'b*". The headquarters of each *sha'b* was called a *hagar* and was more an administrative centre than an urban area. Very few of the "towns" of ancient south Arabia seem likely to have supported much of a population, for most of the people of the *sha'b* lived in villages outside, although the *hagar* would contain fine, substantial buildings and an associated temple. There are many *hagar* (or *hajar*) sites in south Arabia today, and while one refers to them as ancient towns, or even as cities, most really consisted of little more than the administrative buildings of the *sha'b* headquarters, with a small, permanent population provided by groups of artisans and traders.[30] Only the capitals seem to have had residential populations of any size, although ordinary homesteads made of mud-brick, the most common building material, would of course erode quickly when deserted.

One of the purposes of the *hagar* may have been to provide the necessary shelter and facilities for travellers, as well, perhaps, as the wherewithal to tax them on their way. We may therefore suppose that the incense caravans coming through the Mablaqah pass would have staged at or close to Haribat. Traffic using Nagd Marqad would have entered the wadi much further to the north and its natural route to Wādī Gūbah would then have crossed the valley from east to west, with a staging point likely to have been at the ruin site now

known as Hagar Ḥarīb. But one purpose of the Mablaqah
pass may have been to allow Qatabanian irrigation engineers
to build a dam which effectively blocked the most direct route
across the valley and imposed a wide detour for caravans
using Nagd Marqad. In consequence the latter pass would
seem to have gone out of use as the main incense route.[31]
Having crossed Wādī Ḥarīb from Mablaqah, the caravans
moved north-west to reach the ZRM pass, which would seem
to be the road now called Tarīq Manqal (the word *"manqal"*
relates to the modern Arabic word *"naqīl"*, meaning "pass"),
and so descended into Wādī Gūbah near a ruin site now called
Hagar Nagā. It is supposed that these ruins, partly covered by
a modern village, may mark the site of the city of the
Gebbanitae named "Nagia" which was recorded by Pliny
(see page 80 above).

This combination of road construction and irrigation
works must have featured elsewhere along the incense route,
for the massive canal systems of the ancient South Arabians
would have affected the high-roads everywhere. It reveals a
highly organised state system capable of working out comprehensive economic plans.

It was a day's march from Nagia to Mārib, the greatest of
all the south Arabian cities and probably the only one
comparable in size and splendour with the illustrious cities of
Mesopotamia and Asia Minor. A great deal of mystery still
surrounds Mārib. In the nineteenth century Arnaud and
Halévy were able to visit it briefly and Glaser to spend a
month there, when a large number of inscriptions were copied,
but for long thereafter the mediaeval suspicions of the
Imams about the intentions of foreigners closed it to all
outsiders. In 1947 an Egyptian archaeologist, Ahmed
Fakhry, became the first twentieth-century visitor to the area
in the course of a brief official survey of the antiquities of the
Yemen. He found the old ruins being used as a quarry for a
large complex of new buildings being constructed by the local
'Āmil, as a result of which at least fifteen ancient monuments
had been destroyed. "(The Āmil) was very proud of his
work", Fakhry wrote, "and boasted that he was ruining the
remains of the dead pagans for the welfare of the living
Moslems."[32]

In 1951 the Imam of Yemen made an exception and

allowed the American expedition which had been working at Tumna' to undertake the first and, so far, the only professional excavation of the site. Professor Frank P. Albright, who headed the party, described the modern village of Mārib as "situated at the north-east end of a mound about 500 m. long by roughly 350 m. wide, which lies on the left bank of Wadi Dhana. Nearer to the wadi, on a second elevation, is a modern compound with a watch-tower, which served as the headquarters of our expedition, while, to the south-west, a third elevation holds the 'Nazerah', or fortress. To the west of the Nazerah is a circular depression of perhaps 100 m. in diameter. All of these places show evidence of ancient habitation. The edge of the mound itself has been deeply cut away by the spring torrents, revealing very deep stratification, the watch-tower elevation has been heightened by an artificial fill of at least 8 ft., the circular depression suggests an ancient market place, while at the south-west part of the Nazerah the upper parts of piers, with their capitals preserved, still project above the sand. We thus realize that the little village of Mārib is all that remains of a city which extended over the entire area, ancient Mariaba . . ."[33]

The American expedition to Mārib was short-lived, because local hostility developed against it until its members were driven out at gun-point, their equipment and finds being abandoned.[34] During the brief time it was there it was able to excavate a portion of the great temple of Awām, known today as Maḥram Bilqis and traditionally the temple or palace of the Queen of Sheba, which lies a short distance from the city site on the other side of the wadi flood-bed.

From Mārib the incense caravans headed north through territory, partly the desert called al-Khabt, about which very little is at present known. In what is now a barren area in Wādī Raghwān, a day's journey away, they would have reached a town identified by an inscription as YLṬ, which is today called Kharibat Saʿud. Philby discovered this site on his south Arabian journey, shortly after he had viewed Mārib from a safe distance, together with a number of other sites close by which indicate that the area was well populated in ancient times.[35] From here the caravans struggled on for another two days into a fertile area in the eastern part of Wādī Gawf, which was the homeland of the Minaean traders.

We are still dependent on the reports of Glaser and Halévy for much of our knowledge of the Minaean ruins and this mostly takes the form of the inscriptions they copied, although Ahmed Fakhry toured it briefly and there have been short visits in recent years under the sponsorship of the new Department of Antiquities of the Yemen Arab Republic. A confusing factor in defining Ma'īn is that the recognisable Minaean dialect of the Early South Arabian language, of which other dialects were spoken by the Sabaeans, Qatabanians and Hadramis, was confined, from the evidence of inscriptions, to a very small area indeed in the immediate vicinity of Qarnaw (or Ma'īn as it is also called), the Minaean capital. The dialect of the cities a little further up the valley such as Nashq, which is thought to be the Asca or Nesca captured by Aelius Gallus, is Sabaean.[36] Moreover, there are two noticeable differences between Ma'īn and the other south Arabian kingdoms: the design of the main Minaean temple is totally unlike the temple designs elsewhere, being nearer to the early Israelite sanctuary, while their system of nomenclature suggests they had a different social structure.[37] All of this adds to the mystery of the Minaeans, who may have been an elite ruling class of rather different origins to most of their subjects. That they regarded themselves as important and different is evidenced by the statement of Pliny already quoted that it was believed they originated from King Minos of Crete (see page 178 above), although there is no archaeological or other evidence for this intriguing claim.

Another problem arises from Pliny's reference to "the Minaei, through whose territory the transit for the export of frankincense is along one narrow track" (see pages 148 and 177 above). Topographically the wide, open plain of the area strictly recognisable as Ma'īn is the least likely part of the incense route where such restrictions would apply. Moreover, Pliny related this specifically to frankincense and not to the other produce which also travelled along the incense road. What we may have here is a reference to the whole of south Arabia as the "territory" of the Minaeans, recognizing their privileged and widespread trading position throughout the region; in such case the "one narrow track" is either the frankincense route from Qana to Shabwah, off which it was a capital offence to diverge, or perhaps the whole long road from Qana through Shabwah, Markhah, Mablaqah, Nagia and Mārib which has been described.

The most northerly point to come under the influence of the incense kingdoms was the rich oasis valley of Nagrān (Najrān). Here, in the sixth century AD, the Judaized king of Himyar massacred the Christian inhabitants after a long siege when they refused to abjure their faith, a crime which brought an Abyssinian army into south-west Arabia in retribution. The ruin-site of the ancient city of Nagrān is to this day known as "al-Ukhdūd", meaning "the trenches", after the pits in which the massacred population was burned to death. Inscriptions in south Arabian script have been found in Nagrān dating from shortly before that event.[38] The name NGRN is attested epigraphically and Pliny mentioned the town of "Negrana", while Strabo referred to Aelius Gallus "arriving at the city of the Negrani and at a country which was both peaceful and fertile" (see page 74 above).

The hold of any of the southern kingdoms over Nagrān seems however to have been a tenuous one, for it was a remote, self-contained frontier district, over a hundred miles in a direct line from Qarnaw and perhaps half that distance again along the trade route. Our knowledge of the road the incense caravans followed when they left Qarnaw is particularly hazy, for this area is still little known. Striking north through a gap in the mountains they would seem most likely to have clung to the eastern fringes of the mountain range, edging the high sand-dunes of the Rub' al-Khālī, with occasional short-cuts through some of the mountain spurs. This route would have provided easier going for desert camels than any more direct routes through the mountains. They would then reach Nagrān from the desert mouth of that wadi, a journey of some six or seven days travelling from Qarnaw.

By the time they reached the shade and water of Nagrān the frankincense caravans which had set out from the "emporium" at Shabwah would have been nineteen days to three weeks on the march and travelled some 430 miles. Much of the produce they carried, coming from the trans-montane groves of Ẓufār, had already been transported 500 miles, mostly by sea, to Qana and a further 160 miles across the mountains to reach Shabwah. This Ẓufāri frankincense had thus travelled over a thousand miles before it reached the frontier of the incense lands. But an enormous distance yet remained. From Nagrān it was still some 1200 miles to the Mediterranean coast at Gaza and a further 250 miles to Alexandria where, in Pliny's time, sorting and processing were carried out. For the incense going on to Rome another 1300 miles remained. The frankincense burned so lavishly by the Roman population in their temples and households would have been carried a total distance of little less than four thousand miles. In the next chapter we shall consider the long route which lay ahead from Nagrān.

Chapter 10

North to
Europe

In addition to Sabaean inscriptions, the frontier area of
Nagrān contains other inscriptions in a different writing,
epigraphically related to the south Arabian one but recording
a very different language. These are in Thamudic, the script
of a people known as the Thamudites who inhabited the
central part of the west side of the Arabian peninsula.

There may be a mention of the Thamudites from as early as
715 BC in an inscription of Sargon II recording his subjug-
ation of the tribes of Tamud. Agatharchides, in the passage
preserved by Photius, refers to a long, rocky coastline which
was "the land of the Thamoudenian Arabs" (see page 69
above) and the same description was drawn on by Diodorus
Siculus ("This coast . . . is inhabited by Arabs who are called
Thamudeni").[1] Pliny records the "Tamudaei (town Bac-
lanaza)" in a list of tribes beyond the Nabataeans.[2] Ptolemy
mentions the "Thamyditae" as a tribe inhabiting the more
northerly part of the Red Sea coast and also the "Thamy-
deni" as one of the inland tribes, while a foundation
inscription on the remains of an isolated Nabataean temple at
Rawwafah, some 50 miles south-west of Tabuk, which can be
firmly dated to AD 166–169 by its reference to the reigning
Roman emperors, refers to the "nation" or "federation" of
the Thamudeans.[3]

By the time of the Prophet Muhammad, the Thamudites
had completely disappeared and in various passages the
Qur'ān tells of their destruction, after they had refused to
accept the words of a prophet, by earthquake or thunderbolt.
Traditionally one of the main places with which the ancient
people of Thamud are associated is Madā' in Ṣāliḥ and there

may be a connection in this legend with the volcanic outbreaks revealed by the lava fields in that area.

Almost as hazy is modern knowledge of Lihyan, a state which developed in the northern parts of the same area. The Lihyanites too developed their own script, which they continued to use when their language, northern Arabic in origin, had become almost pure classical Arabic. Pliny mentions the "Lichieni" in one of his tribal lists.[4] Many Lihyanite inscriptions have been found, particularly at Dedān (al-'Ula), some 20 kilometres south of Mada'in Ṣāliḥ, the centre of the earlier kingdom of Dedān which the Lihyanites supplanted.[5] From these records an incomplete king-list of ten Lihyanite monarchs is known, suggesting that the kingdom must have extended over more than a century, straddling the last century BC and first century AD. It is apparent from Minaean inscriptions found in al-'Ula that a Minaean commercial colony thrived there, but the extent to which this was contemporaneous with the Lihyanite kingdom is uncertain; its establishment would seem to go back to some time in the fourth century BC but it may have ceased to operate by about 100 BC.[6] Logically, however, because of the complete control over the trade route which the Lihyanites could exercise by dint of their geographical position, the Minaeans might be expected to have had trading representatives of some sort in the territory.

So little is known about the Thamudites and the Lihyanites that we cannot say any more about their relations with the Minaean traders who brought the incense caravans through their territory. Unlike the South Arabians, most of the people of central Arabia would appear to have been nomadic, but here and there were oases with settled communities and townships. The culture of the Thamudites and Lihyanites was by no means primitive, as is shown not only by their script but also by their religious system and by the quality of some of their relief sculpture. However, there is no real reason to think that the Thamudic people achieved an administrative domination over the whole of the huge area from Nagrān northwards to the main centre of their culture seven hundred miles away in the region of Dedān and Ḥijrā. In the account of the expedition of Aelius Gallus provided by Strabo (see page 74 above) the country traversed before

Nagrān was reached was called "Ararene", belonging to the nomads, ruled by a king Sabos and mostly "truly desert". More probably the culture, starting somewhere around 500 BC, spread among the many independent nomadic tribes inhabiting that region without in any way involving Thamudic control over them.[7] Over the long period of the overland incense trade, power and influence will have shifted among the different tribes of central Arabia and it seems likely that the Minaeans organising the trade will always have been much concerned in dealings to ensure the safe passage of their caravans through the territories of tribal chiefs with varying and fluctuating degrees of authority. A general measure of law and order must have been maintained, however, for the trade to have continued over the centuries without, so far as we know, any major interruption, and for the Thamudic culture to have spread so widely. The thousands of Thamudic graffiti on rocks in central Arabia reveal a widespread literacy. The diplomatic endeavours of the Minaean merchants may have been a major factor, together with the influence of the stronger civilisations to the south and north, in preserving this stability.

In the early centuries AD, when the incense trade was dwindling, when the Roman Empire was tottering and when both the south Arabian and the Nabataean states were fading, security in Arabia as a whole began to break up, leading to frequent wars of plunder and inter-tribal feuding and to the setting up of a number of short-lived dynasties, most notable being the third to fifth century kingdom of Kindah.

Set among the nomadic tribes in central Arabia were certain towns and settlements with a special importance because they lay in favoured oases or housed religious shrines to which local tribesmen would make annual pilgrimages. Foremost among these were Makkah and Yathrib. At Makkah, possibly the "Macoraba" of Ptolemy, was a shrine approached in importance only by that at Nagrān[8]. Yathrib, listed by Ptolemy and mentioned in Minaean inscriptions, later took the name al-Madīnah, or more correctly Madīnat an-Nabī—"the town of the Prophet", although in earlier days it was an oasis occupied by several scattered communities. Such places provided safe havens for trading caravans, and their religious fairs were the occasions for markets.

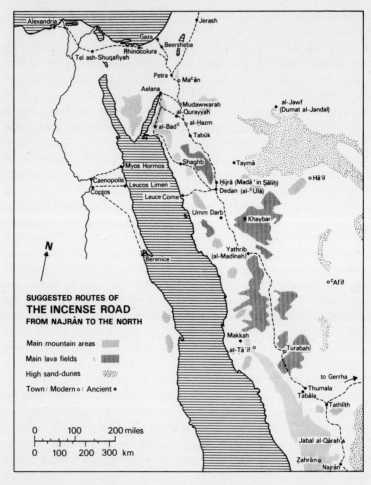

SUGGESTED ROUTES OF
THE INCENSE ROAD
FROM NAJRĀN TO THE NORTH

Main mountain areas

Main lava fields

High sand-dunes

Town: Modern o : Ancient ●

| 0 | 100 | 200 miles |
| 0 | 100 | 200 | 300 km |

We have few pointers to the route taken by the incense caravans through the Thamudic region between Nagrān and Yathrib and it is not proposed here to attempt any analysis of the available facts in order to suggest the likely staging posts. There are arguments that a number of different routes would have been used, rather at the whim of the cameleers, but the probability would seem greater that for the most part there was a single route for the main stream of traffic, as can be inferred from Pliny. To some extent the way is determined by the dictates of topography, but the need for organised watering points, protection and taxation posts would also trend the system towards a single road. The fixed trade route or pilgrim route is a tradition of Arabia brought about by the nature of the country. But the route may have altered at different periods with fluctuations in the stability of the different areas through which it passed.

On the first part of the journey from Nagrān the pilgrim routes to Makkah of later times offer some clues, although the main route for pilgrims from the Yemen, moving from San'ā' through Sa'dah and Zahrān and then skirting the edge of the 'Asīr mountains, was probably well to the west of the incense road in higher ground. The "Road of the Elephant", which Abraha took on his way to attack Makkah[9], also followed this route through Zahrān. The incense route seems likely to have been closer to the western edge of the central desert, where the terrain was less rocky and hence more suitable for camels, passing through the area of Jabal Qāra and Tathlīth.[10] Tathlīth may be Ptolemy's "Laththa". But the two routes probably converged at Tabāla or Thumala, in the modern region of Bīshah, a direct distance of about 200 miles northeast from Nagrān. The distance travelled over this stretch would be about 280 miles, or some 12 stages. At Tabāla was a famous temple and the name still exists as one of the tributaries of Wādī Bīshah, while the name Thumala, recorded by Pliny and Ptolemy, survives in Jabal ath-Thamalah nearby.[11] From Tabāla it was about 350 miles direct to Yathrib, but the distance travelled was probably much greater owing to the need to skirt round the great lava fields of central Arabia; this part of the journey may thus have taken some fifteen to eighteen stages. The incense route seems unlikely, for topographical reasons, to have gone through Makkah, which lies on the coastal side of the northern tip of the mountain range stretching upwards from Yemen, but more probably it passed about 100 miles to the east of it, perhaps through or close to the present-day town of Turabah. Some incense would of course have been taken to Makkah for local trading.

From Yathrib the main route seems likely to have followed what was to become the Islamic pilgrim route as far as the Lihyanite capital of Dedān, now al-'Ula, and the town of Ḥijrā (al-Ḥigr), now Madā'in Ṣāliḥ, close nearby. In Islamic times this route passed through Marwah, now the ruin site of Umm Dharb, about 110 miles north-east of al-Madīnah; this is thought to have been Ptolemy's "Mochura".[12] At Ḥijrā the Minaeans had an important trading colony and here, throughout the most important centuries of the overland incense traffic, it was not the Thamudites or the Lihyanites who held sway but the Nabataeans, whom we shall discuss later. This stretch of the journey, from Yathrib to Ḥijrā, is about 215 miles and would have taken nine to eleven days of travelling.

It has sometimes been supposed that alongside the Minaeans there travelled another group of merchants for part of the way who came from a city with a harbour on the Gulf side of the Arabian peninsula called Gerrha. While the existence of the Gerrhaeans as an important trading community is firmly established, the evidence that they collected incense from south Arabia is less certain.

Pliny has a brief mention of Gerrha in his description of the Arabian Gulf, where he refers to "the bay of Gerra and the town of that name, which measures five miles round and has towers made of square blocks of salt".[13] But our principal information about Gerrha is quoted by Strabo from Eratosthenes and thus dates from no later than the third century BC:

> "After sailing along the coast of Arabia for a distance of two thousand four hundred stadia one comes to Gerrha, a city situated on a deep gulf; it is inhabited by Chaldeans, exiles from Babylon; the soil contains salt and the people live in houses made of salt; and since flakes of salt continuously scale off, owing to the scorching heat of the rays of the sun, and fall away, the people frequently sprinkle the houses with water and thus keep the walls firm. The city is two hundred stadia distant from the sea; and the Gerrhaeans traffic by land, for the most part, in the Arabian merchandise and aromatics, though Aristobulos says, on the contrary, that the Gerrhaeans import most of their cargoes on rafts to Babylonia, and thence sail up the Euphrates with them, and then convoy them by land to all parts of the country."[14]

Aristobulos, mentioned in this extract, took part in the campaigns of Alexander the Great, and his history of them was also one of the main sources used by Arrian (AD 96–180); Arrian noted that Alexander's ships "anchored in the mouth of the Euphrates near a village of Babylonia, called Diridotis; here the merchants gather together frankincense from the neighbouring country and all other sweet-smelling spices which Arabia produces."[15]

Strabo also mentions the Gerrhaean merchants in other paragraphs. Drawing his information from Agatharchides through Artemidorus, he talks of: "The Palestine country, where Minaeans and Gerrhaeans and all the neighbouring peoples convey their loads of aromatics."[16] Elsewhere he notes from the same source that: "from their trafficking both the Sabaeans and the Gerrhaeans have become richest of all" (page 67 above), a passage also recalled by Photius in the statement: "No race seems to be more prosperous than the Sabaei and the Gerrhaei, since they act as the warehouse for everything from Asia and Europe which goes under the name of distinction" (page 71 above).[17] A further important but fragmentary reference to Gerrha is found in the work of the historian Polybius, who described a naval expedition in about 205 BC of the Seleucid king, Antiochus III, when the Gerrhaeans bought off his attack with a gift of 500 talents of silver, 1000 talents of frankincense and 200 talents of "stacte" myrrh.[18] Ptolemy listed Gerrha among the Arabian Gulf ports together with two other coastal towns which also belonged to the Gerrhaeans.

The site of Gerrha has still to be identified. The principal clues are the statements that it was two hundred stadia (about sixty miles) from the sea and that it was opposite the island of Tylus (Pliny says "Tyros" in error), which can now with certainty be identified with Baḥrayn. A location recently favoured has been the large site at Thāj, where archaeological examination has revealed a city with imposing walls which was occupied during the right period over about four centuries, but inscriptions have now been found which indicate that this was probably Ptolemy's "Phigea". Al-'Uqayr, on the coast, which Philby and others believed was the site, has since been excavated and found to be of Islamic origin.[19] The most probable answer would seem to be that Gerrha was in the Ḥasā oasis, perhaps where the city of Hufūf now lies, with a port known by the same name somewhere not far from al-'Uqayr, The place-name Qārah which occurs several times both in al-Ḥasā and on the coast south of al-'Uqayr could be a survival of the ancient name.[20]

Strabo also recorded the statement of Eratosthenes that the

merchants trading in incense travelled to Minaea from Aelana (near Eilath) in seventy days, but "the Gabaioi arrive at Chatramotitis in forty days" (see page 64 above). The precise meaning of this reference to the Gabaioi is obscure. Believing that "Gabaioi" was a corruption, editors have substituted "Gerrhaei" in the text and the sentence has then been held as evidence that the Gerrhaeans made a direct journey from Gerrha to Shabwah or even to Zufār. Such journeys would have required a crossing of the formidable Empty Quarter and, although both Bertram Thomas and Wilfred Thesiger have traversed it with camels, regular journeys by trading caravans over this great sand-dune desert would hardly have been possible unless climatic and related topographical changes have been considerable since those days. Thomas described the crossing as follows:

> ". . . Our party would be reduced to twelve picked men and mounts and five pack animals, all in perfect condition. . . . to loiter in these sands meant death. Perfect health in camel and man was essential; marches must be long and sharp; loss of camels, sickness, treachery or tribal opposition involving a hold up of ten days or too slow progress might spell disaster. The great consideration was to get out of the hunger-stricken wastes as soon as possible. . . . A successful crossing was by no means certain; if the pastures in our way failed, we should have to face the question whether to tempt the Fates further by going on, or to turn back to certain sustenance . . ."[21]

Although the direct distance was only about 500 miles, Thomas' journey in 1930 took him 48 days between Shisūr, in the frankincense-growing region north of Zufār, and ad-Dawhah, in Qatar (which is a little closer than Hufūf), since he was obliged to follow a winding course between the dunes from one waterhole to the next. A journey by the incense caravans which skirted round the eastern edge of the Empty Quarter would have been no easier, in particular because of the huge areas of salt-desert to be passed, and would have taken very much longer.

If the merchants of Gerrha collected frankincense from Shabwah at all, rather than buying it from trading centres like Makkah and Yathrib for the Arabian Gulf markets, it seems most likely that their route would have followed that of the Minaeans until they were north of Nagrān, when they would strike across the Arabian peninsula along one of the lateral trade routes of central Arabia. Most probable, because it is the most direct, would be the route which leaves the main incense road near Tathlīth, follows the Wādī Dawāsir through the gap in the Tuwayq range at as-Sulayyil and then heads north-east along the eastern flank of that range as far as as-Sulaymiyah and hence to Gerrha. Excavations currently being carried out by Professor Ansari of Riyadh University at Qaryat al-Faw, near as-Sulayyil, testify to the importance of this route in antiquity. The last stretch of such journey, involving a crossing of the waterless Dahna desert, would have been difficult, but every east-west route must face that crossing.

The total distance travelled on this route would have been about 750 miles between Gerrha and Nagrān, assuming Gerrha to be Hufūf (which is the nearest of all the possible sites). This would take a minimum of 30 to 34 days, but probably much longer. If nine days are added for the Nagrān–Mārib stretch and at least seven days for that between Mārib and Shabwah, then the total journey time would have been at least 46 to 50 days.

When read in its context, Eratosthenes' statement about the Gabaioi may be held to signify that the Gabaioi arrived in Chatramotitis in forty days from Ma'īn, but this is far too long a time, since even the journey from Ma'īn through Shabwah to Qana should not have involved much more than 21 days of travelling. Who in any case were the Gabaioi? Professor Beeston has suggested that Strabo, like Pliny, may have been referring to the Gebbanitae (see pages 178–180 above), in other words the Minaean merchants. The figure could perhaps refer to the distance to the furthest frankincense-producing area, in Zufār, although it is by no means certain that the Minaeans went so far for their frankincense at the time of Eratosthenes, whom Strabo was quoting. Otherwise the figure may be corrupt.[22]

It is easy to imagine the Minaean merchants heaving a sigh of relief as they approached the cities of Dedān and Ḥijrā in their narrow valleys and reached the protection of the Lihyanites and Nabataeans. For some six weeks of travel, since they left Nagrān, they had moved through harsh tribal areas inhabited by nomads, where unpredictable squabbles could put both their profits and, perhaps, their lives at risk. The major centres, Yathrib in particular, would have provided safe havens, but elsewhere, in the absence of strong rule, law and order must have been precarious. "Of these innumerable tribes," said Pliny, "an equal part are engaged in trade or live by brigandage."[23]

We do not know many details about the administrative aspects of the incense trade, but it is reasonable to assume that at various points along the route, speculatively one might suggest at intervals of between ten days and three weeks,[24] the cargoes would be transferred to fresh camels, probably locally owned and handled by local cameleers. Almost certainly this would have happened at Ḥijrā, capital of the Nabataean southern province, which became the main Minaean centre during the Nabataean period. One can imagine the tired merchant seeking out his Minaean agent, a relative perhaps, who would need to make elaborate arrangements for guarding the precious loads while they were transferred to new teams of camels, for obtaining clearance and safe-conducts from the Nabataean authorities after payment of taxes and for paying off the previous cameleers and escort. From Ḥijrā the incense would have been carried on the backs of Nabataean camels.

Of course, this was the position during only a part of the long history of the incense trade, for the Minaeans had been carrying frankincense and myrrh northwards for centuries before the Nabateans came on the scene.[25] The northern end of the route had been controlled by Assyria in the seventh century BC and captured by Nebuchadnezzar of Babylon at the end of that century. Fifty years later Cyrus of Persia had conquered it. Over this period the Nabataeans, whose origin is not yet certain but is thought by some to be central Arabia,[26] had begun to move northwards into the ancient but, by that time, depopulated land of Edom, settling and integrating with the surviving Edomites. Nabonidus, the last king of Babylon (555–539 BC), who set up residence in the oasis of Tayma for reasons concerning his religious convictions, had made some effort to bolster his fading empire by trying to secure a firm grip on the rich trade routes in his western borders between Tayma and Yathrib.[27] When Babylon fell to the Persians the land of Edom was left undisturbed.

This set the stage for the flowering of a brief but brilliant civilisation, which began to make its mark from about 300 BC and which established at Petra a major city, with a population eventually reaching some 30,000 persons. From Petra, the Nabataean kingdom at its full extent stretched northwards, encircling Judaea and the other Palestinian states, to Damascus and Coele-Syria, westwards into the eastern half of Sinai, eastwards as far as the oasis of Jawf and southwards to the cities of Ḥijrā and Dedān. From those latter cities a trade route led east through Ḥayl and Tayma to Gerrha as well as south to the incense lands.

The first dateable mention of the Nabataeans is provided by Diodorus Siculus, whose work is particularly valuable as a source on this subject. He gives an account of an unsuccessful attempt in 312 BC by Syrians under Antigonus Cyclops, one of Alexander the Great's former generals, to capture Petra. The booty at first seized by the Syrians but later recovered consisted of most of the frankincense and myrrh found there, as well as five hundred talents of silver. Clearly the Nabataeans were an effective power with established commercial links by that date.

Ḥijrā is probably the "village called Egra" of the Nabataeans through which, in Strabo's report, Aelius Gallus passed on his way back from south Arabia. This provides 25 BC as the earliest reference to the Nabataean occupation of that place, for all the dated Nabataean inscriptions at Ḥijrā come from the first century AD, when the city reached its apogee. But the area seems to have been taken over by the Nabataeans in the second or first century BC after a Nabataean adventurer called Mas'udu had overthrown the Lihyanite kingdom and was himself ousted by the Nabataean king.[28] Ptolemy showed Egra in his map.

Diodorus, probably with Agatharchides as his source, described the Nabataeans at a very early stage in their development, when strict disciplines still governed their way of life:

> "They live in the open air, claiming as native land a wilderness that has neither rivers nor abundant springs from which it is possible for an army to obtain water. It is their custom neither to plant grain, set out any fruit bearing tree, use wine, nor construct any house; and if anyone is found acting contrary to this, death is his penalty . . . Some of them raise camels, others sheep, pasturing them in the desert. While there are many Arabian tribes who use the desert as pasture, the Nabataeans far surpass the others in wealth although they are not much more than ten thousand in number; for not a few of them are accustomed to bring down to the sea frankincense and myrrh and the most valuable kinds of spices, which they procure from those who convey them from what is called Arabia Eudaemon."[29]

Diodorus went on to describe the underground reservoirs constructed by the Nabataeans to provide secret water supplies in the desert. But since no grain was being planted, the brilliantly conceived irrigation schemes which were to become a marked feature of the Nabataean economy may not have commenced. Plutarch mentioned a campaign by Demetrius, the son of Antigonus, who "was sent to subdue the Nabataean Arabs, in performing which service he incurred great danger by journeying through waterless deserts; but his intrepid courage overawed the barbarians, and he returned loaded with plunder, having captured seven hundred camels."[30]

Strabo's *Geography* contains three passages about the Nabataeans. In the first he quoted Artemidorus, who reported that Nabataea was:

> "a country with a large population and well supplied with pasturage. They also dwell on islands situated off the coast

nearby; and these Nabataeans formerly lived a peaceful life, but later, by means of rafts, went to plundering the vessels of people sailing from Aegypt. But they paid the penalty when a fleet went over and sacked their country."[31]

In the second passage Strabo provided an account obtained at first hand:

"The first people above Syria who dwell in Arabia Felix are the Nabataeans and the Sabaeans. They often overran Syria before they became subject to the Romans; but at present both they and the Syrians are subject to the Romans. The metropolis of the Nabataeans is Petra ("rock"), as it is called; for it lies on a site which is otherwise smooth and level, but is fortified all round by a rock, the outside parts of the rock being precipitous and sheer, and the inside parts having springs in abundance, both for domestic purposes and for watering gardens. Outside the circuit of the rock most of the territory is desert, in particular that towards Judaea . . . Petra is always ruled by some king from the royal family; and the King has as Administrator one of his companions, who is called "brother". It is exceedingly well governed; at any rate Arthenodorus, a philosopher and companion of mine, who had been in the city of the Petraeans, used to describe their government with admiration, for he said that he found both many Romans and many other foreigners sojourning there, and he saw that the foreigners often engaged in law suits, both with one another and with the natives, but that none of the natives prosecuted one another, and that they in every way kept peace with one another."[32]

In the third passage, which one supposes may also have derived from his friend Arthenodorus, Strabo has more to say about the Nabataeans themselves during the time when their civilisation was at its zenith:

"The Nabataeans are a sensible people, and are so much inclined to acquire possessions that they publicly fine anyone who has diminished his possessions and also confer honours on anyone who has increased them. Since they have but few slaves, they are served by their kinsfolk for the most part, or by one another, or by themselves; so that the custom extends even to their kings. They prepare common meals together in groups of thirteen persons; and they have two girl singers for each banquet. The king holds many drinking bouts in magnificent style, but no one drinks more than eleven cupfuls, each time using a different golden cup. The king is so democratic that, in addition to serving himself, he sometimes even serves the rest himself in his turn. He often renders an account of his kingship in the popular assembly; and sometimes his mode of life is examined. Their homes, through the use of stones, are costly; but, on account of the peace, the cities are not walled. Most of the country is well supplied with fruits, except the olive; they use sesame oil instead. The sheep are white fleeced and the oxen are large, but the country produces no horses. Camels afford the service they require instead of horses. They go without tunics, with girdles about their loins, and with slippers on their feet—even the kings, though in their case the colour is purple. Some things are imported wholly from other countries, but others not altogether so, especially in the case of those that are native products, as, for example, gold and silver and most of the aromatics, whereas brass and iron, as also purple garb, styrax, crocus, costaria, embossed works, paintings and moulded works are not produced in their country. They have the same regard for the dead as for dung, as Heracleitus says: 'Dead bodies more fit to be cast out than dung'; and therefore they bury even their kings beside dung-heaps. They worship the sun, building an altar on the top of the house, and pouring libations on it daily and burning frankinsense."[33]

Comparison of Strabo's contemporary description with the information provided by Diodorus Siculus demonstrates the remarkable changes in the Nabataean way of life as their civilisation developed under Greek and Roman influences. Contrary to their earlier customs, they began to grow grain, to build houses and to drink wine. There are also interesting affinities with the way of life of modern tribal Arabia, for example in the "democratic" behaviour of the king. Modern archaeological investigations have corroborated much of Strabo's account, although some of his statements are still debated. Arthenodorus is believed to have been blind (a reason, perhaps, for the absence of any description of the unique architecture of Petra) and it is possible that he did not understand everything he was told. The most perplexing point is the reference to the disposal of dead bodies, for funerary rituals must have played as important a part in the life and religion of the Nabataeans as of all other ancient peoples, but as yet no cemetery has been discovered for the common people of Petra.[34]

It is the usual practice to date the end of the Nabataeans to AD 106, when the Romans incorporated Nabataea into their

Provincia Arabia, but this action seems to have had little effect on the Nabataean civilisation, which continued to thrive as long as there was trade. Some of the finest Nabataean buildings are dated after this event. In any case most of the southern territory of the Nabataeans was not occupied militarily. But the development of sea transport was already beginning to squeeze the overland incense trade out of existence, while political changes north of Petra were beginning to favour the economic ascendency of Palmyra. Petra remained a place of some importance in the fourth and possibly into the fifth century AD, long after the incense trade had declined, but there are no inscriptions in the distinctive Nabataean script after the fourth century and by that time the city may no longer have had a Nabataean population.[35]

The picture presented always shows the Minaeans bringing their aromatics from south Arabia into the Nabataean kingdom. Although Nabataean script has been found on potsherds as far south as Qaryat al-Faw, near as-Sulayyil, there is no evidence of Nabataean traders themselves going south to the incense lands to collect their supplies, although Pliny, who in general is remarkably silent on the subject of the Nabataeans,[36] does provide an interesting reference to this

possibility. In discussing cinnamon and cassia he states, in a fragment of a chapter the source for which is not apparent: "From the border of the cassia and cinnamon district gum-resin and aloe wood are also imported, but they come by way of the Nabataean cave-dwellers, who are a colony from the Nabataei."[37] The location of this colony would seem, by deduction from Pliny's slender clues, to have been in the area of western Somalia or southern Ethiopia.

The journey from Ḥijrā to Petra is about 300 miles, although Pliny erratically quoted 600 miles according to available manuscripts. The natural and, because of extensive lava fields, most probable route seems likely to have been that followed by the Hejaz railway through Muʻazzan, Tabūk and Mudawārah.[38] This is also the line of the Islamic pilgrim route known as the Darb al Tabūkiyya. Doughty recorded it on his map as the "old gold and frankincense caravan path to Arabia Felix",[39] although without reference to this in his text. The incense caravans would probably have taken twelve to fifteen days along this part of the route and a further five to seven days for the 125 mile journey from Petra to Gaza.

Pliny spoke of Gaza as the northern terminus of the incense route and noted that it was 65 camel stations from Tumnaʻ. In Pliny's time it was under Roman control, but its strategic importance, both as a Mediterranean terminus of trade routes from Arabia and as the key position on the route from Egypt to Palestine and Mesopotamia, had given it an unsettled and bloody history. One of the five cities of the Philistines, it was already of great antiquity when Alexander captured it, and it stood, as Arrian noted, about two and a half miles from the sea on a high, artificial mound – perhaps a "tell" site even then.

Plutarch states that after Gaza was captured Alexander sent many of the spoils to his friends, including five hundred talents' weight of frankincense and one hundred of myrrh to his old tutor Leonidas. In Plutarch's story: "Leonidas once, when sacrificing, reproved Alexander for taking incense by handfuls to throw upon the victim when it was burning on the altar. 'When', he said, 'you have conquered the country from which incense comes, Alexander, then you may make such rich offerings as these; but at present you must use what we have sparingly.' Alexander now wrote to him: 'We have sent you abundance of frankincense and myrrh, that you may no longer treat the gods so stingily.'"[40]

Gaza was razed by Ptolemy when he pulled back into Egypt after Antigonus had taken Coele-Syria.[41] Later Ptolemy's forces defeated Demetrius, the son of Antigonus, in a battle near Gaza.[42] About two centuries later, after Octavian, who was to become the Emperor Augustus, had wrested Egypt from Cleopatra and Anthony, he assigned Gaza to Herod the Great, after whose death it was incorporated into the Roman province of Syria.[43] Clearly there were times when alternative routes and termini had to be found for the incense traffic.

Strabo, quoting Eratosthenes, observed that aromatics were conveyed by merchants who reached south Arabia from Aelana, near modern Eilath, in seventy days (page 64 above). In another section which dealt with Palestine he stated:

> "Then, near Ascalon, one comes to the harbour of the Gazaeans. The city of the Gazaeans is situated inland at a distance of seven stadia; it became famous at one time, but was razed to the ground and remains uninhabited. Thence there is said to be an overland passage of one thousand two hundred and sixty stadia to Aela, a city situated near the head of the Arabian Gulf. This head consists of two recesses: one extending into the region near Arabia and Gaza, which is Aelanites, after the city situated on it, and the other extending to the region near Aegypt in the neighbourhood of the City of Heroes, to which the overland passage from Pelusium is shorter; and the overland journeys are made on camels through desert and sandy places . . . After Gaza one comes to Rhapia . . . then to Rhinocolura, so called from the people with mutilated noses that had been settled there in earlier times."[44]

These two references in Strabo seem to fit together. It may be noted that at that time, about 200 BC, the harbour of Gaza was operating even though the ruined city was still deserted. Pliny's reference to the "town of Rhinocolura and inland Rhapea and Gaza and inland Anthedon" suggests that by his time the new town round the harbour had taken on the name of the old city.[45]

Strabo shows that there was a trade route between Aelana and Gaza, but he does not specifically state that aromatics were carried along it, only that merchants expected to take

seventy days to reach "Minaea" from Aelana. But there may
well have been an alternative route for incense caravans which
avoided Petra. This may have branched off the main route
near Mudawārah, leading through Aelana to Gaza or Rhinocolura[46]; or it may have left the main route near al-Hazm,
north of Tabūk, and so reached Aelana through al-Qurayyah
(an important ruin site with Nabataean remains) and the
small gulf port of Haql. Alternatively, it may have left the
main route at a much earlier stage: the principal overland
route for Islamic pilgrims from Egypt to Makkah followed
due south from Aelana through the coastal hills of the Gulf of
Aqaba and passing in Wādī al-Ifal the ruins of the important
Nabataean city of al-Bad' (Mughayr Shu'ayb); keeping
inland from the Red Sea, it then led through Shaghb, now a
ruin site some seventy miles east of the harbour of Dubā, and
rejoined the main incense road a little south of Ḥijrā. Ptolemy
knew Shaghb as "Soace" and a number of other stages on this
pilgrim route can be identified in his list of places, indicating
its use in pre-Islamic days.[47]

Aelana (or Aila) was a Nabataean port. Up to the fifth
century BC the settlement at the head of the Gulf of Aqaba was
at Ezion-Geber close nearby. From very early days this place
would have attracted the Minaean merchants as the trading
centre for the rich copper and iron mines of Wādī 'Arabah,
copper being one of the few commodities which the South
Arabians were glad to import in exchange for aromatics.
Fragments of jars incised with letters in the south Arabian
script have been found at Ezion-Geber, indicating a South
Arabian presence there in the fifth or sixth century BC.[48]

At some periods, for example when the Seleucid Syrians were threatening the Nabataeans and already had control of Gaza, the harbour of Rhinocolura, modern al-Arīsh on the coast of Sinai, may have received much of the aromatics traffic, although at other times incense was probably traded from both places, while Ascalon, a little north of Gaza, may also have carried part of the trade. Over a long period Rhinocolura appears to have been under Nabataean control.

In his account of the expedition of Aelius Gallus, and therefore presumably describing the situation in about 25 BC, Strabo wrote:

> "Now the loads of aromatics are conveyed from Leuce Come to Petra, and thence to Rhinocolura, which is in Phoenicia near Aegypt, and thence to other peoples; but at the present time they are for the most part transported by the Nile to Alexandria; and they are landed from Arabia and India at Myus Harbour; and then they are conveyed by camels over to Coptos in Thebais, which is situated on a canal of the Nile, and then to Alexandria."[49]

A few sentences before this Strabo also referred to:

> "Leuce Come, in the land of the Nabataeans, a large emporium . . . camel traders travel back and forth from Petra to this place in safety and ease, and in such numbers of men and camels that they differ in no respect from an army."[50]

The statement here that the aromatics were conveyed to Petra from the port of Leuce Come is particularly puzzling, for it suggests that they had reached Leuce Come by sea, which contradicts the strong evidence that frankincense came overland through Shabwah. Agatharchides made no suggestion of a seaborne incense traffic, although the Ptolemies were attempting in his time to foster Red Sea shipping by developing ports on the Egyptian coast and clearing the waters of pirates.[51] Moreover Ptolemaic vessels bringing incense from south Arabia could be expected to sail straight to an Egyptian port rather than to Leuce Come. As camel owners the Nabataeans must have been as concerned as the Minaeans to restrict aromatics to the overland route.

Possibly this account by Strabo derived from some earlier date when, for a short period, the overland route was closed or exceptionally difficult. There is no evidence for such an event, but Mas'udu's seizure of power from the Lihyanite king could mark such an occasion. Alternatively, there may be a textual corruption in Strabo's reference, perhaps through a confusion between Ḥijrā and the port of Ḥijrā, which was Leuce Come. But there may always have been a coastal trade to Leuce Come bringing produce, including a trickle of aromatics, from the Red Sea coastal areas of Saba, from Somali shores and from Ethiopia. Ships employed on this trade would avoid going further north than Leuce Come because of the difficult sailing conditions in the extreme north of the Red Sea and most of them would in any case have gone to the other side of the Red Sea, to Myos Hormos and other Egyptian harbours. This situation is reflected considerably later in the *Periplus* – "there is another harbour and fortified place called Leuce Come ("white village") from which there is a road to Petra. . . . It holds the position of a market town for small vessels sent there from Arabia; and so a centurion is stationed there . . ." (see page 90 above).

The importance of Leuce Come once Nabataean trading was fully developed is unquestionable. The Nabataeans profited not only from the incense trade but also from the sale of Dead Sea bitumen, which was in high demand in Egypt, and from the commercial traffic flowing through their territory between Egypt on the one hand and Mesopotamia, the Arabian Gulf (via Gerrha) and India on the other. Regardless of any traffic in aromatics, Leuce Come must have been busy as an entrepôt for goods crossing the Red Sea.[52]

The Nabataean ties with Egypt were considerable. Numerous graffiti, inscribed for the most part in the first three centuries AD, by Nabataean cameleers and traders have been found along the main caravan routes to Coptos and Caenopolis from the three Egyptian Red Sea ports of Myos Hormos, Berenice and Leucos Limen, the greater number being along the road from the latter port. If the site of Leuce Come was at modern al-Wajh then Leucos Limen was the nearest Egyptian port to it. Funerary inscriptions show that there were many Nabataeans among the guards protecting these routes, while many more served the Ptolemaic governments as customs officials and border guards. A permanent colony of Nabataeans was settled at a site now known as Tell ash-Shuqafiyah, near Tell al-Kabīr, well inside Egypt on the important Wādī Tumilah highway leading into the Nile delta from north Sinai.[53] Nabataeans went further afield, too. A Graeco-Nabataean inscription has been found on the island of Rhodes and there may have been a Nabataean sanctuary at Puteoli, near Naples, while Nabataean merchants are known to have visited such distant places as Miletus, in Asia-Minor, and Hatra, on the Euphrates in Parthia.[54]

Minaeans too seem to have travelled beyond Nabataean territory. A Minaean altar dedicated to their principal deity has been found on the island of Delos. Strabo, describing the region of Damascus, mentioned the southern mountains where lived brigands who "have been robbing the merchants from Arabia Felix, but this is less the case now that the band of robbers under Zenodorus has been broken up through the good government established by the Romans and through the security established by the Roman soldiers that are kept in Syria."[55] There is also inscriptional evidence to suggest that there were Minaeans in Egypt in the third or second century BC.[56]

Egypt's significance in the incense trade derived not only from its own consumption of incense but also from the special position of Alexandria as the sorting and processing centre for

produce destined for Rome. "At Alexandria . . . where
frankincense is worked up for sale," Pliny wrote, "no
vigilance is sufficient to guard the factories. A seal is put upon
the workmen's aprons, they have to wear a mask or a net with
a close mesh on their heads, and before they are allowed to
leave the premises they have to take off all their clothes."[57] As
the main industrial centre of the Empire, Alexandria received
cargoes from India, Mesopotamia and the Red Sea countries,
while it was also the central granary for the exports of
Egyptian corn. Shipments followed a seasonal pattern. The
huge corn ships and other cargo vessels which plied between
Alexandria and Puteoli tended to sail between May and
September to obtain the right winds, while from mid-
November to mid-February few voyages were attempted.[58]
Suetonius records a compliment paid to the Emperor Augustus by one of these ships when he was sailing through the gulf
of Puteoli: "An Alexandrian ship had just arrived, the
passengers and crew of which, clad in white, crowned with
garlands and burning frankincense, lavished good wishes and
the highest praise on him, saying that it was through him they
sailed the seas and enjoyed their liberty and fortunes. So
pleased was he at this that he gave forty gold pieces to each of
his companions, exacting a pledge under oath from them to
spend the money entirely on buying wares from
Alexandria."[59]

At first the greater part of the frankincense and myrrh
destined for Alexandria must have reached it through Gaza or
Rhinocolura, arriving from there either by boat or on camels'
backs. But as seaborne trade in the Red Sea developed under
the Emperors, increasing amounts will have arrived from the
ports on the Red Sea coast, at first Myos Hormos, which lay
near the present Port Safaga, and later Berenice, some 200
miles further south. Well organised routes, first set up by the
Ptolemies, were maintained for the long journey between
these ports and Alexandria and Pliny has provided a detailed
description of them in describing the route to India, for it was
principally in connection with the Indian trade, and in
particular the trade in pepper, that this journey was made.[60]
From Berenice there was a twelve-day overland journey to the
Nile, usually covered at night owing to the extreme heat. The
road was divided into stages with fortified stations where

there were "Hydreumata", or water cisterns, and the Nile was reached at Coptos (modern Keft). The journey from Myos Hormos took six or seven days along a similar road which ended at Caenopolis (modern Kenah), not far from Coptos. The cargo was then loaded into river boats which sailed down the Nile, reaching Alexandria by taking the Canopic arm of the river, with a final journey along a canal to Juliopolis, two miles from Alexandria itself. The river journey took twelve days when travelling up river with the right winds, so may at times have taken considerably longer, although down-river traffic would have benefited from the current.[61]

In describing the various stages of the long route which the incense caravans followed on their way to the Mediterranean, an estimate has been made of the number of days of travel between the principal towns through which they passed. These figures, a summary of which is set out in the table on page 213, show minimum and maximum travelling times on the basis of a day's journey of between 20 and 25 miles. The total journey from Shabwah to Gaza works out at 69 to 87 days, or a mean figure of 78 days of travelling.

We have three estimates of the length of the journey in the classical sources: Strabo's 70 days from Aelana to Minaea; Pliny's 65 stages from Tumna' to Gaza; and Strabo's statement that it took Aelius Gallus 60 days to reach "Egra" from "Marsiaba". Strabo's "70 days", derived from Eratosthenes, was clearly a "rounded-off" and hence only an approximate figure, but represented the total travelling time, whereas Pliny's figure quoted the number of staging posts. At some points there may have been more than one day's travel between the recognized staging posts, with their wells or cisterns. Moreover, at various places, more particularly in the major towns, longer halts would have been called for watering, rest, repair of equipment or the hiring of fresh camels (occasioning a redistribution of the loads). We do not known how frequently this might have happened, but one day of rest for every six days of travelling would have added 13 days to the mean travelling time between Shabwah and Gaza. On the figures calculated, the mean travelling time between Minaea (Qarnaw) and Petra (which is only a little further than Aelana) is 60 days, but with one day of rest after every six days of travel the total travelling time becomes 70 days.

Strabo's passage relating that it took Aelius Gallus 60 days to reach "Egra" is not easy to comprehend without knowing from where the journey commenced. The "Egra" referred to seems likely to be Ḥijrā; Strabo described it as "situated on (or "near") the sea", however,[62] so this could be a reference to Leuce Come as "the port of Ḥijrā", since in classical times ports were often known by the names of the cities they served; it was at Leuce Come that Gallus had left his fleet and therefore it was likely to have been from that port that he embarked to sail back to Myos Hormos. The journey time from Mārib (which may not have been "Marsiaba") to Ḥijrā would have been 43 to 55 days of travel in accordance with the table. We do not know the route Gallus followed, since not all the places listed in his itinerary can be identified, but if he travelled to Ḥijrā and thence to the coast it may have taken him an additional 5 or 6 days to reach Leuce Come. Aelius Gallus was in any case leading a despondent army, suffering from sickness, fatigue, hunger and heat and his journey may therefore have been a slow one.

Having examined all aspects of the journey to Europe, the whole trading cycle for south Arabian incense, and in particular for frankincense, can now be set down and this is done schematically in the chart on page 147. The timings shown in this chart cannot be very precise, because the harvest and the trading journeys were all undertaken over periods which depended, among other factors, on the monsoons and were subject to considerable variations between one year and another. But in relating the sea voyage to India with the frankincense seasons in this way, the separate nature of the Roman trade with India is very apparent. In effect ships journeying to India left Egypt in July and passed south Arabia with the south-west monsoon winds behind them, which was before the bulk of the main frankincense harvest, the "autumn" crop, could be brought down to the coast and conveyed to Qana. If they called at Qana at all—and the *Periplus* contains no statement that they did—it was to collect frankincense, such as was available, for trading in Indian ports.[63] On the return journey they might call at Moscha (the *Periplus* (section 32) noted that returning ships would winter there if the season was late), when they would obtain frankincense from the inferior "spring" crop of Ẓufār, which was just beginning to reach that port. The journey to Qana to obtain supplies of the best quality "autumn" crop had to be organised separately—"the voyage to this place is best made at the same time as that to Muza, or rather earlier," states the *Periplus* (section 28), having previously noted September as the best time to travel from Berenice to Muza. On this timetable the ships reached Qana as the monsoon was dying out and the frankincense sheds beginning to fill up. They left with the first gusts of the north-east monsoon, before the spice ships set out from India and at about the same time that the first Minaean incense caravans were beginning to reach Petra and Gaza. This may be one reason why the overland trade was able to survive for so long against the competition of Greek and Roman trading vessels.

Table Showing Distances and Journey Times on the Incense Road

	miles	days' journey
(Ẓufār to Shabwah—overland	400 (direct)	16–30)
Qana to Shabwah	160 (either route)	7– 8
Shabwah to Tumna'—via Aiyadim	110	4– 5
—via Markhah	170	7– 8
Tumna' to Mārib—via Nagia	65	3
Shabwah to Mārib—via Markhah and Mablaqah	230	9–11
Mārib to Qarnaw	60	2– 3
Qarnaw to Nagrān	150	6– 7
Nagrān to Tabala	280	11–14
Tabala to Yathrib	350 (direct)	15–20
Yathrib to Ḥijrā	215	9–11
Ḥijrā to Petra	300	12–15
Petra to Gaza	125	5– 7
Total (Shabwah to Gaza)	1710 miles	69–88 days

Chapter 11

Climate and History in Arabia

Comment has already been made on the unusual situation of Shabwah, remote from the main populated area of Ḥaḍramawt and the mandatory emporium for all frankincense even though it did not lie on the most direct route from Qana to Mārib.

At Shabwah, on Pliny's information, a tithe was "taken by the priests for the god they call Sabis . . . and on a fixed number of days the god graciously entertains guests at a banquet." Ancient south Arabian inscriptions provide evidence of ritual meals at temples during periodic pilgrimages,[1] corroborating Pliny's statement, and the temple at Shabwah was dedicated to the national god of Ḥaḍramawt, SYN (vocalization not known), the sun-god (not Sabis). Clearly Shabwah was a place of great religious importance to the people of Ḥaḍramawt, an importance perhaps enhanced by its role as the centre for the frankincense trade: frankincense itself had a religious significance, so that its very harvesting involved certain taboos—the harvesters were not, according to Pliny, allowed to be polluted by meeting women or funeral processions. Yet it would appear that frankincense was not the original cause of Shabwah's religious importance. We can deduce this from the existence of a small, isolated rock, covered with inscriptions and surmounted by the remains of a building, which lies some ten miles west of the city ruins in the Ramlat Sabʿatayn, the sand-dune desert also known as the Ṣayhad.[2] This place is called al-ʿUqlah. Its inscriptions, first recorded by Philby, reveal that the coronation of the kings of Ḥaḍramawt and other ceremonies were held there, sometimes involving fairly substantial animal sacrifices.[3] One of these inscriptions refers, according to a new interpretation proposed by Professor Serjeant, to the killing in a ritual hunt of 35 ibex, 82 wild cows, 25 gazelles and 8 lynx.[4] Although these inscriptions are late in origin, they indicate that the rock of al-'Uqlah and hence Shabwah itself were associated with traditional religious ceremonies unconnected with the frank-incense trade.

Both Mārib, the capital city of the Sabaeans, and Tumna', the capital of Qatabān, lay on the desert edge of their kingdoms, but these cities were both at the delta mouth of major wadis and could have become established there from economic causes. At Shabwah there was no major wadi, although some agriculture by irrigation was practiced from the wadi on which it lies, while the salt-mine, though a valuable asset, can hardly have led to it becoming the temporal and religious capital of the kingdom. The expla-nation for the ceremonies performed at al-'Uqlah seems likely to lie in some traditional association with that part of the Ṣayhad desert originating long before the incense trade was of any real significance. This leads one to consider whether the climate might not have changed over the centuries to account for such an association with what is now a barren and waterless area and to explain Shabwah's evident ability to support in earlier days a much larger population than is possible now. Obviously this also has a significant bearing on the problem of the area in which incense trees flourished in ancient times.

Until recently scholars describing the ancient remains of Arabia have tended to assume that the climate of the sub-continent has not changed in historical times and that, in consequence, the people of the earliest historical days were, in general, competing with conditions little different from those of today. This has sometimes provided awkward problems in explaining ancient habitations where there is no longer any water supply, but only in recent years has such explanation become really difficult when, with the pronounced increase in archaeological exploration, particularly in the south-eastern and Arabian Gulf regions, more and more sites have come to light in what are now entirely waterless areas.

The classical authors do not seem to have regarded south-west Arabia as a particularly arid area and the very name

Arabia Felix suggests a land which is exceptionally fertile. Theophrastus heard of frankincense growing in mountains which were "lofty, forest-covered and subject to snow, and rivers from them flow down into the plain" (page 63). Eratosthenes talked of the rivers leading into lakes and of the country being fertile, with "an abundance of domestic animals" (page 64). To Agatharchides/Artemidorus the country was "very fertile" with "an abundance of fruits" and Mārib was on a "well-wooded mountain" (page 66). Diodorus/Agatharchides stated that "throughout the interior of the land there are thick forests."[5] Photius/Agatharchides, describing the voyage down the Arabian Red Sea coast, referred to "an extensive and exceedingly well watered shore" south of the Thamoudians, together with a prominent mountain "clothed in forests of every kind of tree" (page 69); south of this in what was probably modern 'Asīr there were "soft, thick clouds from which come showers and temperate storms even in summer" (page 69); in the area of the Sabaeans the land "produces everything which we regard as important for our lives", having in its interior "large, unbroken tracts of forest" (page 70). The hills in Pliny's frankincense-producing district called Sariba had "natural forests on them running right down to the level ground" (page 111). Even to the writer of the *Periplus* the frankincense country was "wrapped in thick clouds and fog", while Socotra was both "desert and marshy, having rivers in it" (page 92).

These various statements of the classical authors are to some extent derived one from another, while much of the description may have been provided by Greeks from Egypt, to whom deserts were not unusual, so too much significance cannot be attached to the absence of comment about the aridity of the land. Yet if the intensely humid heat of the southern coastal areas, which many of the Greek sailors must have experienced, was as great then as it is today it is perhaps a little surprising that nothing was said about it. Certainly the reference to forest-covered regions is a consistent one but applicable to no more than a very few parts of Arabia today.[6]

Whether the statements of the classical writers can be held to imply a climatic change or not, the indications that there were once considerable populations in what are now waterless tracts lend weight to the opinion now receiving scientific support that there have been much greater climatic and environmental changes in Arabia than had been supposed. Looking back to pre-historical times, indeed, some of these changes have been dramatic.

Modern meteorology, benefited by satellites and other technology, is now able to attempt some scientific determinations about the effect which phenomena such as sun-spot cycles and lunar and planetary pull on the tides have on climatic conditions. One important deduction reached from such study concerns the cycle of tidal fluctuations and the concomitant increase in rainfall. Maximum tidal force, with likely peaks of rainfall, is now seen to have occurred in cycles of about 1670 years with maxima in 3500 BC, 1900 BC, 250 BC and AD 1433 and with minima in 2800 BC, 200 BC and AD 550.[7] But this cycle has to be seen against the wider background of the Ice Age (the Pleistocene) which concluded around 8300 BC, by when the ice-sheets had retreated to their present position. In the context of northern Europe, the Post-Glacial age has been divided into a number of periods of changing climate: a slow rise in temperature up to about 5500 BC (the Pre-Boreal and Boreal periods); an exceptionally moist period of maximum warmth from 5500 BC to 3000 BC (the Atlantic period); a period when the climate was drier and more "continental" from 3000 BC to 500 BC (the Sub-Boreal period); and one when the climate became in general wetter and colder, lasting from 500 BC to the present day (the Sub-Atlantic period).[8]

Important work which has a bearing on the Arabian climate has been carried out by Butzer and Twidale, who have examined the climate of the Sahara.[9] Here ancient rock drawings show animals and vegetation which can no longer exist in the regions concerned, while pollen grains have been found in western Sahara rock shelters of cypress, pine and oak trees which have a radio carbon dating of between 3450 and 2730 BC. Their evidence leads to the general deduction that between 5500 BC and 2350 BC the climate was very moist and that from 2350 to 800 BC it became intensely dry before settling down to a more average level. Their broad conclusion is that the moist interval from the late sixth to the late third millennium BC and the pronounced aridity in the second millennium BC may both be of fairly general validity. But they also show how a comparatively minor climatic variation can bring about substantial ecological changes.

In another study, of climate in the Near East, Butzer concluded that moist conditions from 6800 BC to 5000 BC were followed by a Neolithic moist interval with a distinctly higher rainfall and, in some areas, higher temperatures between 5000 and 2400 BC, though from 3600 BC there were also temporary cycles of aridity. From 2400 to 850 BC was a period of greater warmth and lesser rainfall, except for a major wet spell *circa* 1200 BC. From 850 BC to AD 700 the climate was broadly similar to that of today, but with marked temporary drought cycles towards the end of the period. Thereafter until the present day it has remained similar but with many short term fluctuations.[10] Other climatologists have also drawn attention to the major wet spell. It has been noted that western Asia enjoyed a short wet period reaching a peak in about 1250 BC, followed by increasing dryness and then by a wet period from about 700 to 250 BC and Dayton has shown how this fits in with the occupation pattern of certain ancient sites in north Arabia.[11] Yet the movement of Hittites off the Anatolian plateau into northern Syria around 1300 BC and of people from Libya into Egypt around 1200 BC have been held to indicate lack of rainfall in these areas, while it has even been proposed that the decline of the Mycenaeans at the same time was due to drought.[12] Clearly one cannot be conclusive and within the general proposition one must allow for local anomalies (or look for other explanations).

These various sets of dates are not easily correlated and exemplify the complexity of the subject, but they help to provide basic material for our purpose. A broad conclusion of general validity would seem to be in line with Butzer's deduction, that in Europe, the Sahara and the Near East the climate was generally rather wet from the fifth or sixth millennium (we need not be concerned with the period before) to the third millennium and that there followed an exceptionally dry period from the middle of the third millennium to early in the first millennium BC, but there were exceptional periods throughout this span of time, possibly geared to other cycles, most notably the wet spell *c*1200 BC.

Although the studies discussed relate only to the Mediterranean and Near East and not generally to Arabia, they may have an application to northern and eastern Arabia, where the climate tends to be governed by winds from the Mediterranean area. South-west Arabia, however, depends for its rainfall on a different wind system, the monsoons, which has been described earlier (pages 144 to 147). The "inter-tropical front", being the line where the Mediterranean and south-west monsoon winds converge, varies substantially from season to season in the Arabian interior. At the present day, in a year when the south-west monsoon is strong, the rainfall will reach Makkah and even as far north as Tayma and Madā'in Ṣāliḥ; the eastern edge of the rain shadow is more regular and lies east of Ẓufār, so that the main frankincense region in the Qāra mountains receives summer rain but the Omān highlands beyond almost invariably remain dry at this season.[13] Professor Brice recently demonstrated how the general lines of the "inter-tropical front" lay considerably further north up to about 3000 BC (reaching the latitude of Sinai) and receded south during the first millennium BC up to about AD 500, by when only the extreme south-west corner of Arabia received the south-west monsoon, although the winter cyclones from the Mediterranean penetrated correspondingly further south down the Arabian Gulf and into south-eastern Arabia.[14]

No study has yet been made of climate in areas served by the monsoon winds which is comparable to Butzer's studies of the Sahara and Near East; but since the monsoon reaches Arabia from the highlands of Abyssinia, the rainfall there is obviously significant to the study of Arabian climate. It follows that any information about the flooding of the Nile, which rises for the most part in Abyssinia, will also be relevant.

The level of the Nile has been recorded by the Nilometer since AD 641; these readings do not go back far enough to cover the time of the incense trade, but they demonstrate that there have been discernible cycles lasting some two to three centuries during which the annual peak flood level has risen by up to two metres and then dropped again. This indicates low rainfall in the periods around AD 1300, 1000 and 800, but the cycle is insufficiently precise for calculations to be made for earlier periods.[15]

A similar general cyclic variation over about 200 years, superimposed on a broader cycle of 700 to 800 years, has been mentioned in recent studies by Winstanley of rainfall in the Mediterranean, the Middle East, the Sahel zone south of the Sahara and north-west India. Dr Winstanley has observed a strongly-marked inverse relationship between the winter/spring rainfall in the area affected by Mediterranean winds and the summer monsoon rainfall in the Sahel and in north-west India.[16] In the Arabian context this may well mean that, subject to local anomaly and the broader world-wide trends, we might expect to see higher rainfall in south-west Arabia during years of drought in north Arabia and the Arabian Gulf region, and vice versa. This could obviously be a highly important factor in explaining the great migrations which are such a major feature of Arabian tribal history. Butzer and Twidale have noted that during the exceptionally dry period from the middle of the third to early in the first millennium the Nile floods appear, from geological as well as historical evidence, to have subsided;[17] this evidence suggests that the Abyssinian highlands, and by implication south-west Arabia too, may have experienced the same exceptionally dry climate during that period. From an earlier period, archaeological investigation in Sudan of "early Khartum" sites (*c*.6000 BC) on the White Nile have provided convincing evidence of a much wetter climate than at present.[18]

One of the major world-wide results of the ending of the Ice Age was an enormous increase in the height of the ocean, by something like 120 metres, as the ice cap melted. Brice has pointed out that the whole of the Arabian Gulf was formerly land well above sea level, with the ocean confined south of the Straits of Hormuz, which then formed a lip of land; by about 9000 BC the melting ice had so increased the ocean level that water began to pour over the lip, flooding the inland plain. The sea waters continued to rise until about 5000 BC, finally subsiding by some five metres below their peak to settle at their present level in around the third millennium BC.[19]

This major effect of the melting ice was not the only geographical phenomenon to affect Arabia. Recent geophysical research into continental drift has shown that the Arabian peninsula is moving north-eastwards at the rate of about 20 metres in 1000 years[20] and at the same time that its eastern side has been tilting upwards under this pressure. In 1971 a leading American geologist, R. Maby, suggested that most of the huge, low-lying area of the Rubʿ al-Khālī, much of the eastern region of which consists of salt tracts, had risen out of the sea in comparatively recent times.[21]

The interaction of these two epic processes has still to be worked out, but their implications will be readily apparent. In the last few years archaeologists have discovered large numbers of very ancient sites in eastern Arabia which are revealed by their pottery and artefacts to belong to the al-ʿUbayd culture, already known in Mesopotamia and going back as far as 5000 BC. The people of this culture, as well as the more primitive people who preceded them and have left their flints behind, lived before the swollen ocean began to subside to its present level and before it had withdrawn from the rising land which was to become the Rubʿ al-Khālī. Carbon-14 dates for shells and charcoal found in a number of these sites range between roughly 3500 and 5500 BC.[22] The al-ʿUbayd sites so far discovered seem to follow an ancient coastline leading inland from a point opposite Bahrayn and in some of them fragments of plaster have been found bearing barnacles at points which now lie three or four (and in at least one case five and a half) metres above the present high-water level of the sea.[23] Geological research in these parts has shown that great areas of the treacherous salt swamp, or *sabkha*, which line the coast have been above sea level for only about 2000 years.[24] The Arabian Gulf, then, has seen dramatic geographical changes since the first civilizations in that region began.

No similar developments can be described for south-west Arabia. Yet there is already some evidence which suggests that in that part of the peninsula too both climate and conditions may have changed noticeably within the period that man has been living there. In many parts of the Rubʿ al-Khālī Philby found, during his journeys in 1932, superficial deposits containing fresh-water shells. It was not possible to date these shells accurately, but none of them showed any significant deviation from the modern fauna, while some were of types which could only have come from rivers or lakes. At some of these sites neolithic flint implements were found in association with the fresh-water shells on the surface of a gravel-strewn plain.[25] During his 1937 journey, Philby discovered troughs in the sand appearing to mark the bed of an old wadi some twenty miles north of Shabwah and recorded: "In the depressions were occasional patches of solid earth clear of sand. On such, and even on the lower sand slopes, I found masses of small, spiral fresh-water shells over a wide area. Most of these patches were lightly covered with small pebbles and fragments of stone and in many places the ground was littered with the broken fragments of ostrich eggs. . . . Some chips of flint and obsidian implements and bits of bone were also met with here and there."[26] Later on the same journey, some thirty miles to the west at Afalil, Philby again found that the plain was "profusely sprinkled with little fresh-water shells, flakes of obsidian and flint, fragments of ostrich shells and the like".[27] These areas are now entirely waterless.

Philby made a further discovery of considerable interest, also in the region of Shabwah. In the Ramlat Sab'atayn north-west of Shabwah his car stuck in a pit some fifty yards in diameter containing a fine dust. He was told that camels often got into difficulties in similar pits in the area and recorded: "Analysis of the powder has revealed a mixture of organic matter and sand particles . . . the organic matter probably represents the decayed weeds of an ancient lake or marsh."[28]

These discoveries of Philby would seem to provide firm evidence for a considerable climatic change in the region of Shabwah. The assocation of neolithic flints with the fresh-water shells, although not observed close to Shabwah, tends to date this evidence to neolithic times.[29] This is precisely the period of the moist interval with distinctly higher rainfall, between about 5000 and 2400 BC, which Butzer and Twidale have concluded was fairly widespread. The discoveries do therefore provide some provisional indication that south-west Arabia too enjoyed this neolithic moist period.

Parallel with the assumption that climatic conditions have not greatly changed in the historical past, it has also been customary to assume that the desert sands have remained more or less static since the days of the incense trade. This is not necessarily the case.

The movement of sand-dunes is determined by wind and

the overall trend of direction must follow the dominant wind, with modifications imposed by secondary winds. Obviously this leads to a confused and complicated situation in a region such as central Arabia, which is subject both to the Mediterranean wind from the north and to the south-west monsoon; the position will be even more complicated by local factors—strong thermal winds, set up by variations between surface temperatures on rock and sand, for instance, may even check the general progress of the sand stream.[30] But the sands of the south-western area of the Rub' al-Khālī, as well as those of the Ṣayhad, do appear to be moving in a general southerly direction, indicating perhaps that on the inland side of the mountain ranges of south-west Arabia the total force of the south-west monsoon is less than that of the northerly winds which prevail over the rest of the year. The *local* movement of wind-blown sand is of course quite apparent from the fact that so many pre-Islamic ruins on the desert edge are now almost, if not completely, covered by sand, but most of these ruin sites are to be found in wadi areas close to or surrounded by mountains and here sand formed from wadi silt may be blown by local winds to cover them.[31]

The general southerly trend of the desert sands is spoken of in Arab tradition[32] and is demonstrated by the fact that the highest dunes in Arabia are found in the south and that in some places, for example in the Ḥarīb and Bayḥān areas, the dunes have piled up against the mountain sides which impede their southerly progress. In the Ṣayhad high sand-dunes now cover much of the ancient water course which one may suppose formerly led into the Wādī Ḥaḍramawt and which, from the evidence of Philby's fresh-water shells, was still being flooded in comparatively recent times. The march of the dunes has also blocked up previously feasible routes: in Wādī Sarr, a northern tributary of Wādī Ḥaḍramawt, the Bents found a pre-Islamic inscription mentioning a caravan route and were told that a pilgrim route to Makkah which had passed that way had become impassable some centuries ago.[33]

Further east, in Ẓufār, there seems to be more significant evidence of the southward march of the sands. This lies in the existence of what seems to be an ancient camel track, cut into parallel grooves altogether over a hundred yards wide, which heads north-west into the Rub' al-Khālī from the area of

Wādī Athinah, in the north of Zufār. This intriguing relic, first seen by Bertram Thomas and thought by Arabs to indicate the highway to the legendary city of Ubar (or Wabar), could provide a valuable measure of sand-dune movement. It was examined by members of the American Foundation for the Study of Man, who observed where it entered the sands and were able to follow it in the troughs of the dunes for some thirty miles until they could go no further. The dunes which have rolled over this track are reported to be up to six hundred feet high.[34] Philby suggested that the track might be a tenth-century AD pilgrim route,[35] but even if it is much more ancient, it can hardly (if indeed it is a camel track at all) be older than the domesticated camel, which is unlikely to have been employed as a pack animal before the second millennium BC (see pages 33 to 37). Whether the dunes have moved down the whole length of the track or encroached a shorter distance from one side, this appears to indicate an enormous movement of sand within the last 3000 years, both in distance and in volume. The speed of sand movement is strikingly shown in recent findings by the Smithsonian Institution's expedition to Shahr-i-Gholgola in Baluchistan, a fertile area in the middle ages but now a sand desert; here six-metre high dunes moved an average of six inches a day during the four months period of north-west wind.[36] Clearly there is need for a scientific study of the general question of sand movement before conclusions can be drawn about its effect on climate, ecology and communications in historical times, but the effect may have been considerable. Study of the shape and formation of the dunes may also provide evidence of climatic changes; for example, Bagnold reads into the unusual dune formation south of the Trucial coast an indication that the northerly *shamal* now penetrates further inland than it once did.[37]

Strong evidence of recent climatic change in south-west Arabia lies in yet another discovery by Philby. Crossing the northern edge of the Ṣayhad from Shabwah to Wādī Gawf, Philby discovered several signs of ancient habitation, including a very extensive area of tombs. He thought that these tombs of Ruwayk and the 'Alam ridges were probably a Sabaean necropolis.[38] Little attention has been paid to this discovery since and the area has not been re-visited for archaeological investigation.

There are two notable features of these tombs. In the first place they are circular in shape, whereas the normal construction shape of the pre-Islamic south Arabian kingdoms, whether of building or tomb, was rectangular.[39] Philby found another ancient cemetery of rather similar "pill-box" tombs at Rudum Saru, near a pass on the road between Nagrān and Saʿdah (here stones near the track had graffiti inscriptions, but these appear to have been added by later travellers).[40] He noted further similar graves and grave mounds in other places near Nagrān.[41] The graves seem to belong to a different culture to that of the incense kingdoms and remind one of the grave mounds in, for example, Baḥrayn, which have been dated back to about 2500 BC, and the thousands of conical tumuli at Jabrin, some 200 miles inland from the Arabian Gulf on the edge of the Rubʿ al-Khālī, which have been uncertainly dated to the middle of the second millennium BC.[42] In the second place, these tombs of Ruwayk and ʿAlam are sited in what is now an area of uninhabited and waterless wilderness, between 40 and 60 miles from Mārib, far from any well and beyond the point now penetrated by wadi floods. The tombs extend over about thirty miles, so they probably relate to a series of settlements, the sites of which have not yet been discovered. Quite clearly the climate must have been different locally to support these settlements. We would seem to have here the traces of a culture which preceded that of the incense kingdoms.[43] If the conclusion is correct that the neolithic wet period was succeeded by an exceptionally dry period, then this early culture must belong to the wet period, for it could hardly have thrived in what is now a barren area at a time when the rainfall there was even less than it is at the present day. The culture may therefore go back to some time between the third and fifth millennia BC. This corresponds with the spread of the ʿUbayd culture into Arabia from Mesopotamia and the dating of somewhat similar tombs in many areas of eastern Arabia.[44]

The picture conjured up of the Ṣayhad of the fourth and fifth millennia BC is a plain covered fairly thickly with vegetation and watered from the hills surrounding it by floods more prolonged and less violent (because greater vegetation on the hillsides and mountain valleys would hold back the

water) than they are today. Some of the streams would be
perennial and if there was not a lake there would have been
permanent ponds. At times the water may have flowed down
the Wādī Ḥaḍramawt to the sea, as it certainly did in the
geological past. Ecologically the conditions would have
favoured herds of wild animals, oryx, ibex and gazelles, with
wild cattle and wild camels, which in their turn enabled the
predators—lions, leopards, hyenas and lynxes—to exist. The
leopard, if not already hunted to extinction, survives only
precariously in the south Arabian mountains, while the lion,
although testified by the classical authors and in inscriptions
and rock drawings, has long been extinct throughout the
peninsula. These same conditions would also have favoured
settled populations in the Ṣayhad, with a hunting tradition
remaining as their agriculture and animal husbandry developed. But the great period of drought which commenced
in the middle of the third millennium BC would have dried up
the plain and forced the population either to retreat into the
surrounding wadis and mountains, where there was still
water, or to become nomadic. By the time moister conditions
returned a thousand years later the ancient association with
the Ṣayhad, already becoming a sand-dune desert, would be
remembered only in confused traditions that the region was
the homeland of the ancient gods; the kings of Ḥaḍramawt
would remember this when they came to al-'Uqlah for the
coronation ceremonies and it may have lingered in the
tradition of the ritual hunts, performed as a part of the
religious ceremonies. All the pre-Islamic inscriptions concerning ritual hunts lie on the edge of desert areas.[45] This may
also be the explanation for the legend of Ubar; the eleventh-
century Arab historian Nashwān bin Sa'īd al-Himyari spoke
of Ubar as "the name of the land which belonged to 'Ad in the
eastern parts of Yemen; today it is an untrodden desert owing
to the drying up of its water. There are to be found in it great
buildings which the wind has smothered in sand."[46]

Clearly in the broad span of Arabia's history climatic
changes have had an important influence, but the whole
subject needs to be examined closely by archaeologists and
others before one can do more than speculate in this way
about its effect.

There is no doubt at all that over the last 1500 years,

perhaps commencing somewhere around AD 300 when the incense kingdoms began to wane at a time of persistent drought, Arabia has suffered from continuing and intense desiccation.[47] The factors contributing to desiccation are numerous, but the periods of exceptional aridity in the early centuries AD may have had a catalytic effect, leading to tribal migrations and the abandonment of some agricultural areas. Shabwah itself seems to have been deserted at this time and the population, according to early Arab writers, went to live in Shibām, in Ḥaḍramawt.[48] The very growth of population, both animal and human, could have been one of these factors, leading to a consumption of fuel, food and fodder greater than the natural rate of regeneration, so that marginal areas would become stripped of their natural foliage and erosion set in. Herding of camels in the plains and of goats in the hills may have been a critical feature of this process. Destruction of the vegetation cover, by making the flash floods more abrupt and difficult to control, would lead to damage to the irrigation systems and erosion of the wadis, sometimes with some lowering of the water table. In many places the established irrigation technique of south Arabia clearly began to defeat its own ends, because the silt layers increased the height of the fields, making it necessary to raise the level of the feeder canals until it eventually became impossible to take the canal entrances further back up the wadi, when the system would have to be abandoned;[49] a common feature of the inland-flowing wadis of south Arabia is the cliffs of ancient silt, some thirty or forty feet high, marking the eroded edges of ancient fields, while in some places inscriptions commemorating the construction of irrigation works can be found quite high up the hillsides where the canals had been built. Elsewhere the intensity of irrigation brought salt to the surface (a problem also faced in modern irrigation schemes) and the land became uncultivable—this is a marked feature in Nabataean areas of north Arabia. In eastern Arabia the rise of the land mass has in some places stemmed the flow of underground water to an extent that settlements and related agricultural systems have had to be abandoned. The adoption of the nomadic life on a large scale also adds to the process of defoliation, while another significant defoliant, the desert locust, becomes a greater menace during times of drought: this derives from its ability to maintain its species by physical changes which turn it during seasons of drought from a grass-hopper type of insect, harmless to crops, into a true swarming locust.[50]

Many of these influences were at work before the incense kingdoms came to an end, but they have continued inexorably ever since. The inscription at al-'Uqlah shows that the Ṣayhad then supported a substantial wild animal population, far greater than could survive in the sandy wastes of the present day. Over the centuries the effect of desiccation has been quite marked and south-west Arabia, like the rest of the peninsula, has become very much more arid. One outcome of this, as we have noted in a previous chapter, is that the frankincense and myrrh trees, which must once have existed in very great numbers, are now rare and confined to more limited areas, the vanishing reminders of south Arabia's ancient prosperity.

Chapter 12

A Summary of Main Conclusions

In the course of this book a number of conclusions have been reached, some of them at variance with existing tenets, which are of importance to a proper understanding of the Arabian incense trade and its position in the perspective of history. The following pages do not attempt to summarize all that has been written in this book, but they cover the principal points and attempt to show how they are woven in together.

Chapter 1

Incense has been associated with religious ceremonial all over the world from time immemorial. In classical times the Greeks began to use it as a substitute for sacrifice in the sixth century BC and it was adopted by the Romans from at least the beginning of the second century BC. As well as a means of propitiating the gods it was also recognized from early times as a purifier and practical fumigant with which the bad smells of primitive urban life could be disguised.

Frankincense was held by the Romans to be the incense *par excellence* and its high price reflected the enormous demand for it. Myrrh was of particular value as a base for perfumes and unguents. Both frankincense and myrrh had considerable uses in medicine and for other purposes.

Frankincense and myrrh grew only in southern Arabia, Somalia and parts of Ethiopia, and the trade to Europe and Mesopotamia was controlled by south Arabians. This contact with the civilisations of the north benefitted the development of a sophisticated civilisation in south Arabia, although the belief held since classical times that Arabia Felix gained its wealth from the incense trade is not correct; the basic wealth of the south Arabian kingdoms derived from agriculture through skilled irrigation schemes.

Strictly speaking, frankincense and myrrh are "gum-resins", but the terms "gum", "resin" and "gum-resin" are used loosely and often synonymously.

Chapter 2

The earliest reference to frankincense and myrrh has been held to be found in the inscriptions of 1500 BC in Queen Hatshepsut's temple near Thebes, which record an expedition sent out to collect incense from the Land of Punt. (Other Egyptian inscriptions refer to earlier expeditions to that Land). It is very improbable that the incense (*'ntyw*) collected by the ancient Egyptians was in fact frankincense; it could have been myrrh; it was more likely "perfumed bdellium", the product of the tree *Commiphora erythraea*. The Land of Punt was not south Arabia, as is sometimes supposed, but its geographical position may never have been very determinate to the ancient Egyptians; most probably the incense was collected from what is now southern Eritrea. These Egyptian inscriptions provide no evidence for concluding that any organised commerce existed between south Arabia and Egypt at that time.

The use of incense in Palestine and Mesopotamia in very early times is attested in inscriptions and archaeologically, but it is probable that locally grown plants, such as galbanum, were used. The Sumerian incense was probably an aromatic wood. There is no evidence that frankincense was used.

The domestication of the camel provides a *terminus post quem* period for the overland incense trade from south Arabia to Palestine, since the view that donkeys may have been used as pack animals on this route before camels is not acceptable. Albright's view that the domesticated camel did not exist in northern Arabia before the end of the 12th century BC has to be modified. Domestication was a very long process and it was a long time before domesticated camels were used as pack animals. Although domesticated in south Arabia by the second millennium BC, it is improbable the camel was brought into significant use to transport incense northwards before the first millennium BC.

Chapter 3

The early Bible references to incense and the incense lands cannot be held as historical evidence for a date later than the Books concerned were compiled, which was often many centuries after the times they described. In consequence none of the biblical texts usually put forward to support an early date for the incense trade can be accepted as evidence of this. In any case many of these texts have other explanations. None of them bring the commencing date for the incense trade to any time earlier than is attested by other sources.

A careful examination of the biblical account of Solomon suggests that Ophir was probably (like Punt) Eritrea and no greater distance away. A number of reasons can be advanced for suggesting that the Queen of Sheba was not the ruler of the south Arabian kingdom of Saba as has always been supposed, but was probably the chief of a north Arabian tribe of Sabaeans engaged in the carriage of goods on the east-west trade route between Palestine and the Arabian Gulf. There is no evidence for the existence of direct trade between south Arabia and Palestine at that time.

Chapter 4

The earliest classical author to provide evidence for the use of frankincense and myrrh from Arabia is Herodotus, from whom it becomes apparent that a substantial trade existed by 500 BC. This ties in with the earliest archaeological evidence, lettering in south Arabian script on sherds found in Eilath which are dated to the fifth or sixth centuries BC.

The first eye-witness account of incense trees growing in south Arabia was provided by Theophrastus (*c.*295 BC), using the reports of reconnaissance vessels sent out by Alexander the Great.

Chapter 5

Cinnamon and cassia, as known in modern times, come from plants found only in the Far East. Yet the evidence in Pliny

231

and the *Periplus* that these products came from plants growing in the Horn of Africa is too strong to dismiss. The theory that they were brought direct to Madagascar from Indonesia and thence northwards to Somalia seems improbable. More likely the cinnamon and cassia of the ancient world came from African plants of other species until the similar but superior product of the Far East replaced them.

Chapter 6

Frankincense comes from trees of the genus *Boswellia*, the Arabian species being *B. sacra*. In Somalia it is collected from the *Mohr madow* tree (*B. carteri*) and *Yegaar* tree (*B. frereana*); considerable doubt exists over the identification of a third tree in Somalia called *Mohr Add* (*B. bhau-dajiana*), which has not been found again since its classification in 1860. Inferior forms of frankincense come from *B. papyrifera*, found in Ethiopia, Sudan and East Africa, and from the Indian species *B. serrata* (or *B. thurifera*). A frankincense-producing tree called *Boido* recorded in Somalia may be *B. papyrifera*. Other species of frankincense-producing *Boswellia* have been found in Socotra.

The belief that Arabian frankincense of classical times came only from Ẓufār is incorrect. From Ẓufār the ancient frankincense-growing region extended as far west as the Wadī Ḥagr area of Ḥaḍramawt where it has recently been found growing. The contention that it grew only at an elevation over 2000 feet is also incorrect, although the quality of gum from trees on the coastal plains may be inferior. Loose use of the Arabic word *lubān* to signify "incense" rather than in its true meaning of "frankincense" makes investigation of this problem difficult.

Myrrh is found growing to this day all over south and south-west Arabia, including 'Asīr, as well as in Somalia and Ethiopia. It comes from a number of different species of the genus *Commiphora*, but principally *Commiphora myrrha*. Ptolemy's "interior" and "exterior" myrrh-growing regions probably signified the regions respectively north and south of Wādī Gawf, the homeland of the Minaean merchants who controlled the trade.

Chapter 7

A number of bdelliums are produced in Arabia and Somalia which come from other species of *Commiphora*, some of them strongly resembling myrrh. These include the "perfumed bdellium" from *Commiphora erythraea* which was probably the *'ntyw* of the ancient Egyptians and the "scented myrrh" of Pliny. Related species grow in India and elsewhere. In classical times some of these may have been regarded as myrrhs.

The Arabian balsam tree *Commiphora gileadensis* (not to be confused with the "balm of Gilead" of Genesis, which probably came from a terebinth tree) is found widely but appears to be a different plant to the "balsam of Judaea" described by Pliny; in classical times its product was probably counted as a myrrh.

Chapter 8

Modern and classical accounts of the harvesting of the incense trees tally and from these the seasonal nature of the trade is apparent. The main frankincense crop of Arabia was harvested between April and June and stored locally until the monsoon finished in September to November. It was then taken to Shabwah, the crop from Somalia, Socotra and Ẓufār being first brought to Qana by sea. The secondary (spring) crop was collected in about February. Ships sailing to India with the south-west monsoon wind passed Qana before the main crop reached that port, but might load frankincense from the secondary crop on their return journey.

The incense trade expanded very considerably in the first two centuries AD, so that Pliny's description does not show it at its height. The development of Ẓufār as the main Arabian frankincense region may have come late to keep pace with that expansion. The trade ended fairly abruptly in the fourth century, principally due to the spread of Christianity, to the Roman economic decline and to warring between the south Arabian states.

The demand for frankincense was substantially greater than that for myrrh. Rough calculations on the basis of figures provided by Pliny suggest that in his time the total production was some 2500 to 3000 tons of frankincense and 450 to 600 tons of myrrh.

Chapter 9

It seems unlikely that frankincense from Ẓufār was ever taken
to Shabwah overland on any scale, the sea route to Qana
described in the *Periplus* being used instead. There was one
main route from Qana to Shabwah, passing through Wādī
Ḥagr, which was probably the high road of Pliny off which it
was a capital offence to deviate.

From Shabwah the main route went westwards through
Tumnaʿ and Mārib. During the hegemony of Qatabān it
probably followed a well organised road through Wādī
Markhah, the Mablaqah pass, Ḥarīb and Gūbah (where the
city of Nagia was located). But at times, especially during
periods of war, caravans travelled from Shabwah along a
more difficult northern route directly to Wādī Gawf.

Chapter 10

Because of the problems of organising staging posts and
ensuring security it is likely that there was a single route for
the main stream of traffic travelling north. To some extent
this route would have been dictated by topographical and
other considerations. But the route may have varied at
different periods with fluctuations in the state of security of
the different areas through which it passed.

From Nagrān the normal route probably went through the
area of Tathlīth and Bīshah (Ptolemy's Laththa and
Thumala) to Yathrib (now al-Madīnah), without passing
through Makkah, and thence to Ḥijrā (now Madā'in Ṣāliḥ)
and Petra.

The Gerrhaean merchants who had collected frankincense
from Shabwah probably took the same route as far as Tathlīth
and then followed the Wādī Dawāsir route to Ḥufūf (the most
likely site for Gerrha). Direct overland journeys between
Gerrha and Ẓufār, as suggested by some modern writers,
would have been quite impracticable.

Gaza was the main Mediterranean terminal for the incense
traffic in Pliny's time, but at other times Rhinocolura and
Ascalon were used. An alternative route branched off north of
Ḥijrā to Gaza through Aelana (near modern Eilath), where
south Arabian inscriptions of the fifth or sixth centuries BC
have been found. From these ports incense was taken to

Alexandria for processing or direct to Rome.

Once incense began to be collected by ships from south Arabian ports it was taken to Myos Hormos and other Egyptian ports (Berenice at a later period). Despite the statements of Strabo it is improbable that the Nabataean port of Leuce Come was much used for the incense trade.

Chapter 11

Recent studies of climatic change suggest Arabia may have shared with the Mediterranean, north Africa and the Middle East a moist interval from the late sixth to the late third millennium BC, which was followed by a period of pronounced aridity in the second millennium BC up to about 850 BC (except for a wet spell around 1200 BC).

Discoveries by Philby in south-west Arabia provide a number of indications of climatic change which fit into the above periods. Sand movement may also have had a considerable effect on the ecology of south Arabia.

A large area of ancient tombs north of Mārib may be the remnants of a culture of the sixth to third millennia moist period in the Ṣayhad, which is now a sand-dune desert. Religious ceremonials in pre-Islamic south Arabia may reflect this ancient ancestry and origin in the Ṣayhad and account for the legend of the lost city of Ubar.

General desiccation, attributable to a number of causes, has considerably reduced the vegetation of Arabia over the last two thousand years, with consequent significant ecological changes, and provides one reason why the incense trees of Arabia are now so rare.

Notes

Books or articles quoted in these notes by author and publication date only are listed with full title and details under author's name in the Bibliography.

Chapter 1: Incense, the Food of the Gods

1. On the general use of incense for religious purposes see Atchley, 1909, pp. 1–77
2. Miller, 1969, p. 85 (quoting *Orientis Graeci Inscriptiones Selectae*, 214. 40)
3. Athenaeus *The Deipnosophists* Bk 5, chs 8 and 9
4. Strabo *Geography* Bk 16, ch 1, para 20
5. In fact only Mark refers to myrrh on this occasion. Matthew has "vinegar mixed with gall". John records: "they filled a sponge with vinegar, and put upon it hyssop and put it in his mouth."
6. See Lucas, 1937, p. 27
7. Lucas, 1937, quotes an oil content of about 7 or 8 per cent in fresh myrrh, but more modern measurements give it a higher content. The *British Pharmaceutical Codex, 1973* quotes the constituents of myrrh as "25 to 40 per cent of resin, 57 to 61 per cent of gum, 7 to 17 per cent of volatile oil and 3 to 4 per cent of impurities". Perfumiers recognize the odorous components of frankincense as Pinene, Camphene and *dl*-Limonene and of myrrh as Pinene, *dl*-Limonene, Cumenic aldehyde, Bisabolene, Eugenal and *m*-Cresol (R. W. Moncrieff, 1967, *The Chemical Senses* Leonard Hill Books, London as quoted by Kennett, 1975)
8. Van Beek, 1960, p. 82. See also p. 131 above
23. Müller, 1976
10. Pliny *Natural History* Bk 12, ch 41, sec 83
11. Plutarch *Lives* ("Life of Sulla", para 38)
12. Miller, 1969, p. 7, quoting Dioscorides *De Materia Medica* trans. J. Goodyer, London, 1655
13. Theophrastus *Enquiry into Plants* Bk 9, ch 20
14. Schmidt, 1927, p. 8
15. Budge, 1913
16. Lane *Arabic–English Lexicon*
17. Müller, 1976
18. Drake-Brockman, 1912, p. 257
19. Thompson R., 1949, p. 346
20. See article on "Flora in the Aden Protectorate" in *The Aden Port Trust Annual, 1952/53*. Also Stark, 1942, Appendix, pp. 272–3.
21. Müller, 1976
22. Serjeant, 1960

23. Müller, 1976
24. Bent, 1900, p. 113
25. Bent, 1900, p. 121
26. Bent, 1900, p. 232
27. Wyman Bury, 1911, pp. 281–2
28. Scott, 1942, p. 69
29. Theophrastus *Concerning Odours* paras 11–13
30. Thompson R., 1949, p. 340
31. Pliny *Natural History* Bk 13, ch 2
32. Lionel Casson *Travel in the Ancient World* (Allen & Unwin, 1974) p. 177, quoting A. Hunt: *Catalogue of the Greek Papyri in the John Rylands Library at Manchester* (Manchester, 1891)
33. Exodus 30. 22–30
34. Athenaeus *The Deipnosophists* Bk 11, sec 464 and Bk 2, sec 66
35. Herodotus *Histories* Bk 2, para 86
36. Diodorus *Library of History* Bk 1, para 7
37. Thompson R., 1949, pp. 339–40
38. Budge, 1913
39. Lane, 1863, entry under *"Murr"*
40. Drake-Brockman, 1912, p. 247
41. Bent, 1900, p. 415
42. See under "Myrrh" in (1) Martindale *The Extra Pharmacopoeia* 26th Ed., 1972, Pharmaceutical Press, London and (2) *Pharmaceutical Formulas* Chemist and Druggist, London, 1956

Chapter 2: When the Trade Began

1. The principal references used for this chapter are Schoff, 1912; Thompson, 1948; Drake-Brockman, 1912; Naville, 1898; Breasted, 1906; Doresse, 1959; Hourani, 1951; and Bulliet, 1975
2. Breasted, 1906
3. V. Loret *La Résine de Terebinthe (Sonter) chez les anciens Egyptiens*, Cairo, 1949, as quoted by Dixon (Dixon, 1969) has identified *sntr* as a terebinth resin which grew in the deserts of Egypt itself. This identification is accepted by Dixon, but he can then suggest no reason to explain why *sntr* should have been imported from Punt. Dixon quotes an inscription of Rameses III which also refers to the importation of both *sntr* and *'ntyw* trees from Punt. Loret's identification would seem debatable.
4. Lucas, 1937, quotes E. Naville, L. J. Lieblein and G. Jequier as those translating it as frankincense. This matter is also touched on in Hepper, 1969
5. Lucas, 1937
6. Drake-Brockman, 1912, pp. 245 and 303–5

7. See Hepper, 1967 and Schoff, 1912

8. Breasted, 1906, Vol II, sec, 848 (p. 339)

9. Hourani, 1951, p. 7

10. See para 20 of the *Periplus of the Erythraean Sea*, quoted at page 90

11. Barnett, 1958, has reckoned their size at about 70 feet long, 17 or 18 feet wide and 4 or 5 feet deep.

12. Breasted, 1906, Vol II, sec 892 (p. 361)

13. ibid., sec 447

14. ibid., sec 491

15. ibid., sec 473

16. ibid., secs 509 and 518

17. Miller, 1969, p. 102

18. Van Beek, 1960, quoting J. A. Knudtzen *Die el-Amarna Tafeln I* (Leipzig, 1915) 22 III/29 and 25 IV/51

19. Pliny *Natural History* Bk 13, ch 2, para 9

20. ibid., Bk 13, ch 2, para 18

21. Theophrastus *Enquiry into Plants* Bk 9, ch 2, paras 1–2

22. Pliny *Natural History* Bk 12, ch 54, para 124

23. ibid., Bk 12, ch 56, para 126 and ch 59

24. See, for example, Wilkinson, 1854, Vol 1, p. 265

25. Exodus 30. 22–5

26. See also Black's *Bible Dictionary* under "Incense":— "references to incense are characteristic of source P. not source J., a fact that suggests the late introduction of incense, which was condemned by certain prophets because of its association with idolatrous rites."

27. It is of interest that the Persian country prescriptions listed (Budge, 1913, p. 688) in a supplement to the *Syriac Book of Medicine* include one: "to make serpents and reptiles flee from the house . . . pound and mix together the root of galbanum, the seed of sapesta, and the horn and hoof of a stag, and dregs of opium, and pour strong vinegar into the mixture, and then set it on fire inside the house, and all the reptiles will flee and make their escape from it."

28. Theophrastus *Enquiry into Plants* Bk 9, ch 9, para 2

29. See Atchley, 1909, p. 5; Usher, 1974 (under "Ferula"); Smith *Bible Dictionary* (under "Galbanum"); and Miller, 1969, pp. 99–101

30. Thomas D. W., 1967; see chapter on "Hazor" by Y. Yadin and on "Megiddo" by J. N. Schofield. Also illustration to article on "Incense" in Black's *Bible Dictionary*

31. Saggs, 1962, p. 354

32. Thompson R., 1949, pp. 337–40

33. Albright W.F., 1940; and Albright W.F., 1949, pp. 206–7.

Also Phillips, 1966, pp. 37–8. The Midianite raids are referred to in Judges 6.5

34. Tosi, 1974, pp. 162–3

35. Moscati, 1959, p. 35 (text and footnote); Thomas D.W., 1967, chapter on "Alalakh" by D. J. Wiseman, p. 134, note 54 (Camels known at Ugarit in the nineteenth century BC) Kitchen, 1966, pp. 79–80. Bulliet, 1975, pp. 58–64

36. Bulliet, 1975

37. See Kitchen, 1966

38. The evidence for knowledge of the camel in Egypt in Abraham's time and back to the pre-dynastic period is listed in Joseph P. Free "Abraham's Camels" (*Journal of Near Eastern Studies*, Vol 3, No 2, April 1944, pp. 110–36) and commented on in Bulliet, 1975

39. See note 33

40. Anati, 1968

Chapter 3: Bible Stories and the Queen of Sheba

1. For a more detailed account of the early history of the development of the Bible see Kenyon, 1958, from which the above paragraphs are principally derived. Kitchen, 1966, discusses the contribution of Middle Eastern scholarship and archaeology to the study of the Old Testament.

2. See Miller, 1969, p. 102, fn 2. Also page 126 above and n. 20, ch 7 below

3. This is now generally accepted. See for instance entries for "Myrrh" in Black's *Bible Dictionary* and Smith's *Dictionary of the Bible*. Curiously, however, the New English Bible has retained the translation "myrrh" (while substituting "gum tragacanth" for "spicery").

4. Neither cloth nor blue dye (indigo) appear in the list of exports from south Arabian ports which are given in the *Periplus of the Erythraean Sea*, although the *imports* included "purple cloths, fine and coarse" (see page 90)

5. South Arabians of today regard the time of 'Ād as a pre-Islamic period when the people of 'Ād occupied their country, and they believe that these people were a race of giants who perished because of their misdeeds. Eber the son of Saleh is held to be the prophet Hūd whose tomb is today a sacred place in Wādī Haḍramawt and who is reputed to have warned the people of 'Ād of their impending doom.

6. See the articles under "Sheba" and "Dedan" in Smith's *Dictionary of the Bible*. The genealogical tables are also discussed in some detail in Montgomery, 1934 (ch 3)

7. See Hitti, 1970, p. 37. The information derives from the texts of inscriptions to be found in Pritchard, 1950, pp. 284, 285 and 286

8. Pliny *Natural History* Bk 6, ch 32, para 151

9. Strabo *Geography* Bk 16, ch 4, sec 21

10. Pritchard, 1974, contains a series of essays by eminent scholars which consider the Queen of Sheba story from different aspects, together with a good bibliography on this subject.

11. Philby, 1939, p. 11, observed that in the carving at Chartres cathedral, where the Queen of Sheba is shown with Solomon and Balaam, her right foot is discreetly hidden by her clothing. Watson, 1974, discusses the extension of this legend of the hairy foot into the European belief that she was goat-footed.

12. See Hamdani *al-Iklil* sec 29. The complicated Islamic traditions are discussed in the chapter by W. Montgomery-Watt on "The Queen of Sheba in Islamic Tradition" in Pritchard, 1974

13. See chapter by Edward Ullendorrf on "The Queen of Sheba in Ethiopic Tradition" in Pritchard, 1974

14. Their source for these stories may have been the document described as "the book of the acts of Solomon" in I Kings 11. 41 and ascribed in 2 Chronicles 10. 29 to Nathan, Ahijah the Shilonite and Iddo the Seer.

15. American excavations during 1938–40 produced traces of shipbuilding at the Solomonic site of Ezion-Geber. See Hourani, 1951, p. 9

16. Harden, 1971, p. 150. Pritchard, 1974, plate 12. H. von Wissmann, article on "Bedw" in *The Encyclopaedia of Islam* (new ed.) Vol 1, p. 881

17. Harden, 1971, p. 209, quoting R. D. Barnett *A Catalogue of the Nimrud Ivories . . . in the British Museum* (London, 1957)

18. Thompson O., 1948, p. 30

19. Josephus *Antiquities of the Jews* Bk 8, ch 7, sec 2.2 and Bk 8, ch 6, sec 14. The term "Ethiopians" frequently embraced all Africans, but it has been suggested that Josephus may have misread the Hebrew word *tukiyyim*, meaning "peacocks", for *kussiyim*, meaning "Ethiopians" in the sense of "black slaves", when he described the goods brought back from Ophir as "silver and gold . . . and a great quantity of ivory, Ethiopians and apes".

20. Miller, 1969, pp. 264–5

21. Harden, 1971, pp. 159–60. Ezekiel, referring to Tyre, states: "Thy rowers have brought thee into great waters" (Ezekiel 27.26)

22. Herodotus *Histories* Bk 6

23. ibid., Bk 2, sec 11

24. H. von Wissmann, article on "Bedw" (see n. 16 above)

25. Pritchard, 1974, p. 9

26. Josephus *Antiquities of the Jews* Bk 8, ch 6, sec 5

27. Principally various publications by Mlle J. Pirenne

28. An inscription of the second or third century AD records a war by the king of Saba against the king of Ḥaḍramawt when the Sabaeans rescued "the queen of Ḥaḍramawt", who was the king of Saba's sister. (See Beeston, 1976/A, p. 47)

29. Cf. Pritchard, 1974A, p. 35: "The general impression gleaned from a survey of the archaeological remains that have come down from the tenth century—and they are considerable—is that cities were built on a small scale, that buildings were simple and modestly constructed from materials locally available, and that the standard of living was far from luxurious when compared to that prevailing in other parts of the ancient Near Eastern world. Solomon is mentioned in no Egyptian, or Mesopotamian, or Phoenician document. Only from the Bible do we learn that he lived."

30. See n. 14 above

31. Hitti, 1970, pp. 37–8. See also Nadia Abbott: "Pre-Islamic Arab Queens", *American Journal of Semitic Languages and Literature* Vol. 58, No 1, Jan 1941. Also Pritchard, 1950, pp. 283, 285 and 286

Chapter 4: The Greek Geographers

1. Strabo *Geography* Bk 6, ch 1, secs 2–4 and 10

2. It was at Pergamum that the paged book, written on parchment, was developed to replace the papyrus scroll.

3. On the Alexandria Library see Hitti, 1970, p. 166; Bean, 1966, p. 75; and Akurgal, 1973, p. 80

4. Herodotus *Histories* Bk 4, sec 44. Athenaeus also mentions Scylax's exploration of the Indus River, but furnishes no information about the voyage round Arabia.

5. Herodotus *Histories* Bk 3, secs 108–15

6. See Anati, 1968, Vol 2, Pt 1, "Fat Tailed Sheep in Arabia"

7. Herodotus *Histories* Bk 3, sec 108

8. Ingrams H., 1945, noted the highly poisonous red viper, which attacks by leaping in the air at its target, in the Wādī Ḥagr, west of al-Mukallā. Lane, 1863, refers to a snake called in Arabic "aṣalah": he describes it as "a very malignant and noxious serpent, short (like a piece of rope) and broad, red, but not intensely red, very deadly, which springs upon a man or horseman like the shaft of an arrow and kills everything upon which it blows." Both the Horned Viper and Puff Adder are common in south Arabia. The "flying snakes" of India and south-east Asia are various tree snakes of the *Chrysopelea* species, which can glide short distances to earth; this species is not known in Arabia and does not seem compatible with the snake described by Herodotus.

9. Strabo *Geography* Bk 16, ch 4, sec 19. Theophrastus (*Enquiry into Plants* Bk 9, ch 5, sec 2) refers to "Numerous snakes which have a deadly bite" found in the Arabian valleys in which cinnamon grew. Diodorus Siculus (*Library of History*, Bk 3, ch 47, sec 2) noted that in the "most fragrant forests" of the Sabaeans "is a multitude of snakes, the colour of which is dark red, their length a span, and their bites altogether incurable; they bite by leaping upon their victim, and as they spring on high they leave a stain of blood upon his skin." This information of Diodorus derived from Agatharchides and a similar account coming from the same source is contained in the extract from Photius quoted on page 70. "This kind of snake has a red colour, is about a span in length and has an incurable bite if it draws blood higher than the flanks. It inflicts its wounds by leaping in the air."

10. See Baron, 1972, especially ch 8

11. Gleuck, 1939

12. Strabo *Geography* Bk 16, ch 1, sec 11

13. Arrian *Campaigns of Alexander* Bk 7, sec 20

14. ibid., Bk 7, sec 21

15. See Herodotus *Histories* Bk 2, sec 158

16. Theophrastus *Enquiry into Plants* Bk 9, ch 4, sec 4

17. See N. G. L. Hammond *A History of Greece to 322 B.C.* (Oxford University Press, 2nd Ed. 1967), p. 636. Also Pirenne, 1961, p. 69

18. Strabo *Geography* Bk 16, ch 4, sec 4

19. Theophrastus *Enquiry into Plants* Bk 9, ch 4, secs 2 and 5

20. Pirenne, 1961, p. 69

21. Bean, 1966, pp. 31 and 273, describes this.

22. Strabo *Geography* Bk 16, ch 4, secs 2–4

23. One suggestion is that this refers to the Minaean trading colony which was formed at Dedān, in northern Arabia, at about this time. See Pirenne, 1961, p. 80

24. Pirenne, 1961, p. 81

25. Strabo *Geography* Bk 16, ch 4, sec 19

26. Hourani, 1951, p. 18

27. The Greek text and a Latin translation of these portions of Photius have been published with notes in Latin by C. Muller (Carolus Mullerus) in *Geographi Graeci Minores* (Paris, 1855). A translation of this into French is contained in Pirenne, 1961. The English translation published here has been made from the revised text of Photius published by R. Henry in 1974 which corrected certain inaccuracies found in Muller's text. Mr Hutchinson's translation has, at the author's request, kept closely to the original Greek syntax and sentences, providing a fairly literal rendering.

28. Botting, 1958, p. 160

29. In the Strabo/Artemidorus text quoted earlier, the sentence appears: "those who live close to one another receive in continuous succession the loads of aromatics and deliver them to their neighbour as far as Syria and Mesopotamia." This does not appear in either the Photius or Diodorus texts and seems more likely to be an interpolation drawn by Artemidorus from another source.

30. Strabo *Geography* Bk 16, ch 4, sec 24

31. ibid., Bk 16, ch 4, sec 22

32. Arguments about how far Aelius Gallus penetrated into south Arabia are discussed in detail in Pirenne, 1961, pp. 98–124. One possibility she does not mention is raised by the tradition of an army of Europeans which reached a ruin site now known as Māriba, near Niṣāb, in the Awlaqī area about 100 miles south-east of Mārib; this is described in Belhaven, 1955, and in a novel on the theme, *The Eagle and the Sun*, by the same author. Cassius Dio (*Roman History*, Bk 53), possibly with Livy as his source, states that the expedition advanced as far as "Athlula" (cf. Strabo's "Athrula"), which conforms better with the identification Yathul. For Beeston's proposal that "Marsiaba" was al-'Abr see Beeston, 1979

33. Strabo *Geography* Bk 16, ch 4, sec 24. Cassius Dio *Roman History* Bk 53

Chapter 5: Pliny, Ptolemy and the "Periplus"

1. See Pirenne, 1961, quoting Strabo Bk 16 ch 4 sec 25. Also Wolfgang Aly: "*Strabon von Amaseia. Untersuchungen uber Text, Aufbau und Quellen der Geographika*", Bonn, 1957. It may also be noted that Cassius Dio gives a brief description of the campaign (*Roman History*, Bk 53) possibly derived from Livy.

2. Strabo *Geography* Bk 17, ch 1, sec 13

3. Pliny *Natural History* Bk 6, ch 26, sec 101. The Rackham translation from which this passage is quoted gives Ocelis, Muza and Muziris as Cella, Mokha and Cranganore respectively. These identifications are disputable. It is the former names which appear in Pliny's text. Inscriptional evidence has provided another name for ancient Mokha, while Muza may either be an inland town now named Mawza', with a port bearing the same name, or else, perhaps more probably, it may lie a little to the north of Mokha.

4. Strabo *Geography* Bk 6, ch 4, sec 5

5. Pliny *Natural History* Bk 6, ch 32, secs 154 and 155. This translation incorporates several amendments proposed by Professor Beeston to the translation by Rackham.

6. Pliny *Natural History* Bk 6, ch 32, secs 160–62

7. ibid., Bk 12, ch 17, sec 32. "*Tabashir*" is well known to early Arab sources and occurs in a list of mediaeval commodities traded

in Aden (personal communication from Professor Serjeant)

8. Pliny *Natural History* Bk 12, ch 37, secs 73 and 74

9. Miller, 1969, p. 114, suggests *Cistus ladaniferous*. Nigel Hepper (personal communication) notes that this is found in Spain and north Africa and suggests that the source of Biblical ladanum in the eastern Mediterranean region may have been *Cistus laurifolius* from Turkey. A. W. Anderson: 1956: *Plants of the Bible* (Crosby, Lockwood & Son, London) has suggested *Cistus villosus* or *Cistus salvifolius*.

10. Pliny *Natural History* Bk 12, ch 42, secs 85–8

11. ibid., Bk 12, ch 43, secs 95–7

12. Miller, 1969, pp. 153–72

13. See Stevenson, 1932

14. See Gervase Matthew: "The Periplus of the Erythraean Sea and South Arabia", *Proceedings of the Seminar for Arabian Studies*, Cambridge, 1970

15. Pirenne, 1961

16. Mussel is (by translation) *Myos Hormos*. See page 210

17. White Village—Leuce Come. The site of this is uncertain, but see n. 52, ch 10

18. Burnt Island: thought to be the volcanic island now known as Gabal Tair

19. Saua: Pliny's Save; probably a ruin site just outside modern Ta'izz. See page 80

20. This passage has been regarded as important to the dating, since it may refer to a time when two Roman emperors ruled together (which happened once in the second century (AD 161–169) and three times in the third century (AD 211–212, 253–259 and 286–305) and certainly indicates a late era in south Arabian history, when the Himyarites were becoming paramount.

21. The phrase "Gebanite-Minaean" is an editorial emendation of a corrupted passage in the original text and is based on Pliny's mention of this type of myrrh. Its appearance does not therefore provide any corroboration for the use of the word "Gebanite", which is otherwise confined to Pliny.

22. The Far side: i.e. the coast of Somalia

23. Diodorus: i.e. Perim

24. Eudaemon Arabia: i.e. Aden. Ptolemy also showed this name.

25. "Charibael" has been inserted in the text of the manuscript used in place of "Caesar", which was assumed to be a corruption.

26. Barygaza: thought to be Broach, a port on the west coast of India south of Baroda (latitude 22°)

27. Syagrus: i.e. Rās Fartak

28. Dioscorida: i.e. Socotra

29. Azania: location uncertain

30. Damirica: i.e. the coastal area of Cochin and Travancore, in south India
31. Zenobian: i.e. the Kuria Muria islands
32. Sarapis: i.e. Masira island
33. Apologus: probably the ancient city of Obollah (or Ubulu)
34. Ommana: site uncertain
35. See Pirenne, 1975. Also Phillips, 1966
36. In Bk 1. 17 Ptolemy stated: "(Marinus) places the bay of Sachalita on the western shore of the promontory of Syagrus, but all who navigate these parts unanimously agree with us that it is toward the east from Syagrus and that Sachalita is a region of Arabia and from it the Bay of Sachalita takes the name."
37. See Thompson, O., 1948, especially pp. 274 and 304

Chapter 6: The Trees and Where They Grew

1. Theophrastus *Enquiry into Plants* Bk 9, ch 4, secs 2–3
2. ibid., Bk 9, ch 4, secs 7–9
3. Pliny *Natural History* Bk 12, chs 33 and 34
4. ibid., Bk 12, ch 31
5. Carter, 1848
6. Birdwood, 1870
7. In Birdwood's spelling
8. Despite the findings of Carter and Birdwood this belief persisted. It appears, for example, in A. K. Nairne *The Flowering Plants of Western India*, published in 1894, and in Smith's *Dictionary of the Bible. Boswellia balsamifera* is another species name now equated with *B. serrata*.
9. See Lucas, 1937, and Hepper, 1969. Birdwood, 1870, gave the Ethiopian name of *Boswellia papyrifera* as "*makker*" or "*angouah*". The former is more correctly transliterated *mäqär*. The latter name should more correctly be spelled "*anqūa*" and designates a myrrh tree (personal communication from Professor W. W. Müller).
10. See Usher, 1974—entry under "Boswellia"
11. Dr Flückiger of Bern in an article in "Schweizerische Wochenschrift für Pharmacie" for 13 May 1864
12. Hunter, 1877, using information from Miles, 1872
13. Miles, 1872
14. Professor W. W. Müller has suggested (personal communication) that the word "*boido*" may simply have been a distortion from the Somali word "*beyo*" (fem. "*beyadi*"), meaning a frankincense tree in general.
15. Drake-Brockman, 1912, pp. 256–60 and 305–6
16. See Thomas Wright (Ed.) *The Travels of Marco Polo*, Bohn, London, 1899, ch 41 and 42 (pp. 440–42)

17. See Gibb, 1929, p. 13. "Hasik" is identified there with Hasikiyah, an island in the Kuria Muria group, but the mainland port of Hasik appears far more probable.

18. Bent, 1900, pp. 253-5

19. ibid., p. 380

20. Botting, 1958, p. 160. The species thus described may be one peculiar to Socotra called *Boswellia ameero*. This is referred to on p. 208 and photographed at Fig. 128 of the Naval Intelligence Division handbook, 1946

21. Thomas, B., 1932, p. 122 and photograph. The latter is reproduced in Hitti, 1970, p. 35

22. Phillips, 1966, p. 183

23. Van Beek, 1960

24. Miles, 1872, p. 64

25. Hepper, 1969. Hepper obtained information and photographs from Dr Ray Cleveland, who visited Ẓufār in 1958 and 1960 in an expedition of the American Foundation for the Study of Man organised by Dr Wendell Phillips, and also from Mr J. Lavaranos, who collected specimens from Ẓufār in 1966

26. Grohmann, 1922, p. 136

27. In a paper published since this book was written Professor Monod reports (Monod, 1979) finding frankincense trees in many parts of the Ḥadramawt region, including trees north of al-Mukallā growing to a height of up to 8 metres. All the trees sighted were the one species and he concludes that *Boswellia sacra* is the only species which grows in Arabia. See also p. 113 above and n. 42, ch 6, below

28. Grohmann, 1922, pp. 141 and 147

29. Drake-Brockman, 1912, pp. 260-61. But see also the reference on page 120 above to a possible myrrh called *Qarān*.

30. Phillips, 1966. The American Foundation for the Study of Man excavated the citadel area of the site at Khor Rori and found the first inscriptions. Others have been discovered since and discussed by Dr Jacqueline Pirenne (Pirenne, 1975), who proposes a date in the 1st century BC on palaeographic grounds. Beeston (Beeston, 1976B) prefers a century or two later for linguistic reasons.

31. Pliny *Natural History* Bk 12, ch 30, secs 51-3. Passages italicized are amendments from the Rackham translation which have been proposed by Professor Beeston.

32. Quoted by Stark, 1942, Appendix. See also Sprenger, 1864

33. This reference to the name Sarīr has been drawn to my attention by Professor Beeston; Professor Serjeant, however, prefers a derivation from *Sirr/Sarr*, meaning a valley. On the general question of the frankincense region see Groom, 1977, and also Wissman, 1977

34. Carter, 1848, p. 388

35. Ingrams, D., 1949, p. 118. See also Naval Intelligence Division Handbook, 1946. Mrs Ingrams names these ports as, from west to east, Qishn, al-Gayda, Judhib, Rakhyut, Risut, 'Auqad, Salālah, Hafah, Taqa Marbut, Sudh and Hadhbaram (her spellings). From Qishn to Hadhbaram is a direct distance of about 300 miles. The first three ports listed are all in Mahrah territory, Qishn being about 120 miles from the border with Ẓufār. On Niebuhr's evidence frankincense was being exported from Mahrah in the eighteenth century; the fact that it was still being exported from Mahrah ports in the twentieth century must mean that this trading had continued through the nineteenth century; the information supplied to the Bents that the Mahrah trees were no longer tapped must therefore have been incorrect.

36. Stark, 1942, Appendix

37. Thomas, B., 1932, p. 123

38. Von Wissmann and Van der Meulen, 1933, photographed opposite p. 25. Serjeant, 1974, p. 221 observes that *lubān* coming from "the upper parts of the mountains in the Shihr region" is still traded in ash-Shiḥr.

39. Stark, 1942, Appendix

40. Ingrams, H., 1945. Earlier Mrs Ingrams was told that there were many "incense trees" in Wādī Mardaha and in the hills north of Qana in the Wādī Ḥagr region (Ingrams, D., 1941). See also Bent, 1894, pp. 318–19 (frankincense and myrrh trees in the gullies of the Jol).

41. Personal communication from Professor Serjeant. See also Serjeant, 1960. Philby even mentioned "frankincense trees" in 'Asīr, known locally as *A'raba* and growing at about 6000 feet, but from his photograph it is clear that this was not frankincense, although some variety of incense, called *lubān* locally, was evidently obtained from it (Philby, 1952, p. 403 and Fig. 31 opposite p. 353)

42. Monod, 1979. Professor Monod's report was published after this book was completed. He found frankincense trees in some sixteen places and was told of their existence at a number of other localities. The most westerly trees he discovered were in side valleys of Wādī Amāqīn, to the west of Wādī Ḥagr.

43. Phillips, 1966, p. 206

44. Hepper, 1969

45. Van Beek, 1958, 1960 and other articles

46. Miles, 1872, p. 64

47. Strabo *Geography* Bk 16, ch 4, sec 14. "Notu-Ceras" was modern Cape Garde-Fui.

48. Strabo *Geography* Bk 15, ch 2, sec 3

49. Arrian *Campaigns of Alexander* Bk 6, sec 22

50. Miller has proposed that, as true nard is not found today in

this area, the nard referred to here may have been "nard-grass" or "sweet-rush" (*Cymbopogon schoenanthus*) (Miller, 1969, p. 90). He makes no suggestions regarding the myrrh.

51. Miller, 1969, p. 104, quoting A. Flückiger and D. Hanbury *Pharmacographia*, London, 1874

52. Grohmann, 1922, pp. 151–2

53. A. Deflers, *Voyages au Yemen*, Klincksieck, Paris, 1889

54. Harris, 1844, Vol 2 Appendix 2 (p. 414) refers to myrrh in Ethiopia, where it was known as *Kurbeta*, growing "on the borders of Efāt, in the jungle of the Hāwash and in the Adel desert", adding that the gum, called *Hofali*, was collected for export. On the general information in this paragraph and following passages see Ingrams D., 1949, p. 119; Naval Intelligence Handboook, 1946, pp. 204 and 533; and Grohmann, 1922, pp. 151–2. A photograph in Van der Meulen, 1947, (Illustr. 22), shows a myrrh tree growing in the mountains north of Dathīnah (at about 5000 feet). Dr Bowen found a myrrh tree in Bayḥān (Bowen and Albright, 1958, p. 62) and discovered traces of what he suggested speculatively might have been ancient myrrh groves in that area. Dr Pirenne has recently found myrrh trees growing on the hills near Shabwah, together with balsam trees (*bashām*) (personal communication).

55. Hunter, 1877, p. 114

56. Grohmann, 1922, p. 151, gives '*Aqor* (or *Akker*) for the name in Zufār, but that would appear to be *Commiphora mukul*, which yields a bdellium (see p. 124 above and notes 12–17, ch 7, below)

57. Drake-Brockman, 1912

58. Personal communication from F. N. Hepper, to whom I am also indebted for other advice used in this section.

59. Botting, 1958, p. 160

60. Drake-Brockman, 1912, p. 243, quoting Johnston: *Travels in Southern Abyssinia*, Vol I, p. 249

61. Drake-Brockman, 1912, pp. 242–5 and 302–5

62. Bury, 1911, p. 173

63. G. J. Letham, 1920: "*Colloquial Arabic: Shuwa Dialect of Bornu, Nigeria and of the Region of Lake Chad*" (Crown Agents for the Colonies, London) lists under the trees of that area the "African myrrh (*Balsamodendron africanum*)" (i.e. *Commiphora africana*) of which he gives the local Arabic name as "*Qafal*". The same tree is also found in Ethiopia and in Sudan, where it is known as *Qafalah* (some authorities have erroneously translated this Sudan Arabic word as meaning a frankincense tree). As noted on page 119 above, *Qafal* is the local name for *Commiphora simplicifolia* in south-west Arabia. Thus the word seems to have been taken from Arabia and applied in Arabic-speaking Africa to other species of *Commiphora*. The *qafal* wood sold in Cairo may therefore have derived from

Ethiopia and Sudan as well as from south-west Arabia, perhaps applying to wood from species of *Commiphora* which produced a similar perfume when burnt.

64. Philby, 1952, p. 597. Philby found "copses of acacia and 'qataf', with a sprinkling of 'basham'" near the coast in mountains on the Yemen-Saudi border region. (Basham = balsam)

65. Grohmann, 1922, p. 151. Professor Müller has informed me that W. Hein, in his unpublished "Nachlass", gives the Mahrah word as *dagayīg*, which seems more likely to be correct.

66. F. N. Hepper—personal communication

67. See entry for *Commiphora* in Usher, 1974. Also n. 56, ch 6

Chapter 7: Incense, Ancient and Modern and "Far-Side"

1. Hunter, 1877, pp. 110–25
2. Naval Intelligence Division handbook, 1946, p. 533
3. See *Colonial Annual Report—Aden—1947*, Her Majesty's Stationery Office, p. 23
4. Hunter, 1877, p. 115
5. See Naval Intelligence Division Handbook, 1946, pp. 204 and 533 concerning this and subsequent details. On "Stacte" see page 13 above
6. Theophrastus *Enquiry into Plants* Bk 9, ch 4, sec 10
7. Theophrastus *Concerning Odours* sec 6, para 29
8. For this and subsequent details about the Somali produce see Drake-Brockman, 1912, pp. 245–9 and 302–5. Also N.I.D. handbook, as in n. 5 above. Also relevant headings in Usher, 1974
9. Quoted by Grohmann, 1922, pp. 153–5
10. Miles, 1872, p. 64
11. Grohmann, 1922, p. 140, n. 4
12. Nairne, 1894, p. 51
13. Naval Intelligence Division Handbook, 1946, p. 533; see also n. 56, ch 6, above
14. Carter, 1848, fn on p. 388
15. Usher, 1974, under "Commiphora Mukul"
16. Quoted in Wohaibi, 1973, p. 159
17. Grohmann, 1922, p. 155 (quoting Glaser)
18. Pliny *Natural History* Bk 12, ch 35, secs 68–71
19. Personal communication from F. N. Hepper
20. Miller, 1969, p. 102 (fn). See page 41 and n. 2 ch 3 above). Nigel Hepper has suggested (personal communication) that Balm of Gilead may have been *Pistacia lentiscus*. See n. 33 below.
21. Ingrams D., 1949, p. 119; this gives the name of the tree as *Timdud*, which is in fact the name in Mahrah (Hirsch gives "*timdūd*", so Professor Müller has observed to me)

22. Drake-Brockman, 1912, pp. 254–5
23. Harris, 1844, Vol 1, p. 11
24. Grohmann, 1922, p. 140
25. ibid. (quoting C. Ritter)
26. Philby, 1952, p. 597
27. This discovery is described in Hansen, 1964, pp. 236–8
28. Lane, 1863, under *"Bashām"*. Lane's main sources for this were the Tāj al-'Arūs and Abu-Hanīfah ad-Dīnawari's *Book of Plants*.
29. Sprenger, 1875, p. 38
30. Josephus, Bk 15, ch 4, sec 2
31. Pliny *Natural History* Bk 12, ch 54, secs 111–12
32. Theophrastus *Enquiry into Plants* Bk 9, ch 1, sec 6 and Bk 9, ch 6, sec 1. Strabo mentions balsam from Arabia, quoting Artemidorus and describing it as a product of the coast of the Sabaeans (Strabo *Geography* Bk 16, ch 4, sec 19). Agatharchides, as quoted by Photius, referred to balsam growing on the coast (para 97, quoted on page 70 above); Diodorus Siculus quoted the same passage (*Library of History* Bk 3, sec 46)
33. Personal communication—see n. 20 above. Other possibilities suggested by Hepper are *Pistacia terebinthus*, *Balanites aegyptiaca* (a balm drawn from seeds), *Liquidamber orientalis* or possibly a species of *Cistus*.
34. See *"The Eastern Key"*, a translation by K. Hafuth Zand and J. and I. Videan of 'Abd al-Latīf al-Baghdādi's "Kitāb al-Ifādah wa'l-'Itibār"; published Allen & Unwin, London, 1965; pp. 41–5
35. Drake-Brockman, 1912, p. 254
36. Personal communication from Dr J. Pirenne
37. Grohmann, 1922, p. 140 (text and footnote). Grohmann wrote: "It is uncertain whether the tree called *bashām* belongs to the frankincense-producing trees. According to Glaser's Diary VI page 29 it is the true Arabian frankincense tree and the gum called *lubān shehri* comes partly from it. Yet according to his Diary VI page 25 it yielded *lubān bedwī*. In Zufār it does not produce any gum and is known as *shiqāf*. One Somali thought it was identical with the *kabrārro*, another doubted this but thought the gum identical with the *ḥaqar*." The *ḥaqar* may be the *Yahar* or *Yegaar* tree (*Boswellia frereana*). In a footnote Grohmann quoted another passage from Glaser (Skizze I page 50) that: "the *bashām* produces a type of frankincense which resembles the genuine product well enough to deceive persons with expert knowledge of Arabian incense". These observations by Glaser were of course the record of remarks made to him by persons he questioned during his time in the Yemen
38. Drake-Brockman, 1912, p. 255
39. Naval Intelligence Division handbook, 1946, pp. 532–3

40. Ibn-Battuta called the frankincense tree "al-Kundooroo". Landberg (*Études sur les Dialectes de l'Arabie Méridionale—I—Hadramoût*, pp. 495–7) has suggested the word *kandar*, used in south Arabia to describe shaving the head, may originate from this act, being a prelude to perfuming the head. An additional word for frankincense is *qunnuq* (Badger *English/Arabic Lexicon*) also found as *kunnuk*; this may derive from Iranian *kunduruk*. (On this and the derivation of *kundur* I am indebted to Professor W. W. Müller.)

41. Birdwood, 1870, quoting information by Cruttenden, Kempthorne and Vaughan. The term *mayti* is still in use in Somalia (personal communication from Mr Neville Chittick).

42. Hunter, 1877, p. 113. Hunter gives "*amshot*", Glaser "*mashatt*". Landberg, 1898, p. 240, noted very tall trees in Wādī Girdān called "*mushaṭ*", the wood of which was very hard and used for making combs, hence the name. He was told this was also the name of an incense. Van der Meulen, 1947, p. 112, recorded this tree in Wādī Girdān as "*meshōt*", Doe and Serjeant ("A Fortified Town House in Wadi Jirdan"—I—*BSOAS* Vol 38, Pt 1, 1975, p. 1) as "*mushṭ (Polypodium crenatum)*", quoting Landberg. There is no evidence that the *mushaṭ* trees of Wādī Girdān produce incense.

43. Drake-Brockman, 1912, p. 256

44. The word "*Shehri*" could possibly derive from "*Shahara*", the local name for the Qarā mountains in Ẓufār and originating from the Shahara tribe which was once dominant in Ẓufār (although now only a remnant is left).

45. See, for example, Birdwood, 1870, p. 135 (quoting Vaughan *Pharmaceutical Journal* Vol 12, 1853,—"luban saharee")

46. Birdwood, 1870

47. Although *muslika* would seem to relate to Arabic *maslak* (= way, road, path) the sense here is not apparent.

48. Drake-Brockman, 1912, pp. 257 and 305. Five different sorts of Somalia-grown frankincense (names not specified) were on sale in the Mogadishu sūq in 1980; a Somalia decree of 1972 lists two categories, *Beyo* and *Maydi*, each with three qualities (personal communication from Miss Ann Bamford).

49. The "*Ṭabaq*" tree listed by Grohmann (see p. 109 above) seems likely to be a corrupt rendering of "*Habbak*".

50. Grohmann, 1922, p. 147 (quoting Flückiger)

51. Neither did Grohmann list names for the product of other possible frankincense-producing trees he recorded, as detailed on p. 109 above; (it is evident that some of these trees cannot in fact be frankincense trees at all).

52. Thomas, B., 1932, p. 123. J. R. L. Carter has since confirmed that these terms are still in use (personal communication).

53. Bent, 1900, p. 252. *Lakt* may derive from *laqaṭ* (= to pick up),

perhaps inferring frankincense collected from trees growing wild and not owned by individuals. *Resimi* appears to be *rasmi* (= official, formal, regular), possibly here inferring cultivated frankincense or frankincense collected from private estates.

54. The Naval Intelligence Division Handbook, 1946, recorded four kinds of frankincense (p. 206 and also quoted by Stark, 1942, p. 14) said to be used by Aden merchants; source not indicated. These were *"hoja'i"*, *"shehri"*, *"samhali"* and *"rasmi"*. However *hoja'i* looks as if it may be a confusion with the Somali *hodai* (spelt by Miles *"hodthai"*) or *haddi*, both bdelliums, while *samhali* may simply be a corruption of "Somali".

55. Personal communication from J. R. L. Carter

56. Miles, 1872, p. 64. Hunter, 1877, p. 113. Grohmann, 1922, p. 147, recorded one type of frankincense included under *lubān shehri* as "the gum of the *moḥr* tree *(fuṣūs)*". *"Fusus"* is clearly the plural form of Arabic *fuṣṣ* (= gemstone) i.e. *fuṣūs*. *"Safee"* is presumably Arabic *ṣāfi* (= clear). *"Muḥamdal"* appears to be Arabic *mujandal* (= stone-like)

57. Drake-Brockman, 1912, pp. 256 and 305. See also Naval Intelligence Division Handbook, 1946, p. 206.

58. Miles, 1872, p. 64

59. Bent, 1900, p. 252

60. Drake-Brockman, 1912, p. 257

61. Birdwood, 1870, p. 134 (quoting Cruttenden (1837))

62. Bent, 1900, p. 253

63. Naval Intelligence Division Handbook, 1946, p. 206

64. Ingrams, D., 1949, p. 204. This figure is quoted for imports from ports of the Aden Protectorate alone, but seems more likely to cover the imports from Ẓufār as well.

65. Cf. Theophrastus *Enquiry into Plants*—"All frankincense is gathered in the rough and is like bark in appearance" (Bk 9, ch 4, sec 10)

66. Cf. Theophrastus *Enquiry into Plants*—"Some say that the frankincense tree is more abundant in Arabia, but finer in the adjacent islands over which the Arabians bear rule; for there it is said that they mould the gum on the trees to any shape they please." (Bk 9, ch 4, sec 10)

67. Cf. Theophrastus *Enquiry into Plants*—"Some of the lumps of gum are very large, so that one is large enough in bulk to fill the hand and in weight is more than a third of a pound." (Bk 12, ch 4, sec 10)

68. A "mina" would be about 1lb 9oz (Aeginetan weight) or 1lb 5oz (Attic weight).

69. Pliny *Natural History* Bk 12, ch 32, secs 58–62 and 65

70. Schoff, 1912

71. For the most part these identifications follow Schoff, 1912, pp. 73–87

72. Pliny *Natural History* Bk 12, ch 16

73. Miles, 1872, p. 65

74. See Grohmann, 1922, and G. Ryckmans "Inscriptions Sud-Arabes" 3rd Series (No 136), *Le Museon*, 1935

Chapter 8: The Harvest and the Trade

1. Cf. Pliny's information about this in the passage quoted in pages 136–137 above

2. Theophrastus *Enquiry into Plants* Bk 9, ch 4, secs 4–6

3. Bent, 1900, p. 252

4. Thomas B., 1932, p. 122

5. Miles, 1872, p. 65

6. The starting dates of the seasons are worked out by the star calendars, which vary in different regions. The dates used in the Ta'izz region of Yemen and in Wadi Ḥaḍramawt, which are similar, are 22 March, 22 June, 23 September and 23 December. See Serjeant, 1954 and 1974B

7. See Serjeant, 1963, pp. 174 and 178

8. Beeston, 1956, p. 19

9. See Thomas B., 1932, p. 123. Passing through a grove of frankincense trees, Thomas recorded: "Its Qara owners, herdsmen and not pickers, are content to rent it to Kathiri and Mashaiyikh for half the produce."

10. See, for example, Stark, 1943, p. 15; Ingrams H., 1945; Serjeant, 1960; Miles, 1872; Miles and Munzinger, 1871

11. Hunter, 1877, p. 110

12. Bent, 1900, p. 252

13. Pliny *Natural History* Bk 12, ch 30, sec. 54 Italicized words are an alternative proposed by Professor Beeston to the Rackham translation.

14. One may also note a separate description of the incense forests as "divided up into definite portions" which is contained in the passage from Pliny Bk 12, ch 32, quoted at page 137 above

15. See Warmington, 1928, pp. 43–6. The great warehouses for pepper and other spices (the *Horrea Piperatarea*) were constructed by Domitian in AD 92.

16. Cf. Rostovtzeff, 1957, p. 66: "Commerce with neighbours and with far-distant lands like China and India played no very important part in the economic life of the early Empire. This type of commerce struck the imagination of contemporaries as it strikes that of some modern scholars, and both of them have exaggerated its importance."

17. Phillips, 1966, p. 201
18. Pirenne, 1975, p. 91. See also page 110 above and n. 30, ch 6
19. Miles, 1872, p. 65
20. Pliny *Natural History* Bk 12, ch 32, secs 63–5. In this passage the Rackham translation reads "through the country of the Gebbanitae". Professor Beeston has suggested this would be better translated "by the Gebbanitae".
21. Miller, 1969, pp. 25 and 279. Schoff, 1912, p. 289
22. Van Beek, 1960, p. 87
23. Pliny *Natural History* Bk 12, ch 41, sec 84
24. ibid., Bk 6, ch 26, sec 101. This figure has also been quoted as "55 million" (see, for example, Miller, 1969, p. 223)
25. Based on the reckoning, which survived from 217 BC until Nero's time, and was presumably used by Pliny, of 4 *asses* to one *sestertius* and 15 *asses* to one *denarius*
26. See Miller, 1969, pp. 223–4 and 227–8
27. Warmington, 1928, p. 272 *et seq*
28. Miller, 1969, p. 223, n. 2
29. Gibbon's *Decline and Fall of the Roman Empire*, chapter 17, quotes the tribute as 2822 gold crowns weighing 20,404 pounds; Caesar had them melted down.
30. Rostovtzeff, 1957, p. 471
31. When Warmington wrote, no silver coins after Nero's reign had been found in India except in the north and in Ceylon, suggesting that the export of silver was being discouraged. See Warmington, 1928, p. 285, and also p. 294, where he stated: "the development of barter and the cessation of unwise exportation of silver, and even gold, to the East from Vespasian's time onwards seem to me to be established facts." Miller, 1969, p. 207, suggests "gold plate" was mistranslated by Schoff; in the *Periplus*, sec. 56, the same Greek word appears with the unmistakable meaning of "coin".
32. Atchley, 1909, p. 43. Also Polybius *Histories* Bk 13, ch 9 (see page 195 below)
33. Hunter, 1877, p. 71
34. Bowen, 1958A, p. 35
35. See Naval Intelligence Division Handbook, 1946, p. 509. But Warmington, 1928, assumes a load of 400 pounds.
36. Bulliet, 1975, p. 20, quoting A. H. M. Jones *The Later Roman Empire, 284–602* (Blackwell, Oxford, 1964) Vol 2, p. 841
37. The following examples demonstrate this point:
    (i) at a ratio of 45 per cent frankincense, 45 per cent myrrh, the total Roman import would be:

    frankincense at $2\frac{1}{2}$ denarii—1326 tons
    $\qquad\qquad\quad$ 2 denarii—1657 tons

myrrh   at   8   denarii— 414 tons
                      6   denarii— 552 tons

(ii) at a ratio of 30 per cent frankincense, 60 per cent myrrh, the total Roman import would be:

frankincense   at $2\frac{1}{2}$ denarii— 888 tons
                         2   denarii—1105 tons
myrrh   at   8   denarii— 552 tons
                      6   denarii— 737 tons

38. See, for example, R. B. Serjeant: "Hūd and other pre-Islamic Prophets of Ḥaḍramawt" (*Le Museon*, Vol 67, 1954, pp. 121–79), quoting, *inter alia*, Arabic sources which describe the fair at Hūd, in eastern Ḥaḍramawt, which was attended by merchants from the Arabian Gulf.

39. On the perfume trade in Byzantium see Kennett, 1975

40. Pliny *Natural History* Bk 12, ch 40, sec 81

Chapter 9: The Road through the Incense Lands

1. See Thesiger, 1959, especially pages 179–84. Military vehicles have of course made these journeys since Thesiger, but detailed military reports have not been published. No archaeologist has yet followed these routes. Vehicular traffic does in any case have to follow a very different route to the camel.

2. Phillips, 1966, described the ancient storage point excavated in the centre of a frankincense-growing area at Hanūn as a place from which frankincense could be carried either to the coast at SMHRM or to Shisūr for conveyance overland. While Hanūn is conveniently positioned for SMHRM there is no real reason for connecting it with Shisūr, which does not itself contain any pre-Islamic remains as far as is known.

3. See Sprenger, 1864, pp. 141–5

4. Despite the attraction of their name the wells at Bīr Thamūd, a key point on this route, have revealed no signs of ancient use.

5. Phillips, 1966, p. 220

6. Ingrams, H., 1945, p. 173 and Ingrams, D., 1941

7. Beeston, 1975. Qalat is more accurately written QLT, since this name is only known epigraphically and therefore unvowelled.

8. Now Naqab al-Hagar, one of the major ruin sites in south-west Arabia

9. Preliminary findings were described to the *Seminar for Arabian Studies* at Cambridge in 1976. A summary of the work has since been published by Dr Pirenne in *Raydān—Journal of Ancient Yemeni Antiquities and Epigraphy* Vol 1, 1978, together with a note on the architecture by Dr Jean-François Breton, who was in charge of the excavations and has since made significant studies of major

buildings in other south Arabian sites. Owing to local border troubles the Shabwah excavations have been temporarily halted at the time of writing (1979).

10. Philby, 1939, ch 4

11. Wendell Phillips, in a quick visit to Shabwah, thought it a larger site than Tumna' with superior buildings (Phillips, 1966, p. 234). On the size of Qana see Doe, 1971, p. 183, where there is a good sketch map of the site.

12. Harding, 1964

13. Belhaven, 1949, pp. 162–3 and Belhaven, 1942

14. For a description of this site and of most of the other major sites in the former Aden Protectorate see Doe, 1971.

15. Pliny *Natural History* Bk 12, ch 32 (see also page 154 above)

16. On the question of how long a camel can go without water see Thesiger, 1959, p. 114 and Thomas, B., 1932, p. 201. But much depends on the climatic conditions, the breed of the animal and the weight it has to carry.

17. Bury, 1911, p. 246

18. See Philby, 1939, p. 54. When Philby visited Mushayniqah the well, an ancient shaft sunk through the rock, had been dry for as long as anyone could remember. It has since been re-opened. (Toy, 1968, p. 72)

19. This pass is today called Rahwat ar-Rib'ah; on the north side of it is a large and ancient well named Bīr ad-Dimnah which was probably a bivouac point. Belhaven, 1943, p. 116 gives the name as "Bir Dhumna".

20. This route is described in more detail in Groom, 1976. Local modern place-names and some details of ancient sites in this region are well covered in Landberg, 1898.

21. Beeston, 1959/71

22. Pliny *Natural History* Bk 6, ch 32, sec 157

23. Albright, 1950

24. See Doe, 1971, p. 72

25. Pliny *Natural History* Bk 12, ch 42, sec 93. See also page 84 above

26. Beeston, 1972

27. Apart from the story of the Queen of Sheba, the Qur'ān contains only this one slight reference to pre-Islamic south Arabia which is of historical interest. This is the 34th Sūrah (chapter), entitled "Saba", which is concerned with the punishment inflicted on the people of Saba because of their wickedness. The text of this reference is as follows:

"The descendents of Saba had heretofore a sign in their dwelling: namely, two gardens on the right hand and on the left, and it was said unto them, Eat ye of the provisions of your Lord, and give thanks unto him; ye have a good country and a gracious Lord. But they turned aside from what we had commanded them; wherefore we sent against them the inundation of Al Arem, and we changed their two gardens for them into two gardens producing bitter fruits and tamarisks and some little fruit of the lote-tree." (Translation of George Sale, 1857)

28. Translated from the transcription into French by Mon. G. Ryckmans of my original copy of this inscription published in *Le Muséon*, Vol 52, 1949 (Louvain), sec 390, pp. 77–8

29. Beeston, 1971(A), pp. 7–8

30. Beeston, 1971(B)

31. See Groom, 1976, where this matter is discussed in greater detail. Also Wissmann and Hoffner, 1952, pp. 40–45. Also Landberg, 1898, pp. 105–6

32. Fakhry, 1951/52

33. Albright, F. P., 1958

34. An account of this expedition and its explusion is given in Phillips, 1955

35. Philby, 1939, pp. 403–9 and other indexed references

36. Strabo referred to "Asca, which had been forsaken by its king", Pliny to "Nesca", as one of the towns which Aelius Gallus destroyed.

37. Beeston, 1972

38. Philby, 1952, p. 209

Chapter 10: North to Europe

1. Diodorus *Library of History* Bk 3, ch 44, secs 2–6

2. Pliny *Natural History* Bk 6, ch 32, para 156

3. Parr, Harding and Dayton, 1970

4. Pliny *Natural History* Bk 6, ch 32, para 156

5. Genesis 10.7 and other biblical references seem to indicate that Dedān was flourishing in the sixth century BC. See Winnett and Reed, 1970, p. 113

6. Winnett and Reed, 1970, p. 118–19

7. This argument, proposed by J. Ryckmans, is discussed in Moscati, 1959, where detailed references are given (pp. 124–6).

8. Hitti, 1970, p. 103, suggests the name Macoraba derived from a Sabaean word *makoraba* meaning "sanctuary", but no such Sabaean word is known. The name may relate to the word *mikrab*, which is of Ethiopic origin and means "assembly place" and hence "synagogue". (Personal communication from Professor Beeston)

9. After the Abyssinian occupation of south-west Arabia following the massacre of Christians in Nagrān (see p. 187 above) a cathedral was established in San'ā'. The Quraysh of Makkah,

seeing this as a challenge to the Kaaba of Makkah as a shrine of pilgrimage, are alleged to have defiled this building, in revenge for which the Abyssinian viceroy, Abraha, set out in AD 570 to subdue Makkah itself, which was by then under considerable Persian influence. Abraha used elephants in his army (some say one, others thirteen) and the route he followed is known to this day as "the road of the elephant". The expedition failed, legend has it because the invaders were attacked and killed to a man by a flock of birds which dropped stones on them (it is thought this description may conceal an outbreak of smallpox).

10. See Philby, 1952. Also Anati, 1968

11. See Stark, 1942, Appendix, p. 260, quoting Dr Ditlef Nielson *Handbuch der Sudarabischen Alterthumskunde*, p. 232. While Ptolemy manuscripts show "Thomata", this is probably "Thomala". Sprenger, 1875, p. 156, equates this philologically with "Tabala", but the surviving geographical names of Wadi Tubāla and Jabal ath-Thumalah suggest two distinct places. (Philby, 1952, pp. 26 and 109, gives "Thimala"). Wissmann, 1964, pp. 184 and 185 and map on p. 64, shows "Tabāla" south-west and "Thumāl" north-east of Bīshah and notes that there was for a time a state of "Thumāl".

12. Sprenger, 1875, p. 154. Also al-Wohaibi, 1973, p. 157

13. Pliny *Natural History* Bk 6, ch 32, sec 147

14. Strabo Geography Bk 16, ch 3, sec 3. The contradiction in this evidence between Gerrha being a port and an inland town will be noted, and provides a major difficulty in determining the site of Gerrha.

15. Arrian *Indica* sec 41

16. Strabo *Geography* Bk 16, ch 4, sec 4

17. See also Photius, sec 87 (page 68 above) which corresponds with the reference in n. 16 above.

18. Polybius *Histories* Bk 13, ch 9

19. Bibby, 1970, especially pp. 319–20, 368–9 and 372–4. Also Philby, 1933, p. 3

20. This problem is discussed in detail in Groom "Gerrha—a 'Lost' Arabian City" (awaiting publication in *Al-Atlāl*)

21. Thomas, 1932, p. 210

22. Since this passage was written, Beeston has suggested (Beeston, 1979) that Strabo's description may have implied a 70-day journey by merchants from Aelạna to "Minaea", where they purchased aromatics from the Gabaioi (Gebbanitae), who had themselves travelled a 40-day journey with it from Shabwah, thus making a total journey time of 110 days. He sees Minaea in this context as meaning no more than the limits of South Arabian trade, which had contracted with the end of the Minaean colony in Dedān

in about 100 BC. Thus the handing-over point might have been Nagrān or further north short of Dedān. But this interpretation would seem to be uncertain, since Strabo appears to have been using Eratosthenes as his source and hence describing the situation in about 200 BC, when the Minaean colony in Dedān was still thriving. (see page 63 above)

23. Pliny *Natural History* Bk 6, ch 32, sec 162

24. Those who have travelled with baggage camels will know the problem of sorting out loads appropriate for each camel and of balancing them and securing them to the saddles. No caravan organiser would wish to repeat this more frequently than he could help.

25. South Arabian pottery thought to date from the fifth or sixth century BC has been discovered at Eilath. See page 206 and n. 48 below.

26. It has been held that, because of a fundamental spelling difference, neither the "Nabayot" of Genesis nor the "Nabaiateans" of Arabia against whom the Assyrian king Ashurbanipal (668–663 BC) waged war can be equated with the Nabataeans. See Glueck, 1965, p. 4 and Winnett and Reed, 1970, pp. 99–100. The Nabataeans wrote in Aramaic, but it is generally held, because of the "Arabisms" in their Aramaic, that they spoke some sort of Arabic, (Beeston—personal communication).

27. See Lambert, 1972

28. Winnett and Reed; 1970, pp. 120 and 130

29. Diodorus *Library of History* Bk 19, sec 94

30. Plutarch *Lives* "Life of Demetrius", ch 7

31. Strabo *Geography* Bk 16, ch 4, sec 18

32. ibid., Bk 16, ch 4, sec 21

33. ibid., Bk 16, ch 4, sec 26

34. See Browning, 1974, pp. 41–2

35. Browning, 1974, p. 58

36. Almost the only mention of the Nabataeans in Pliny is in the brief statement in Bk 6, ch 32, sec 144: "next are the Nabataeans inhabiting a town named Petra; it lies in a deep valley a little less than two miles wide, and is surrounded by inaccessible mountains with a river flowing between them. Its distance from . . .(Gaza) . . . is 600 miles. . . . At Petra two roads meet, one leading from Syria to Palmyra and the other coming from Gaza."

37. Pliny *Natural History* Bk 12, ch 44

38. The Hejaz railway mileage from Madā'in Ṣāliḥ to Ma'an was 308·2 miles. The caravan route to Petra would probably have turned off the route which the railway follows shortly before Ma'an, which is a modern settlement about 20 miles from Petra.

39. See the map "North West Arabia and Negd" in Doughty, 1888

40. Plutarch *Lives* "Life of Alexander", ch 25. This story is related by Pliny in Bk 12, ch 32: "Alexander the Great in his boyhood was heaping frankincense on the altars in lavish fashion, when his tutor Leonides told him that he might worship the gods in that manner when he had conquered the frankincense-growing races; but when Alexander had won Arabia he sent Leonides a ship with a cargo of frankincense, with a message charging him to worship the gods without any stint."

41. Diodorus *Library of History* Bk 19, ch 93, sec 6

42. Plutarch *Lives* "Life of Demetrius", ch 4

43. Josephus *Antiquities of the Jews* Bk 17, ch 11, sec 4

44. Strabo *Geography* Bk 16, ch 2, secs 31–2

45. See Pliny *Natural History* Bk 5, ch 14, sec 63. Strabo may have incorporated a reference to the razing of Gaza by Alexander Jannaeus in 96 BC. (See Glanville Downey *Gaza in the Early Sixth Century* University of Oklahoma Press, Norman, Oklahoma, 1963)

46. When the writer Barbara Toy motored along these parts of the incense route in 1967, she was informed by the Amir of Tabūk that there were two ancient routes, one heading northwards towards Ma'an and the other turning north-west through Midian to the Gulf of Aqaba. See Toy, 1968, p. 153

47. See Sprenger, 1875; also al-Wohaibi, 1973. From Aelana this route passed through Madyan, Kilābah, Shaghb and Badā, all stations on the pilgrim route recognised by mediaeval Arab geographers and identifiable in Ptolemy's list as respectively Madiama, Laba, Soace and Badais (although Sprenger had not appreciated that all these places lay on the same route).

48. Glueck, 1939

49. Strabo *Geography* Bk 16, ch 4, sec 24

50. ibid., Bk 16, ch 4, sec 23

51. Agatharchides stated of the Nabataeans, in the text of Diodorus:

"This tribe occupies a large part of the coast and not a little of the country which stretches inland, and it has a people numerous beyond telling and flocks and herds in multitudes beyond belief. Now in ancient times these men observed justice and were content with the food which they received from their flocks, but later, after the kings in Alexandria had made the ways of the seas navigable for their merchants, these Arabs not only attacked the shipwrecked, but fitting out pirate ships preyed upon the voyagers, imitating in their practices the savage and lawless ways of the Tauri of the Pontus; some time afterwards, however, they were caught on the high seas by some quadriremes and punished as they deserved."

(Diodorus Siculus *Library of History* Bk 3, ch 43, sec 5)

52. A problem exists over the location of Leuce Come (Leuke Kome). Oddly enough this place does not appear in Ptolemy's list, although its existence is testified before Ptolemy by Strabo and after him by the *Periplus*. It does not appear that Ptolemy listed this place under another name and Sprenger (1875, p. 20) believed there was a gap in Ptolemy's information here. Schoff (1912) placed Leuce Come at al-Hawrah, which is near Umm Lajj, about 125 miles S.S.E. of Ḥijrā; Leuce Come translates as "white village" and "Hawrah" also denotes whiteness. But this location would seem too far south for a Nabataean port feeding Petra, despite the difficulties of navigation in the northern Arabian waters of the Red Sea. Futhermore it is consistent neither with Strabo's description (page 207 above) nor with the inference from Strabo that Aelius Gallus passed through Ḥijrā (Egra) on the way back to his sea transport, which he had left at Leuce Come. A natural port for Ḥijrā would have been at or near modern al-Wajh, about 100 miles E.S.E. of Ḥijrā and the same distance from al-Hawrah. From here Petra could also have been reached without passing through Ḥijrā. Glueck shows it at this position in his map (1965, p. 632) without discussing why, but confuses the issue by several references in his text to Leuce Come as a port in the Gulf of Aqaba. Grohmann (1968, pp. 4, 29, 44 and map) alternates between al-Hawrah and the surely much less likely port of Yenbo, considerably further south. Other authorities on the Nabataeans are silent about this problem. In my map on page 192 I have placed Leuce Come at al-Wajh. A more exact clue to the location may lie in the surviving place-name "Rās Karkumā" (also recorded as Rās Karkumah) for a headland some thirty miles south of al-Wajh close to where Wādī al-Ḥamḍ enters the sea. The current name Marsa Martabān for the adjacent bay indicates that it is an anchorage. This is the nearest point on the coast which can be reached from Ḥijrā. The name Leuce Come used by the Greek navigators could well have been a pun on a Nabataean place-name resembling "Karkumā".

53. Littmann and Meredith, 1953. Also Glueck, 1965, especially pp. 529–34.

54. Glueck, 1965, pp. 69 and 361

55. Strabo *Geography* Bk 16, ch 2, sec 20

56. The inscription concerned is RES 3022. See Winnett and Reed, 1970, pp. 117–19. This provides the evidence of Minaean presence in the 21st year of one of the Ptolemies and must hence relate to the third or second centuries BC.

57. Pliny *Natural History* Bk 12, ch 32, sec 59

58. Warmington, 1928, p. 5

59. Suetonius *Lives of the Caesars* "Augustus", sec 98

60. Pliny *Natural History* Bk 6, ch 26, secs 102–3. See also page 79 above

61. Warmington, 1928, pp. 6 and 7

62. Strabo *Geography* Bk 16, ch 4, sec 24. This part of Strabo's text is omitted from the extract at page 75 above. The Jones translation of Strabo translates the passage as "situated *on* the sea", but Professor Beeston has pointed out (personal communication) that the original Greek also has the sense of "near", which may well have been intended here.

63. The *Periplus* mentions the conveying of frankincense to Indian ports only in respect of Barbaricum, in the north, which was reached after a coasting voyage to Omān. It is not listed at all among the imports of Muziris or any other of the southern ports from which pepper and other spices were obtained. Pliny mentioned the possibility of a call at Qana by ships bound for India, but added that the best way was to go direct from Ocelis (see page 79 above).

Chapter 11: Climate and History in Arabia

1. See Ryckmans J., 1973

2. The word *Sab'atayn* derives from the Arabic for "two Saturdays" and hence "two weeks". This desert is not "The sands of the two Shebas" (Saba'tayn) as has been popularly supposed. See Serjeant, 1976, p. 89 (n. 37)

3. Beeston, 1939

4. Serjeant, 1976, p. 70

5. Diodorus *Library of History* Bk 3, sec 46

6. For example, Philby (*Arabian Highlands*, pp. 458–9) talks of "savannah jungle", "jungle" and the "densely wooded bed of the wadi" in the area of Wādī Baysh, on the Tihamah coastal plain, while the tropical growth on the southern slopes of the mountains of Ẓufār is well known.

7. See Dayton, 1975, pp. 35 and 45, quoting O. Petterson and R. W. Fairbridge

8. See, for example, the summary on pp. 186–7 of W. Day and D. Trump *The Penguin Book of Archaeology* Penguin Books, London, 1972.

9. Butzer and Twidale, 1966

10. Butzer "Climate in the Near East", quoted in Fisher, 1971

11. See Dayton, 1975, especially p. 48. Dayton also quotes C. E. P. Brooks *Climate through the Ages* New York, 1970

12. See R. A. Bryson, H. H. Lamb and D. L. Donley "Drought and the Decline of Mycenae" *Antiquity*, No 189, March 1974

13. See Brice, 1960, especially pp. 35–44. Also Dayton, 1975, pp. 40–41.

14. In a talk to the *Seminar for Arabian Studies* on 14 July 1976. Since this book was completed this matter and various further

problems of climate in the ancient Middle East have been covered in contributions by Brice, Butzer and others in Brice, 1978.

15. Dayton, 1975
16. Winstanley, 1973
17. Butzer and Twidale, 1966, p. 137
18. See article on "Excavations at Khartum prove revealing" in the Sudan supplement of *The Times* for 26 Feb 1977
19. Professor Brice in addresses to the *Seminar for Arabian Studies* in 1975 and 1976. See also n. 14 above
20. *New Scientist*, 27 January 1966
21. In a talk to the *Seminar for Arabian Studies* in London in 1972
22. Golding, 1974
23. ibid.
24. See Bibby, 1970, especially pp. 374–5. Also the same author's summary of a paper on "The Al-Ubaid Culture of Eastern Arabia" in *Proceedings of Sixth Seminar for Arabian Studies*, London, 1972 (pub. Seminar for Arabian Studies, London, 1973) pp. 1 and 2
25. Philby, 1933, Appendix, pp. 387–9
26. Philby, 1939, p. 73
27. ibid., p. 364
28. ibid., p. 369
29. See Caton-Thompson and Gardner, 1939. Miss Caton-Thompson found "geometric microliths", of a type which existed in Europe and the Mediterranean area long before 3000 BC, in tombs which could hardly be dated earlier than 600 BC. She suggested that this "established beyond question" that such microliths "were still flourishing in South Arabia at this late date", but this point seems open to question pending further investigation—they could, for example, have been regarded by the people of the tombs as talismans making them desirable funerary ware.
30. On the general subject of sand movement see Bagnold, 1951
31. In the central and southern desert areas the golden hue of the desert sands is quite distinct from the paler wadi silt sands.
32. See Thomas, B., 1932, p. 162
33. Bent, 1900, p. 129
34. Phillips, 1966, pp. 228–9
35. ibid., p. 224. Perhaps the track led to a salt-mine.
36. See Robert K. Vincent, Jr: "The Lost Kingdom of Tamurlane" in The *Sunday Times Magazine*, 18 November 1979.
37. Bagnold, 1951, p. 84
38. Philby, 1939, particularly pp. 379 and 380
39. Rare exceptions to this include the surround of the great Sabaean temple at Maḥram Bilqis, close to Mārib, which is oval in shape, and the temple at Ṣirwāh, which also lies on a very ancient site.
40. Philby, 1952, p. 304

41. ibid., pp. 221, 226 and 332

42. Bibby, 1970, p. 380

43. The general term for the culture of the incense kingdoms is Early South Arabian (ESA). Professor Beeston has recently used the term "the Ṣayhad culture" to describe that part of the ESA culture centred on the Ṣayhad.

44. See Tosi, 1974, for a valuable summary of information about the development of cultures in the eastern part of Arabia up to about 2000 BC

45. Serjeant, 1976, p. 73

46. Quoted by Thomas B., 1932, p. 143

47. See Dayton, 1975, p. 52

48. See Bent, 1900, p. 143

49. See Bowen, 1958

50. See Fisher, 1971, fn on p. 207 (quoting Dr Uvarov of the Desert Locust Survey)

Bibliography

The following are the principal works consulted during the preparation of this book.

AKURGAL Ekrem *Ancient Civilisations and Ruins of Turkey*, Haşet Kitabevi, Istanbul 1973

ALBRIGHT Frank P. "Excavations at Marib in Yemen" Article in BOWEN and ALBRIGHT, *"Archaeological Discoveries in South Arabia"* (q.v.) 1958

ALBRIGHT Frank P. and BOWEN Richard *Archaeological Discoveries in South Arabia*. See under BOWEN

ALBRIGHT W.F. *From the Stone Age to Christianity*, Baltimore 1940

ALBRIGHT W.F. *The Archaeology of Palestine*, Penguin, London 1949

ALBRIGHT W.F. "The Chronology of Ancient South Arabia in the Light of the First Campaign of Excavations in Qataban" *Bulletin of the American Schools of Oriental Research*, No 119, October 1950

ANATI E. *Rock Art in Central Arabia*, Bibliothéque du Muséon, Louvain 1968

ARRIAN *Indica*. See ROBSON

ARRIAN *The Campaigns of Alexander*. See Aubrey de SELINCOURT.

ATCHLEY E.G. *A History of the Use of Incense in Divine Worship* Longmans Green & Co., London 1909

ATHENAEUS *The Deipnosophists*. See GULICK

BAGNOLD Brigadier R.A. "Sand Formations in Southern Arabia" *Geographical Journal*, January/March 1951, pp. 78–86

BARNETT R.D. "Early Shipping in the Near East" *Antiquity*, December 1958, p. 233

BARON Stanley *The Desert Locust* Eyre Methuen, London 1972

BEAN George E. *Aegean Turkey—An Archaeological Guide*, Ernest Benn, London 1966

BEEK Gus W. van "Frankincense and Myrrh in Ancient South Arabia" *Journal of the American Oriental Society*, Vol 78, No 3, 1958A

BEEK Gus W. van "Ancient Frankincense-Producing Areas" in BOWEN and ALBRIGHT *Archaeological Discoveries in South Arabia* (q.v.) 1958B

BEEK Gus W. van "Frankincense and Myrrh" *The Biblical Archaeologist*, Vol 23, No 3, September 1960

BEEK Gus W. van "The Rise and Fall of Arabia Felix" *The Scientific American*, December 1969, pp. 36–46

BEEK Gus W. van "The Land of Sheba" in PRITCHARD *Solomon and Sheba* (q.v.) 1974

BEESTON A.F.L. "On the Inscriptions Discovered by Mr Philby". Appendix to PHILBY *Sheba's Daughters* (q.v.) 1939

BEESTON A.F.L. *Epigraphic South Arabian Calendars and Dating*, Luzac, London 1956

BEESTON A.F.L. "The Mercantile Code of Qataban". Part of *"Qahtan: Studies in Old South Arabian Epigraphy"*, Luzac, London, Fascicule 1 of 1959 and Fascicule 2 of 1971

BEESTON A.F.L. "The Labakh Texts". Part of *Qahtan: Studies in Old South Arabian Epigraphy*, Luzac, London, Fascicule 2, 1971A

BEESTON A.F.L. "The Functional Significance of the Old South Arabian Town" *Proceedings of 4th Seminar, Cambridge, 1970* Seminar for Arabian Studies; London 1971B

BEESTON A.F.L. "Pliny's Gebbanitae" *Proceedings of 5th Seminar, Oxford, 1971* Seminar for Arabian Studies, London 1972

BEESTON A.F.L. "The Himyarite Problem" *Proceedings of 8th Seminar, Oxford, 1974* Seminar for Arabian Studies, London 1975

BEESTON A.F.L. "Warfare in Ancient South Arabia (2nd–3rd Centuries AD)". Part of *Qahtan: Studies in Old South Arabian Epigraphy*, Fascicule 3, Luzac, London 1976A

BEESTON A.F.L. "The Settlement at Khor Rori" *The Journal of Oman Studies*, Vol 2, 1976B, pp. 39–42

BEESTON A.F.L. "Some Observations on Greek and Latin Data Relating to South Arabia" *Bulletin of the School of Oriental and African Studies*, Vol 42, Pt 1, 1979

BELHAVEN Lord (The Hon. R. A. B. HAMILTON) "Six Weeks in Shabwa" *Geographical Journal*, Vol 100, 1942

BELHAVEN Lord (The Hon. R. A. B. HAMILTON) "Archaeological Sites in the Western Aden Protectorate" *Geographical Journal*, Vol 101, 1943

BELHAVEN Lord *The Kingdom of Melchior*, Murray, London 1949

BELHAVEN Lord *The Uneven Road*, Murray, London 1955

BENT Theodore and Mrs *Southern Arabia*, Smith, Elder, London 1900

BIBBY Geoffrey *Looking for Dilmun*, Collins, London 1970

BIRDWOOD Dr G. "On The Genus Boswellia" *Transactions of the Linnean Society*, Vol 27, 1870 pp. 111–48

BOTTING Douglas *Island of the Dragon's Blood*, Hodder and Stoughton, London 1958

BOWEN Richard and ALBRIGHT Frank P. (Eds) *Archaeological Discoveries in South Arabia*, Johns Hopkins Press, Baltimore 1958

BOWEN Richard "Irrigation in Ancient Qataban". Bowen and Albright *Archaeological Discoveries in South Arabia* (q.v.) 1958

BOWEN Richard "Irrigation in Ancient Qataban". BOWEN and ALBRIGHT *Archaeological Discoveries in South Arabia* (q.v.) 1958A 1958B

BREASTED J.H. *Ancient Records of Egypt*, Russell and Russell, New York 1906 (reprinted 1962)

BRICE W.C. *South West Asia*, University of London Press, London 1960

BRICE W.C. (Ed.) *The Environmental History of the Near and Middle East since the Last Ice Age*, Academic Press, London 1978

BROWNING Iain *Petra*, Chatto & Windus, London 1974

BUDGE E.A. Wallis *The Syriac Book of Medicine (Syrian Anatomy, Pathology and Therapeutics)*, Humphrey Milford and Oxford University Press, 1913

BULLIET R.W. *The Camel and the Wheel*, Harvard University Press, Cambridge, Massachusetts 1975

BURY G. Wyman (Abdulla Mansur) *The Land of Uz*, Macmillan, London 1911

BURY G. Wyman *Arabia Infelix—or the Turks in Yemen*, Macmillan, London 1915

BUTZER K.W. and TWIDALE C.R. "Deserts in the Past". In E. S. HILLS (Ed.) *Arid Lands—a Geographical Appraisal*, Methuen, London, and UNESCO 1966

CARTER H.J. "A Description of the Frankincense Tree of Arabia with Remarks on the Misplacement of the 'Libanophorous Region' in Ptolemy's Geography" *Journal of the Bombay Branch of the Royal Asiatic Society*, Vol 2, 1848 pp. 380–90

CARY E. (trans.) *Dio's Roman History*. Loeb Classical Library, Heinemann and Harvard University Press 1927

CATON-THOMPSON Gertrude and GARDNER E.W. "Climate, Irrigation and Early Man in the Hadramaut" *Geographical Journal*, No 93, 1939 pp. 18–38

CATON-THOMPSON Gertrude *The Tombs and Moon Temple of Hureidha (Hadramaut)*, OUP/Society of Antiquaries, London 1944

CRUTTENDEN C.J.: 1846. "Report on the Mijjertayn Tribe of Somallies, inhabiting the District forming the North East Point of Africa" *Transactions of the Bombay Geographical Society*, Vol 7, 1846, pp. 111–27

DAYTON John "Preliminary Survey in N.W. Arabia—1968". See under PARR

DAYTON John "The Problem of Climatic Change in the Arabian Peninsula" *Proceedings of the 8th Seminar, Oxford, 1974* Seminar for Arabian Studies, London 1975.

DIO Cassius *Roman History*. See CARY E.

DIODORUS SICULUS *The Library of History*. See OLDFATHER C.H.

DIXON D.M. "The Transplantation of Punt Incense Trees in Egypt" *Journal of Egyptian Archaeology*, Vol 55, 1969 pp. 55–65

DOE Brian *Southern Arabia*, Thames & Hudson, London 1971

DORESSE Jean (Trans. Elsa Coult) *Ethiopia* Elek, London 1959

DOUGHTY Charles M. *Travels in Arabia Deserta*, Cambridge University Press, 1888; and new edition Jonathan Cape, London 1921

DRAKE-BROCKMAN R. E. *British Somaliland*, Hurst & Blackett, London 1912

FAKHRY Ahmed *An Archeological Journey to Yemen*, Service des Antiquités de l'Égypte (3 vols), Cairo 1951/2

FARIS Nabih Amin *The Antiquities of South Arabia. A Translation of the Eighth Book of al-Hamdani's "Al-Iklil"*, Princeton University Press, Princeton 1938

FISHER W.B. *The Middle East* (6th Edition), Methuen, London 1971

GARDNER E.W. and CATON-THOMPSON G. "Climate, Irrigation and Early Man in the Hadramaut". See CATON-THOMPSON

GIBB H.A.R. (Trans.) *Ibn Battuta—Travels in Asia and Africa—1325–1354*, Routledge & Kegan Paul, London 1929

GLUECK Nelson "The Second Campaign at Tell el-Kheleifah" *Bulletin of the American Schools of Oriental Research*, No 75, October 1939, pp. 8–22

GLUECK Nelson *Deities and Dolphins*, Cassell, London 1965

GOLDING Marny "Evidence for Pre-Seleucid Occupation of Eastern Arabia" *Proceedings of 7th Seminar, Cambridge, 1973* Seminar for Arabian Studies, London 1974

GROHMANN Adolf *Südarabien als Wirstschaftsgebiet*. Part I; 1922; Verlag des Forschungsinstitutes für Osten und Orient; Vienna. Part II; 1933; Verlag Rudolf M Rohrer; Brünn

GROHMANN Adolf *Kulturgeschichte des Alten Orients-Arabien*. C. H. Beck'sche Verlagsbuchhandlung; Munich 1968

GROOM Nigel "The Northern Passes of Qataban" *Proceedings of 9th Seminar, London 1975* Seminar for Arabian Studies, London 1976

GROOM Nigel "The Frankincense Region" *Proceedings of 10th Seminar, Cambridge, 1976* Seminar for Arabian Studies, London 1977

GROOM Nigel "Gerrha: A 'Lost' Arabian City" (awaiting publication in *Al-Atlāl*)

GULICK C.B. (trans.) *Athenaeus' "The Deipnosophists"* Loeb Classical Library, Heinemann and Harvard University Press 1961

HAMDANI Al- *Al Iklil*. See FARIS N.A.

HAMILTON Hon. R.A.B. See BELHAVEN Lord

HANSEN Thorskild *Arabia Felix*, Collins, London 1964

HARDEN Donald *The Phoenicians*, Penguin, London 1971 (First published Thames & Hudson, London 1962)

HARDING G. Lankester *Archaeology in the Aden Protectorate*, H.M. Stationery Office, London 1964

HARDING G. Lankester "Preliminary Survey of N.W. Arabia". See under PARR

HARRIS W.C. *The Highlands of Aethiopia*, Longman, Brown, Green and Longmans, London 1844

HEPPER F. Nigel "Arabian and African Frankincense Trees" *Journal of Egyptian Archaeology*, No 55, 1969, pp. 66–72

HEPPER F. Nigel "An Ancient Expedition to Transplant Living Trees" *Journal of the Royal Horticultural Society*, Vol 92, Pt 10, October 1967

HERODOTUS *The Histories*. See SELINCOURT

HITTI Philip K. *History of the Arabs* (10th Ed.), Macmillan, London 1970

HÖFFNER Dr Maria and WISSMANN H. von "Beiträge zur Historischen Geographie des Vorislamischen Südarabien". See WISSMANN

HOGARTH David George *The Penetration of Arabia*, London 1904 (Reprint Khayats, Beirut, 1963)

HORT A. (trans.) *Theophrastus: "Enquiry into Plants"* and *"Concerning Odours"* (in one volume), Loeb Classical Library, Heinemann and Harvard University Press, 1916

HOURANI George F. *Arab Seafaring in the Indian Ocean in Ancient and Early Mediaeval Times*, Princeton University, 1951 (Reprint Khayats, Beirut, 1963)

HUNTER Captain F.M. *An Account of the British Settlement of Aden in Arabia*, London 1877. New impression Frank Cass, London 1968

IBN BATTUTA See GIBB

INGRAMS Doreen (Mrs Harold) "Excursion into the Hajr Province of Hadramaut" *Geographical Journal*, Vol 98, No 3, September 1941, pp. 121–34

INGRAMS Doreen *A Survey of Social and Economic Conditions in the Aden Protectorate*, Aden Government, 1949

INGRAMS Harold *Arabia and the Isles*, Murray, London 1942

INGRAMS Harold "The South Arabian Incense Road" *Journal of the Royal Asiatic Society*, 1945, pp. 169–85

INGRAMS Harold *The Yemen—Imams, Rulers and Revolutions*, Murray, London 1963

JONES H.L. (trans.) *The Geography of Strabo*, Loeb Classical Library, Heinemann and Harvard University Press, 1930

JOSEPHUS Flavius "Antiquities of the Jews". See William WHISTON

KENNETT Frances *History of Perfume* Harrap, London 1975

KENYON Sir Frederick *Our Bible and the Ancient Manuscripts* (5th Ed.), Eyre & Spottiswoode, London 1958

KIERNAN R.H. *The Unveiling of Arabia*, Harrap, London 1937

KITCHEN K.A. *Ancient Orient and the Old Testament*, Tyndale Press, London 1966

LAMBERT W.G. "Nabonidus in Arabia" *Proceedings of 5th Seminar, Oxford, 1971* Seminar for Arabian Studies, London 1972

LANDBERG Le Compte de *Arabica V* Brill, Leyden 1898

LANE E.W. *An Arabic–English Lexicon* Williams & Norgate, London 1863. (Published in 8 volumes over the period 1863–1893, but referred to here as "Lane, 1863")

LITTMANN Enno and MEREDITH David "Nabataean Inscriptions from Egypt" *Bulletin of the School of Oriental and African Studies*, No 15, 1952, pp. 211–46 and No 16, 1953, pp. 1–28

LONG G. and STEWART A. (trans.) *Plutarch's Lives*. See STEWART

LUCAS A. "Notes on Myrrh and Stacte" *Journal of Egyptian Archaeology*, Vol 23, 1937

MEREDITH David and LITTMANN Enno "Nabataean Inscriptions from Egypt". See LITTMANN

MEULEN D. van der and WISSMANN Hermann von "Hadhramaut: Some of its Mysteries Unveiled". See WISSMANN

MEULEN D. van der *Aden to the Hadhramaut*, Murray, London 1947

MILES Captain S.B. "On the Neighbourhood of Bandar Marayah" *Journal of the Royal Geographical Society*, Vol 42, 1872

MILES S.B. and MUNZINGER W. "An Account of an Excursion into the Interior of Southern Arabia" *Journal of the Royal Geographical Society*, Vol, 41, 1871

MILLER J. Innes *The Spice Trade of the Roman Empire*, Clarendon Press, Oxford 1969

MONOD Théodore "Les Arbres à Encens (*Boswellia sacra* Flückiger, 1967) dans le Hadramaout (Yémen du Sud)" *Bulletin du Muséum National d'Histoire Naturelle, Paris*, 4th series, 1, 1979, section B No 3, pp. 131–69

MONROE Elizabeth *Philby of Arabia*, Faber & Faber, London 1973

MONTGOMERY James A. *Arabia and the Bible*, University of Pennsylvania Press, Philadelphia 1934

MOSCATI Sabatino *Ancient Semitic Civilizations*, Elek, London 1957

MOSCATI Sabatino *The Semites in Ancient History*, University of Wales Press, Cardiff 1959

MÜLLER W.W. "Notes on the Use of Frankincense in South Arabia" *Proceedings of 9th Seminar, London, 1975 (Vol 6)* Seminar for Arabian Studies, London 1976

MÜLLER W.W. "Weihrauch" *Realencyclopadie von Pauly-Wissowa; Supplement, Vol 15* Alfred Druckenmuller Verlag, Munich 1978

MUNZINGER W. See MILES

NAIRNE A.K. *The Flowering Plants of Western India*, London 1894

NAVAL INTELLIGENCE DIVISION *"Western Arabia and the Red Sea"*, Naval Intelligence Division, Admiralty, London 1946

NAVILLE E. *The Temple of Deir al-Bahri* Memoirs of Egypt Exploration Fund, Vol 16, Pt 3, London 1896–7.

NIEBUHR Karsten *Travels Through Arabia*, London 1792

OLDFATHER C.H. (trans.) *Diodorus (Diodorus Siculus): The Library of History* Loeb Classical Library, Heinemann, London, and Harvard University Press, 1935

PARR P.J., HARDING G.L. and DAYTON J.E. "Preliminary Survey in N.W. Arabia, 1968" *Bulletin of the Institute of Archaeology*, Nos 8 & 9, Institute of Archaeology, London 1970

PATON W.R. (trans.) *Polybius: Histories*, Loeb Classical Library, Heinemann, London, and Harvard University Press, 1922

PHILBY H. St J.B. *The Empty Quarter*, Constable, London 1933

PHILBY H. St J.B. *Sheba's Daughters*, Methuen, London 1939

PHILBY H. St J.B. *Arabian Highlands*, Cornell University Press 1952

PHILLIPS Wendell *Qataban and Sheba*, Gollancz, London 1955

PHILLIPS Wendell *Unknown Oman*, Longmans, London 1966

PIRENNE Jacqueline *Le Royaume Sud-Arabe de Qatabān et sa Datation*, Publications Universitaires, Bibliothèque du Muséon, Louvain 1961

PIRENNE Jacqueline "The Incense Port of Moscha (Khor Rori) in Dhofar" *Journal of Oman Studies*, Vol 1, 1975

PLINY *Natural History*. See RACKHAM.

PLUTARCH *Lives*. See STEWART and LONG

POLYBIUS *Histories*. See PATON

PRITCHARD James B. *Ancient Near Eastern Texts Relating to the Old Testament*, Princeton 1950

PRITCHARD James B. (Ed.) *Solomon and Sheba*, Phaidon, London 1974

PRITCHARD James B. "The Age of Solomon" and "Conclusion". (Chapters in Pritchard, 1974A)

RACKHAM H. (trans.) *Pliny's Natural History*, Loeb Classical Library; Heinemann, London, and Harvard University Press, 1945

REED W.L. and WINNETT F.V. "Ancient Records from North Arabia". See WINNETT

ROBSON E. Eliff (trans.) *Arrian's History (Anabasis) of Alexander* and *Indica*. Loeb Classical Library, Heinemann, London, and Harvard University Press, 1966

ROSTOVTZEFF M. *The Social and Economic History of the Roman Empire*. Clarendon Press, Oxford 1957

RYCKMANS G. "Inscriptions Sud-Arabes—8me Série" *Le Muséon*, Vol 62, 1949, pp. 55–124

RYCKMANS G. "Inscriptions Sud-Arabes—9me Série" *Le Muséon*, Vol 64, 1951, Nos 1–2

RYCKMANS Jacques "Petits Royaumes Sud-Arabes d'Après les Auteurs Classiques" *Le Muséon*, Vol 70, 1957, pp. 75–96

RYCKMANS Jacques "Ritual Meals in the Ancient South Arabian Religion" *Proceedings of 6th Seminar, London 1972* Seminar for Arabian Studies, London 1973

SAGGS H.W.F. *The Greatness that was Babylon*, Sidgwick & Jackson, London 1962

SCHMIDT Dr Alfred *Drogen und Drogenhandel in Altertum*, Barth, Leipzig 1927

SCHOFF Wilfred H. *The Periplus of the Erythraean Sea* (trans. and commentary), Longmans, Green, New York 1912

SCOTT Hugh *In the High Yemen*, Murray, London 1942

SELINCOURT Aubrey de (trans.) *Herodotus: The Histories*, Penguin, London 1954

SELINCOURT Aubrey de (trans.) *Arrian: The Campaigns of Alexander*, Penguin, London 1971

SERJEANT R.B. "Star Calendars and an Almanac from South West Arabia" *Anthropos*, Vol 49, 1954

SERJEANT R.B. "Review of Bowen/Albright: Archaeological Discoveries in South Arabia" *Bulletin of the School of Oriental and African Studies*, 1960, pp. 582–5

SERJEANT R.B. *The Portuguese off the South Arabian Coast*, Clarendon Press, Oxford 1963

SERJEANT R.B. "The Ports of Aden and Shihr (Mediaeval period)" *Les Grandes Escales, Proceedings of the Société Jean Bodin*, Vol 32, 1974A

SERJEANT R.B. "The Cultivation of Cereals in Mediaeval Yemen" *Arabian Studies I*, Hurst & Co, London 1974B

SERJEANT R.B. *South Arabian Hunt*, Luzac, London 1976

SMITH W. (Ed.) *A Dictionary of the Bible*, Murray, London 1861

SPRENGER Aloys *Post- und Reiserouten des Orients*, F. A. Brockhaus, Leipzig 1864

SPRENGER Aloys *Die Alte Geographie Arabiens*, Von Hube, Berne 1875

STARK Freya *The Southern Gates of Arabia*, Murray, London 1942

STARKEY Jean "The Nabataeans: A Historical Sketch" *Biblical Archaeologist*, Vol 18, 1955, No 4

STEVENSON E.L. *The Geography of Claudius Ptolemy* (translation and commentary). New York Public Library, New York 1932

STRABO "The Geography of Strabo". See JONES

STEWART A. and LONG G. (trans.) *Plutarch's Lives*, Bohn Library, Bell, London 1901

THEOPHRASTUS *Enquiry into Plants* and *Concerning Odours*. See HORT

THESIGER Wilfred *Arabian Sands*, Longman, Green and Co., London 1959

THOMAS Bertram *Arabia Felix*, Cape, London 1932

THOMAS D. Winton (Ed.) *Archaeology and Old Testament Study*, Clarendon Press, Oxford 1967

THOMPSON Gertrude CATON-. See CATON-THOMPSON

THOMPSON Oliver *History of Ancient Geography*, Cambridge University Press 1948

THOMPSON R. Campbell *A Dictionary of Assyrian Botany*, British Academy, London 1949

TOSI Maurizio "Some Data for the Study of Prehistoric Cultural Areas on the Persian Gulf" *Proceedings of 7th Seminar, Cambridge, 1973* Seminar for Arabian Studies, London 1974

TOY Barbara *The Highway of the Three Kings*, Murray, London 1968

TWIDALE C.R. and BUTZER K.W. "Deserts in the Past". See BUTZER

USHER George *A Dictionary of Plants Used by Man*, Constable, London 1974

WARMINGTON E.H. *The Commerce between the Roman Empire and India* Cambridge University Press, 1928

WATSON Paul F. "The Queen of Sheba in Christian Tradition". In Pritchard: *Solomon and Sheba* (q.v.) 1974

WHISTON William (trans.) *The Works of Josephus Flavius – Antiquities of the Jews* Thomas Tegg, London 1825

WILKINSON Sir J. Gardner *A Popular Account of the Ancient Egyptians*, Murray, London 1854

WINNETT F.V. and REED W.L. *Ancient Records from North Arabia*, University of Toronto Press, 1970

WINSTANLEY Derek "Rainfall Patterns and General Atmospheric Circulation" *Nature*, Vol 245, 28 September 1973, pp. 190–94

WISSMANN Hermann von and MEULEN D. van der *Hadhramaut: Some of its Mysteries Unveiled*, Leyden 1933 reprinted Brill, Leyden, 1964

WISSMANN Hermann von and HÖFFNER Maria *Beiträge zur Historischen Geographie der Vorislamischen Südarabien*. Akademie der Wissenschaften und der Literatur, Wiesbaden 1952

WISSMANN Hermann von "Himyar Ancient History" *Le Muséon*, Vol 77, 3–4, 1964A, pp. 429–97

WISSMANN Hermann von *Zur Gesichte und Landeskunde von Alt-Südarabien* Osterreichischen Akademie der Wissenschaften, Vienna 1964B

WISSMANN Hermann von *Das Weihrauchland Sa'kalān, Samārum und Mos-cha*. Osterreichischen Akademie der Wissenschaften; Vienna 1977

WREDE Adolf von *Reise in Hadhramaut* H. Freiherr von Maltzen, Brunswick 1870

WOHAIBI Abdullah al- *The Northern Hijaz in the Writings of the Arab Geographers, 800–1150* Al-Risalah, Beirut 1973

Index

Figures in bold type indicate a more important reference. For reasons of space, references in the Notes have been indexed only where there are special circumstances. For a note on spelling see Preface page xi